SoJourn
Volume 6.2

A journal devoted to the history, culture, and geography of South Jersey

SJCHC
South Jersey Culture & History Center

2022

SoJourn is a collaborative effort. Local historians contribute the articles; Stockton students—in this issue, the editing interns of spring and fall 2022—edit the articles, design the layout, and set the type; the directors of the South Jersey Culture & History Center at Stockton University oversee the publication. We are always seeking additional articles. If you have one, or more, or an idea for one, please contact us at the address or emails below.

Editors
Mariah L. Ayala, Chris Curtain, Jennah Figueroa, Travis Finley, Evelyn D. Hunt, Daniel Jacoby, William A. King, Cory D. Krause, Zophia C. Krause, Chris Lopez, Cassius Navarro, Makena Olson, Lauren Parks, Jonathan Porro, Felix Ramos, Katharyn Sagusti, Rose Shaw, Amanda Sciandra, Rachel A. Wronko.

Supervising Editors
Tom Kinsella and Paul W. Schopp

ISSN: 2474-6665
ISBN: 978-1-947889-13-2
A publication of the South Jersey Culture & History Center
at Stockton University
www.stockton.edu/sjchc/

© 2022, the authors, South Jersey Culture & History Center, and Stockton University. All rights reserved.

Filler images at the conclusion of articles, along with historic images in articles not otherwise credited, and cover images courtesy of the Paul W. Schopp Collection.

Cassius Navarro designed the Redknot & Horseshoe Crab glyph that appears at the conclusion of several articles.

To contact SJCHC write:
SJCHC / School of Arts & Humanities
Stockton University
101 Vera King Farris Drive
Galloway, New Jersey
08205

Email:
Thomas.Kinsella@stockton.edu
Paul.Schopp@stockton.edu

About this Issue of *SoJourn*

It has been a busy time for the student-staffed local history press at the South Jersey Culture & History Center. Numerous titles have recently appeared under our imprint, with more on the way.

Since the start of 2021 we have republished Katharine Sabsovich's biography of her husband, *Adventures in Idealism: The Life of Professor H. L. Sabsovich Founder of Woodbine, New Jersey* (1922); Elizabeth B. Alton's *Beauty is Never Enough*, the memoir of the "mother of Stockton" who spent 40+ years associated with the Miss America Pageant in Atlantic City; William J. Lewis and Shane Tomalinas' *Adventure with Piney Joe: Exploring the New Jersey Pine Barrens Volumes I & II*, our first full-color young adult work focused on the plant life and culture of the Pine Barrens; Claude Epstein's masterful *No Wild Rivers in South Jersey: An Environmental Biography*, detailing the cultural adaptation and changes wrought on South Jersey's waterways; our second selection of Dallas Lore Sharp essays, *The Nature of Things*; Harriet S. Sander's *Sketches of Old Port Republic*, published for The Port Republic Heritage Society (you will have to approach them about copies); and finally my own volume in support of the fall 2021 exhibition *Growing American: The Alliance Agricultural Colony of South Jersey, A History*. Add one more to the list, our second edition of Bluma Bayuk Rappoport Purmell's *A Farmer's Daughter: Bluma*, forthcoming in November 2022—all published with significant student assistance—and you will see that we have been busy. So busy that Paul W. Schopp, the Advisory Board members of SJCHC, and I have made the difficult decision to stop publishing *SoJourn* on a twice-yearly schedule. Starting with the current issue we will make our best effort to publish this journal at least once a year. If time permits, we will publish more frequently, but we have taken ourselves off a stated schedule. We hope you will understand.

In your hands is our second Special Issue of *SoJourn*. In summer 2018 we published a thematic issue focused on the impact of the American Revolutionary War on South Jersey. That issue was approximately 50% larger than a standard issue. The current issue focuses on the Jersey Coast, including the Delaware Bay, Delaware River, and tributaries.

The issue opens with Bill Bolger's "Against All Odds: The Judge's Shack at Island Beach State Park"; Bill provides an engaging history of the Shack which has endured for long decades—improbably given its construction and placement near the tip of Island Beach Peninsula—and tells of a community coming together to save the locally iconic structure. Susan Allen, in a beautiful photographic essay, chronicles the interdependent relationship between red knots and horseshoe crabs along the beaches of the Delaware Bay. Norman Goos uncovers the meandering tracks of several attempts to bring "Rails to Brigantine"—these efforts involved large dreams and enormous spending, but little success. Kenneth W. Able and Paul W. Schopp describe the enduring impact of railroads crossing the salt marshes to the barrier islands of New Jersey, from Seaside Park to Wildwood.

John Lawrence shifts attention to the Delaware River and the intriguing history of the Red Dragon Canoe Club, the second oldest, continuously operating boat club in the United States. The club's longevity can be attributed to its willingness to plan and adapt through the years and to sustain a sense of camaraderie among its members. A companion piece of sorts is offered by Paul W. Schopp in his description of the Tammany Pea Shore Company. I had found a wonderful hand-colored lithograph from circa 1852 of the Fishing Company clubhouse (see pages 84–85) and had asked Paul for a brief caption to the piece. A few days later, the "caption" arrived in the form of a complete article, with wonderful supporting materials.

Loretta Thompson Harris preserves the compelling history of Tabernacle Baptist Church in Ocean City whose congregation to this day worships in the oldest church building in that oceanside resort. In "Scullers, Decoy Carvers, and River Rats on the Delaware River," Alice M. Smith describes the colorful watermen residing in twentieth-century Delanco, New Jersey. Zachary Baer revisits the horror of U-boat warfare off the coast of New Jersey in 1918 and provides chilling detail about the US government's control over speech at that time.

We close this issue with articles on life along two of South Jersey's rivers. Horace Somes Jr., with the assistance of Stephen Eichinger and Peter H. Stemmer, provides an expert description of railbirding along the Wading River and describes the environmental changes that have led to its cessation. Our last offering is the fourth installment of Joseph S. Reeves Jr.'s stories, first published in his *Maurice River Memories* (1993). Reeves chronicles his childhood experiences with his family on the Maurice River, describing a bygone era when rivermen could support a family utilizing the natural resources of river and shoreline meadowlands.

We hope you enjoy this issue. We have several articles lined up for its successor and will begin work on them soon. If you have articles to contribute, please contact either Paul Schopp or me.

Tom Kinsella

Director
South Jersey Culture & History Center
Stockton University

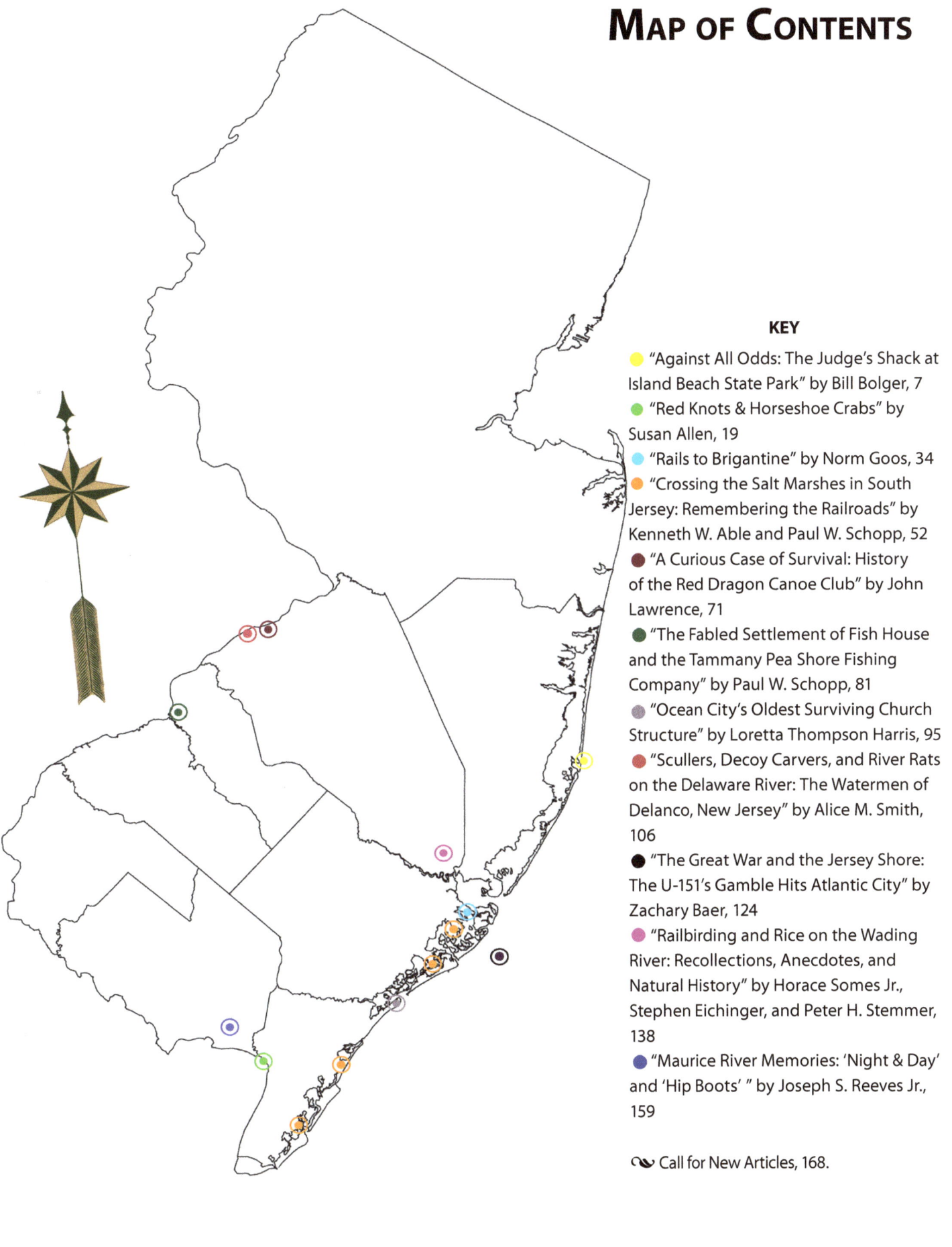

MAP OF CONTENTS

KEY

● "Against All Odds: The Judge's Shack at Island Beach State Park" by Bill Bolger, 7

● "Red Knots & Horseshoe Crabs" by Susan Allen, 19

● "Rails to Brigantine" by Norm Goos, 34

● "Crossing the Salt Marshes in South Jersey: Remembering the Railroads" by Kenneth W. Able and Paul W. Schopp, 52

● "A Curious Case of Survival: History of the Red Dragon Canoe Club" by John Lawrence, 71

● "The Fabled Settlement of Fish House and the Tammany Pea Shore Fishing Company" by Paul W. Schopp, 81

● "Ocean City's Oldest Surviving Church Structure" by Loretta Thompson Harris, 95

● "Scullers, Decoy Carvers, and River Rats on the Delaware River: The Watermen of Delanco, New Jersey" by Alice M. Smith, 106

● "The Great War and the Jersey Shore: The U-151's Gamble Hits Atlantic City" by Zachary Baer, 124

● "Railbirding and Rice on the Wading River: Recollections, Anecdotes, and Natural History" by Horace Somes Jr., Stephen Eichinger, and Peter H. Stemmer, 138

● "Maurice River Memories: 'Night & Day' and 'Hip Boots' " by Joseph S. Reeves Jr., 159

☙ Call for New Articles, 168.

A. M. Heston, *Illustrated Hand-Book of Atlantic City, New Jersey . . .* [Atlantic City, 1891]. Courtesy of the Library of Congress.

Against All Odds:
The Judge's Shack at Island Beach State Park

Bill Bolger

As a work of architecture, it is undistinguished. It will never be included in a survey of American architecture. And yet, by virtue of its history, its setting, its associations, and the people who have loved it over the past century, it has achieved a unique status in New Jersey's maritime culture. The ignominious little frame building known as "the Judge's Shack" (the Shack) has managed to survive severe nor'easters and hurricanes, impending development, and a bureaucratic death sentence to become an icon that resonates with our longings and dreams. The basic facts of its history are simple but the effects that it has had on people who know it, whether it is the fishermen who use it as a landmark or the families who it has sheltered, run deep and personal. There are many such accounts that could be recorded. This is just one.

1. Endurance

The care of the Shack is something that I've been involved in for over thirty years now, beginning in the late 1980s, when I offered to assist the Hartshorne family, who had owned it since 1942. One of the key points

Figure 1. The Shack on the front dune at Island Beach (full wide-angle panorama).

in the annual calendar was closing it up for the winter, which usually occurred in late October or November. In 2012, I planned a weekend gathering of a few friends to do some birding and botanizing, as well as the routine of winterizing. Late October can be one of the most splendid times of year at the Shack, if it is sunny and calm. Reports of a late-season hurricane in the Caribbean in the week prior to our visit were not a concern. Cooling coastal waters in the fall mean that such storms quickly lose their strength as they track along the warm waters of the Gulf Stream, which takes them well out to sea by the time they reach the middle latitudes. The Tuesday forecast confirmed the norm with the predictive models charting a path out to the east. Except for one. The European Model[1] seemed to be malfunctioning with its sharp left turn path that would bring it straight at the Jersey coast. How improbable.

By Thursday the European Model was universally accepted, but most shocking was the fact that the storm had regained hurricane force winds as it moved into the temperate zone and had become one of the largest storms on record with a spiral that spanned the coast from Florida to Nova Scotia. Our revised task for the weekend was to prepare the Shack for a direct hit from one of the most severe storms ever to visit the Jersey coast. Aside from making sure the winter shutters on the windows were tight, and bracing the small windows in the gable ends, and adding battens to the porch shutters, however, there was really nothing we could do to actually protect the frail wooden structure from what was headed its way. And so, our small gathering that Saturday night turned into a bit of an Irish Wake. We knew that this might finally be the end of the Shack after 60 years on the front dune overlooking the North Atlantic. By the time we departed Sunday afternoon, the sustained winds were already 30 knots. Superstorm Sandy was on its way.

Landfall occurred just after sunset Monday, October 29, near Atlantic City, about 35 miles to the south-southwest, which meant that the shore points north were subjected to the strongest winds and greatest storm surge. The full phase of the moon occurred around 3:00 p.m. the same day, adding to the tidal effect. From my home in Mount Holly, coverage of the storm after 9:00 p.m. was limited to a battery powered radio as much of the state's electrical grid suffered failure. The following morning in my office in Philadelphia, the news was even more grim than anyone had predicted, with images of the New York subway system flooding, power stations exploding, breaches in the barrier islands, and most haunting of all, the image of the wrecked rollercoaster at Seaside Heights, just nine miles north of the Shack, sitting out in the surf. Over the course of the next day, Shack followers exchanged their solemn memorials assuming that it was wrecked, if not missing in action altogether. The Island Beach State Park staff was reeling at the devastation they faced and could not be reached. The Park was closed indefinitely, along with the other barrier islands, and under strict police surveillance; getting confirmation on the fate of the Shack was out of the question. And then, sometime Wednesday or Thursday, a friend sent me an email with a United States Coast Guard aerial photograph. The Shack had survived! The 70 feet of healthy sand dune that had stood between it and the beach was gone. The eastern corner of the structure hung over the beach and the cinderblock pier that supported that corner was perilously close to collapsing. The clear evidence of the storm waters showed that at the height of the storm the Shack had been surrounded by the surf. There is little doubt that if the storm had lingered on the coast another few minutes, it would have destroyed the little building, possibly taking it out to sea. Remarkably, the only damage was to the 40-year-old asphalt rolled roof on the ocean side. Otherwise, there wasn't a shingle missing.

In January 2013, the Park was finally ready to have a volunteer workday and hundreds of people turned out to help. The Friends of the Judges Shack, a newly formed group who were working to preserve the building, fielded a crew to install a temporary roof to provide critical protection until a permanent roof could be completed the following summer. The most gratifying experience that day was having several people volunteer to haul fence posts and other materials into the site. We discovered that the Shack had many admirers who were overjoyed to find that it had survived the storm and were delighted to lend a hand. Enduring Sandy proved to be a major turning point. But first I need to explain the Shack's backstory.

2. "The Strenuous Life"

When the Shack was constructed in 1909, it stood five miles north of where it now stands, just one mile in from today's Park entrance, and some 100 yards back from the beach. It was well protected by the primary and secondary dunes but lacked the dramatic views of the ocean and the bay that it would later command. It was characteristic of simple sportsmen fishing shacks with a 12 x 16-foot main room, an eight-foot bedroom shed off to the north side and an eight-foot screened porch on the south. At that time, many of the fishing shack owners were squatting on one of the remaining undeveloped stretches of barrier island in New Jersey. This once common practice along the shore involved sportsmen building simple structures where they could come to duck hunt, fish, crab, and enjoy the wilds of the coast. As that practice gave way to resort developments with streets and avenues laid out for hotels, houses, and commercial facilities, the shacks and shanties disappeared along with the coastal forest and dunes, swept aside by "progress." The ten-mile-stretch of Island Beach remained undeveloped, lacking easy access to rail transportation but that would soon change with the advent of the automobile.

Henry Phipps Jr., former partner of Andrew Carnegie and real estate developer, purchased the entire undeveloped ten miles of Island Beach in 1926 with plans to create a luxury resort town. While gearing up for construction, his development company offered the owners of the fishing shacks an opportunity to legalize their interests as leaseholders, an arrangement that was expected to be temporary. But development plans ran afoul of the Great Depression and the shacks and shanties of Island Beach received a reprieve.[2] This was the situation that 54-year-old Judge Richard Hartshorne encountered in 1942 when he and his wife Ellen decided to purchase the structure that would come to be known as the Judge's Shack.

At that time, Richard, a graduate of Princeton and Columbia University School of Law, was a judge in the Court of Common Pleas in Essex County, New Jersey. His family had a long association with the coast, stretching back to his ancestor, Richard Hartshorne, one of the first European settlers at Sandy Hook and the Atlantic Highlands in the seventeenth century. The family remained in that area through the eighteenth century, and after moving to Newark, would vacation at the shore where the judge spent his summers as a youth. The judge's wife, Ellen Fritz Sahlin (born 1895), was the daughter of a prominent Swedish engineer and the granddaughter of a Pennsylvania steel manufacturer.[3] Richard and Ellen were not people who needed to "rough it"; it was a lifestyle choice based in the belief that a virtuous life needed to engage the natural world with a minimum of civilized comforts, at least in one's leisure time. Theodore Roosevelt had been the embodiment of this principle and its greatest advocate. At the turn of the twentieth century, his speech "The Strenuous Life," which became an American classic, began with this declaration:

> I wish to preach, not the doctrine of ignoble ease, but the doctrine of the strenuous life, the life of toil and effort, of labor and strife; to preach that highest form of success which comes, not to the man who desires mere easy peace, but to the man who does not shrink from danger, from hardship, or from bitter toil, and who out of these wins the splendid ultimate triumph.[4]

Roosevelt's generation of leaders believed that their ancestors, who settled this country, had led lives of hardship and endurance that had built strong character, but that their descendants were becoming soft with the advances of civilization. Central heating, railroads, indoor plumbing, electricity, the telephone, and numerous other advances that gave the nation pride at the same time conspired to make people soft and dependent. The proper antidote was to engage in vigorous spartan endeavors. Rustic accommodations like the Shack offered the perfect opportunity to engage the natural elements with a minimal amount of civilized trappings. The structure was basic shelter, only 450 square feet, little more than a tent that could snugly accommodate their family of six. The conveniences, such as they were, consistent of a hand pump for water, a stove, kerosene lamps, and an outhouse. The objective was to have a place to swim, sail, fish, crab, and enjoy being outdoors, cooking dinner over an open fire and enjoying the sun and moon and stars.

The Hartshornes had four children, including Penelope (Penny), who would play a major role in the Shack's future, and John, who would eventually become the long-time leaseholder. According to Penny, Ellen Hartshorne was a trained interior decorator who made modest improvements to the interior to transform it from a man's fishing shack into something a bit more appealing. The main room had wallboards installed and painted, the bedroom walls were painted, and a patriotic color scheme of red, white, and blue was applied to the doors and window sash. Kitchen cabinets were installed along with basic furniture like the dining table and six ladder-back caned chairs. It remained a stoically simple accommodation, however, and in its location down low behind the dunes it could be especially uncomfortable on a hot summer day.[5]

Following the Second World War, a movement was launched to preserve the Phipps tract. By then, there was a growing awareness of the important role the east coast barrier island ecosystem played and that protecting Island Beach was New Jersey's last best hope to maintain a major portion of that environment. Rachael Carson, who had just published her noted work, *The Sea Around Us*, took an interest in the conservation of Island Beach and visited briefly in 1950. In writing to Richard Pough, the leading advocate for the resource, she noted, "The saving of some such place before it is forever too late is, of course, a subject very close to my heart."[6] There was a proposal to have it become a unit of the National Park Service and then eventually the case was made for it to become a New Jersey state park. Realizing the changes that were about to occur, Judge Hartshorne decided to relocate the Shack to its current location five miles farther south and on top of the primary dune overlooking the Atlantic. He retained a house moving company, who cut a drive to provide access for the move, and at the end of June 1952, the Shack, with some complications, was removed to its new location with Ellen Hartshorne sitting on the porch holding her cat.

There is no record of the Judge's decision to choose the site he did. The ocean view and breezes would have certainly provided the appeal. The obvious vulnerability of the location has always made me wonder, however, if he would be surprised to find that it still remains after 70 years. It was, after all, dismissive of the Evangelist Matthew's passage about ". . . the foolish man who built his house on the sand: and the rain descended, the floods came, and the winds blew and beat on that house; and it fell. And great was its fall" (7:24–29). One curious aspect of its siting is that rather than aligning with the north-south direction of the beach, it sits on a northeast-southwest alignment. The Judge was a sailor, and he certainly was very aware of the winds and their capacity. By placing it in this position, he exposed the smallest elevation to the strongest wind direction. It is the aptly named nor'easter storms that do the most damage on the Jersey coast. If the full 28-foot length of the building with its fourteen-foot-high peak and four windows had faced due east, the weather beatings to which it was subject would have been much worse. The Shack's bold stance on the edge of the North Atlantic is a statement of grandeur, defiance, and vulnerability all at the same time. It is an image that makes this otherwise negligible building a photographic icon.

3. Penny and George

At the time of the Shack's relocation, Penny Hartshorne was completing her degree in architecture at the Illinois Institute of Technology, which architecture program was then under the direction of the famous German modernist, Ludwig Mies van der Rohe. Perhaps she hoped to practice architecture and join a modern design firm, although as a woman at that time, it would have been difficult if not impossible to find a position in what was virtually an exclusively male profession. Fortunately for the field of historic preservation, she decided to take a very different turn. Her mother had maintained close ties with her father's Swedish homeland and Penny had grown up visiting her relatives there and identifying as closely with her Scandinavian heritage as with her Anglo-American side. A close relative, Gerda Boëthius, was a prominent art historian and the director of the Zorn Museum in Mora, Sweden, where she promoted the study of folk art and folkways. Penny spent two years working under Boëthius, studying Swedish folk culture, measuring and drawing the country's vernacular architecture, and documenting the people and crafts in film. When she returned to the United States, she found that her combined skills as architect and historian would serve her well at the newly established Independence National Park in Philadelphia, where the nation's premier restoration project was getting underway at Independence Hall. Penny would spend the next four decades working on that and many other historic architecture projects for the National Park Service and, in the process, become one of the leaders in her field.[7] This proved to be one of the great lucky breaks for the Shack as she was within weekend driving distance and would continue providing expert care for the vulnerable building long after her parents were no longer able to do so.

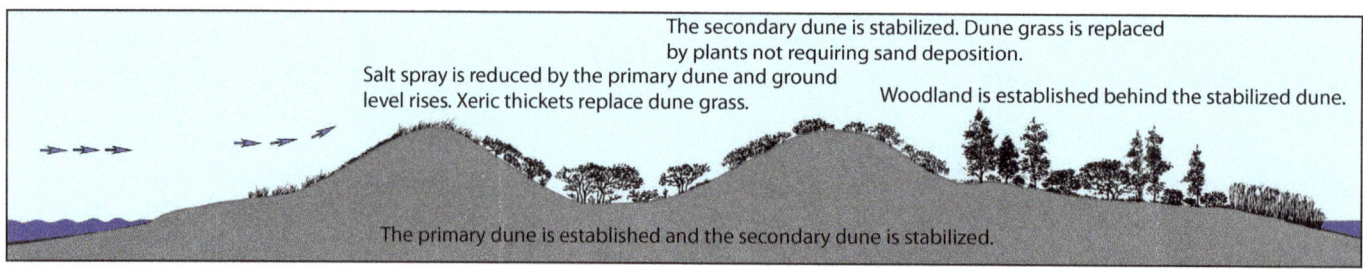

Figure 2. Cross section of the island. Based on a diagram in Ian McHarg's *Design With Nature*.[14]

Figure 3. Panorama from the porch.

In her profession, Penny was noted for her interest in and advocacy for maintenance of buildings, which is often the least valued and frequently neglected aspect of architectural practice. Routine maintenance work can preserve a structure rather than restore or rebuild it. In this respect, she was as much a curator as an architect and the approach would come to serve the Shack very well over the ensuing half century.

In 1968, Penny married architect George Batcheler, a graduate of the University of Pennsylvania's school of architecture and a partner in the firm of Mirick, Pearson, and Batcheler. They met while working to restore houses on historic Elfreths Alley, where George lived, and then purchased a house on South American Street, which they restored. George's professional work with his firm dealt exclusively with modern construction, but he clearly enjoyed dealing with historic structures. There were other friends and colleagues who joined Penny and George at the Shack and helped with the work, especially architects and building contractors, so the Shack benefited by an abundance of top talent. As a result of these efforts, the Judge's Shack survived on the front dune and became something of a legend among those who saw it and marveled at its tenacity.

Buildings that stand next to oceans command our admiration as symbols of strength and endurance. Lighthouses everywhere certainly have this command, as well as fortifications. But those are structures designed to stand against the elements. The Shack's power lies in its frailty. The surprise is that it survives at all. In the early 1980s, photographer Gene Ahern captured an image of the Shack that conveyed all of this. I think of this as the shot seen round the world. It was sold to a photo archive and used by several publications. It served as the cover of the L.L. Bean catalogue for their summer 1984 issue, although the image is horizontally flipped. You can view the catalog cover online.[8] It also appeared on map and atlas covers, but my favorite sighting was by a member of the Hartshorne family who saw it on a calendar at a gas station in Hawaii with the simple caption, "New Jersey."

My first experience at the Shack occurred in the summer of 1983, when I was invited to visit Penny and George and a small group of their friends. My memory of that first brief visit is how stunned I was at finding such a perfect retreat. The approach on foot, which is only 500 feet along a sand trail and takes five minutes, is a dramatic journey. From the private drive, I followed the foot path, first through the shelter of the dense island forest, over a tertiary dune and down through an open field of beach heather, and then, cresting the secondary dune, gaining the first sight of the Shack some 60 yards away, where it sits in solitude on the primary dune, silhouetted against the sea. It seems to me that we spent most of that afternoon sitting outside. (There must have been a sea breeze that day that kept the bugs at bay!) But the most amazing feature was the porch with its distinctive shutters hinged from the top and propped up with sticks to reveal a 270-degree view from the ocean to the east, down island to the Barnegat Light, around to Barnegat Bay, and the mainland to the west, and up-island to Seaside Heights. Over the next five years, I probably spent one weekend a summer there with colleagues and friends. One of the most notable things about Penny is how generous she was in sharing the place and how much joy it seemed to give her to have others enjoy its special qualities.

In the fall of 1989, following a particularly stressful time at work, I asked Penny if I could stay at the Shack for a week. It proved to be a splendid stretch of high fall weather: clear, sunny, breezy, with warm days and cool nights, and perfect ocean water temperatures. A single day there equals at least five or six days anywhere else in my experience. Decompression and relaxation seem to advance at lightning speed. And so, the week seemed like a month. And over the course of that week, I observed many things I had not seen before. The beach goldenrod, one of the few plants that grow on the primary dune along with the dune grass, was in full bloom and it serves as an important fueling stop for the monarch butterflies as they congregate and prepare for their journey to Mexico. There are always a few passing by in the fall, but if you are lucky and you are there on the right days, there might be hundreds in view at one time. There were also the resident foxes on their daily dune patrols. These are the island's "charismatic megafauna" who emerge generally in the evening searching for food. And there was the sun and the moon, the same sun and moon I had known my entire life, of course, but I experienced them as I had never experienced them before. With nothing to obscure their passage from horizon to horizon the order of their movements was fully revealed. The moon was in its fullest phase and so would follow the sun each day, rising over the ocean at dusk as the sun set in the west, arcing across the full sky and setting over the bay at dawn. The sun's progress would start with the filtered cool light of dawn through the ocean mist and, as it ascended, transform the island with its blazing power until late in the afternoon when it cooled and sank into an evening sunset. Some days the atmosphere dimmed the setting sun so that it appeared visually equal to the moon rising above the opposite horizon at the same time. This all reminded me of an orrery with its clockwork motions. This was the original full-scale orrery, all 93 million miles of it. And of course, what I was observing was not the rising and setting of the sun and moon at all, but the view from the spinning Earth.

I also came to understand that week just how dynamic the primary dunes are and how the immediate environment of the shack was quickly changing. The dune to the east of the structure was topping out at a height level with the roof. The northeast winds excavated the face of the dune on the ocean side, so that it looked a bit like an apple after someone had taken several bites out of it. The excavated sand was blowing over the top of the dune and dropping on the back side where it began to bury the Shack. The easternmost corner of the Shack at the ocean side bedroom had sand piled up to the window level and, while the surface of a dune is dry, the conditions a foot or more below the surface are always damp. On the inside of the frame structure, damage was beginning to occur with the spread of wood fungus. Penny and George knew about the problem, but they had too many other obligations to attend to it. Now in their sixties and still working full time, they also had inherited a family farm west of Philadelphia that needed heroic levels of work. They told me that they were thinking that perhaps it was time to let nature take its course. My involvement in the Shack and its survival was about to get a lot more serious.

4. Saving The Shack

My proposal to Penny and George was that rather than letting nature takes its course, I would excavate the Shack in exchange for being allowed to spend as much time there as the job required. They agreed and work began in earnest the following spring. The ensuing five years proved quite challenging. Not only was the huge dune migrating onto the top of the building, but the roof was failing, and the cedar shingles after forty years of sandblasting winds were paper thin. Then, unusually heavy storms began to hit. Others, fortunately, were willing to step up and help. Ted Nickels, an experienced restoration contractor who had worked with Penny and

Figure 4. Orrery with author reflected in the glass.

Against All Odds

Figure 5. The view from the east bedroom.

had been a guest at the Shack, offered to address the roof issues, which were at least as critical as the sand issues. Penny and George took renewed interest in the work, especially in the spring and fall, when they joined me in doing repairs.

It was during these work weekends with Penny and George that I developed a deep affection for them personally and also came to learn their very particular approach to Shack maintenance. Penny, as already noted, was an accomplished restoration architect, and George was an architect who created modern, state-of-the-art buildings, but they had a whole distinct practice that they both shared when it came to the Shack. The first rule was to repair rather than replace, but when replacement was necessary, use only available driftwood or other things lying about. It was, as they were quick to point out when I offered to run into town and buy some lumber for our repairs, "just a shack," which spoke both to a sense of economy but also the appropriate character that should be maintained with such structures. George would scavenge the beach on his morning walks and bring back planks of wood and bits of driftwood that could be used for the repairs.

At the end of October 1991, a cyclone developed off the coast of the northeastern U.S. that became known as the Halloween Gale or "the unnamed hurricane" with winds of up to 75 miles per hour. It remained off the coast for three or four days. It eventually became known as The Perfect Storm, a term a meteorologist coined and then Sebastian Junger used it in his riveting account of events that occurred in the course of the disturbance.[9] The center of the storm did not cross the Jersey coast, but by staying off the coast for multiple days, it did considerable damage. At the Shack, it removed the top of the dune, which had been threatening the Shack and brought about a sudden reversal of fortune. Not only was the Shack fully exposed to the power of northeast winds, but the beach that had separated it from the surf was almost gone. At times in the winter, the beach was so diminished that vehicles could not access it. There was at least one other severe storm, perhaps two, within the next year or so that continued to damage the primary dunes and erode the beach. A small shed attached on the north wall, which was perhaps five by five feet, had taken the worst of the fungal attack, and it finally succumbed to one of the storms. With so much else requiring our attention, we all decided to not rebuild it but focus our efforts on the main structure. Protection efforts suddenly shifted from excavation to dune building. This called for the installation of hundreds of feet of snow fencing over the next two decades in order to stabilize and rebuild the dune on the ocean side of the Shack. One season, after installing about 400 feet of fence to the north and northeast, another major nor'easter hit the coast. The fences are at their most vulnerable when they are newly installed because its full elevation is exposed. I returned the next day to assess the damage and cresting the secondary dune, I could see the area where the fence had been, but now there was nothing but a smooth windswept dune. On closer inspection, however, the fence had survived; it was fully buried. In one single storm, the fence had captured five feet of sand.

It was also during these storms in the early nineties that the schooner A. G. ROPES reemerged at the foot of the primary dune within view of the Shack. The hull's heavy timbers, including the keel and several ribs, had been buried in the beach following its destruction. It was Bill Vibbert, the park's superintendent at the time, who told me the name of the vessel. Bill was a superb guardian of the park who impressed me for his extensive knowledge and enthusiasm for its history. Several years later, when Gordon Hesse published his book about Island Beach, I learned the full story of the Ropes. She was a three-masted, 258-foot-long schooner built in Bath, Maine, in 1884 that had once circumnavigated the world and set speed records for the New York to San Francisco run in the days before the Panama Canal, when sailing around Cape Horn was one of the ultimate tests of ships and sailors. She suffered de-masting in a typhoon off the coast of Japan and ended her days in humiliating service as a coal barge. On December 26, 1913, while being towed off the coast of New Jersey on its way to Rhode Island with another barge, she encountered her final gale. She slipped her hawser and was destroyed as she struck the beach. She was a total loss, and crew faced the same fate.[10] What seemed to me at one time a mere curiosity of timbers and spikes, has become a memorial to a great ship, to her fate, and to the lives lost on her final day at sea.

During the mid-nineties, work efforts intensified when it became clear that the Shack was long overdue for a re-shingling. The original cedar shake siding had withstood forty years of life on the front dune where it was subject to driving winds and rains complete with copious amounts of sand that effectively sandblasted the wood away. The lower six-inch exposure of the 18-inch shakes was entirely gone and the middle six inches reduced to a paper-thin dimension. Even more alarming was the fact that the nails securing the underlying one-inch sheathing boards to the frame were badly corroded and many had completely failed, so that once the remains of the shakes were removed the sheathing simply fell off.

The days devoted to the re-shingling effort over three years provided a greater opportunity to learn about the life on the primary dunes and nearby. The makeshift scaffolding, cobbled together from old fence posts and driftwood planks, provided access to the upper levels of the structure, which proved a perfect vantage point for viewing the bird life from the bay out to the beach and beyond. Three major easily observable domains existed there. The passerines (perching songbirds mainly) ruled the island forest and the primary dune. The pelagic birds dominate the open water with some never coming ashore except to nest. And in-between, working mostly the tidal zone of the beach, were the sandpipers. Some of the pelagic birds could be seen far out to sea in huge flocks while other more solitary species could be seen in the surf. My favorite seagoers were the loons and the cormorants. A surprise species was the brown pelican, a bird whose historic range did not extend north of Virginia. When I spotted the first one with its unmistakable

Figure 6. Gulls on the Roof. Felix Heidgen September 2011.

form cruising the coast, I dropped my hammer. But this was only the first of several. The passerines allowed much closer observation. Some barn swallows even had the temerity to build nests inside the porch early in the season so close to me that I could see their expressions. Everything about the swallows was irresistibly appealing: their sleek form, their rich color, their alert intensity, and their tireless devotion to their young. Even birds familiar to me took on new attributes, like the mourning doves who cruise the dunes in strong winds looking more like raptors than their normal sedentary selves. Then there were the gulls, the group comfortable at sea, in the tidal zone, and the dunes. They were undaunted by my presence and would often congregate on the ridge of the roof. There are over 250 species of birds present along this ten-mile barrier island and I'm like an illiterate man thumbing through books in a library missing most of what is there but being awed by it all.

The famous mammalian of the island is the red fox. There has always been a den close to the Shack and denizens of those dens were not shy. One would often appear in the evening when shingling resumed following the hottest afternoon hours and they would watch me, perhaps hoping for a bite to eat but, sometimes seeming to be curious as to what was happening. They were sometimes within ten feet, so I could see their expressions. They are, for anyone who hasn't observed them, as emotive as any domestic cat or dog. But these are wild animals who make their way by their wits year-round in an environment that is limited in its food sources and extremely harsh in the winter. I came to realize just how brutal their lives, and deaths, can be when we were removing junk stored beneath the Shack. The body of a fox was discovered curled inside a rusted propane cylinder. It was perfectly preserved, mummified by the dry sand. Several years later when a friend offered to articulate the skeleton, he found upon close examination that this female fox had lost its front right leg below the knee as well as the last few inches of her tail. His theory is that she lost her leg and perhaps the tail due to mange, which is horribly painful and can cause an animal to actually amputate its own leg. Whatever the cause, her reason for retreating beneath the Shack to spend her last hours was to avoid infecting her family in the den. And so, she spent her last moments alone, in terrible pain, inside a discarded tank.

5. The Shack's Darkest Hour and Its New Dawn

With the arrival of the new millennium, the Hartshorne family and the other supporters began to

Figure 7. K.K. the fox, who was found beneath the Shack where she took shelter and died.

seriously discuss the formation of an organization that could assume management of the Judge's Shack and pursue an agreement with the Park that would allow it to remain. The lease agreement, which all the shack owners had signed with the state in the early 1950s, required that the structures be removed following the termination of the lease with the provision that the leases could not be transferred to another party. There were over 70 such leases initially and 90 percent of them had run their course by 2000 and the dwellings had been demolished.[11] Securing a post-lease future for the Shack would require a policy exception by the state and while this posed a formidable challenge, superintendent Bill Vibbert had long supported such an action. In a letter to John Hartshorne, Penny's brother, who held the lease, Vibbert expressed his views. "I believe that the leases are an important part of the history of Island Beach and your lease is without question the most representative structure left. In my opinion, it is a landmark at Island Beach and should remain as part of our cultural history."[12] Vibbert's support was crucial and so it was a crushing development when his tenure as superintendent ended in 2002. His successor expressed indifference to the issue, a "short-termer" who held no interest in challenging the rules. Soon, park administration stated that no one was allowed to use the lease without one of the Hartshornes being present. With Penny and George spending most of their summer in New Hampshire by that time, and John Hartshorne living in Massachusetts, they were allowed to appoint one person as a caretaker to look after the property in their absence. So, for the first time in its existence, the Shack was devoid of its regular summer visitors and remained shuttered.

In the midst of that dark decade, Penny made one last and important contribution to her family's legacy by researching and writing a 78-page historic structures report (HSR). Penny had pioneered HSRs for the National Park Service for fifty years, including the report for Independence Hall and its restoration, a project in which she had direct involvement. So the Judge's Shack received the full documentary treatment from one of the leading experts. Drawing from her own 65-year involvement and other family records, she produced a history, measured drawings, a detailed account of changes and work, as well as a set of management alternatives intended to give the Park and the state officials a basis to recognize its importance, justify its preservation, and options as to how it could be preserved. The report was submitted to the Park in March 2006. The Hartshornes were not even given the courtesy of a response or a thank you by the superintendent or any other staff.

Then, in March of 2007, Penny Hartshorne Batcheler suddenly died. George was unable to continue making the trip. John Hartshorne no longer wished to maintain the lease, especially with insurance and property taxes soaring. The nascent friends organization assumed those costs and continued to seek a transition agreement with the state, but to no avail and with virtually no access, the situation was untenable.

In late summer 2011, Hurricane Irene arrived. It seemed like it might be the final blow, but the storm did only minor damage to the Jersey coast. Then, in September, while I was working on repairs to the porch, a vigorous, pleasant young man approached with a park employee. He was casually dressed in loafers, shorts, and a knit shirt and when he got close, I could see that the shirt had a NJ State Parks insignia. It was Ray Butowski, the recently appointed park superintendent. Everything about him told me that I might have a chance to pitch the case for preserving the Shack. He cut me off before a had a chance to begin, however, and proclaimed all the reasons that he had to see it remain as a feature of the Park. Ray had grown up in the area, had known the Shack for his entire life, and when he operated a chartered fishing boat, he told me of one couple who hired him to bring them just offshore of the Shack so they could get married in view of their favorite place. Ray was well aware of the legendary appeal of the Judge's Shack and needed no convincing of the case for preserving it. It is reasonable to believe that a large bureaucracy, ensconced as it is in laws, regulations, hierarchy, and traditions, would leave little latitude for individuals to make a difference, but that is wrong. People like Bill Vibbert and Ray Butowski, who have the capacity to observe and care and act accordingly, can make a great difference.

Of course, the challenge a year later of surviving Superstorm Sandy, one of the worst storms ever to hit the coast, turned out well and revealed just how many people really loved the place. The Friends of the Judge's Shack soon formally organized as a non-profit corporation under the leadership of Hector Griswold, a business owner whose experiences at the Shack dated back to his childhood visits there with the Judge. Ted Nickles and his partner Jack Abgott continued providing their building conservation expertise and hard work. The organization has grown and now includes Gordon Hesse, the author of the definitive account of the history and culture of Island Beach; Bill Cahill, an educator and expert naturalist; Michael Mills, one of the region's leading restoration architects; Mike Gersie, an engineer and building management professional; Allen Crawford, an award-winning graphic artist; Steve Maybury of the New Jersey Department of Environmental Protection and his daughter who manages the website; Bianca Charbonneau, an expert in dune management and conservation; and Debbie Douglass of the National Park Service. In 2017, John Hartshorne transferred the Shack's ownership to the state with the expectation that the FoJSA would continue to manage the property. Soon after, an agreement was signed recognizing the organization as an Officially Recognized Friends Organization (ORFO) for purposes of working with the state to manage the Judges Shack. Also, in 2017 the organization began working with the Park naturalist, Kelly Scott, to provide speakers at the weekly summer After Dark programs, where groups gather for a bonfire on the beach near the Shack. Work on the Shack increased once we had the official sanction to proceed and, by the end of 2021, the maintenance backlog had been nearly eliminated. The building now has a new roof, new porch screens, a new kitchen pump, interior painting, floor repairs, and reconstructed cinderblock piers. It is in better shape now than it has been since I first visited it nearly 40 years ago. None of this would have occurred without the understanding and support of Ray Bukowski and his successor, Jennifer Clayton. Individuals make a difference, and people working together can accomplish great things.

Of course, the Shack continues to lead a precarious existence out on the front dune of Island Beach. Not only is the sea level rising, but the Jersey shore is sinking due to the on-going isostatic rebounding of the continent in what is still the aftermath of the last ice age. (While the interior of northern North America continues to rise, a fulcrum effect causes the coast to sink.) As a result, sea levels over the next century along the Jersey coast may rise as much as three feet. The front dune currently has successfully recovered since Sandy but, as that and other storms have demonstrated, the Shack is imminently vulnerable. We hope to move it back to the secondary dune, which in time will become the primary dune. The beauty of the barrier islands is that they are designed to recede westwards with the rising ocean levels. They have been moving for a very long time and have covered a great distance. At the end of the last ice age the ocean's surface was 400 feet lower and the surf was some seventy or eighty miles east of its current position. The Shack's century-long saga is just a blink of the eye in the island's history, but then so are we all.

> "For a moment of night we have a glimpse of ourselves and of our world islanded in its stream of stars—pilgrims of mortality, voyaging between horizons across the eternal seas of space and time." Henry Beston[13]

Figure 8. The Shack at night with the Milky Way. Courtesy of Natalie Gregorio.

Endnotes

1. The European Model was developed and is operated by the European Center for Medium Range Weather Forecasts (ECMWF).
2. Gordon Hesse, *Island Beach* (Bay Head, NJ: Jersey Shore Publications, 2017), 68–76.
3. Penelope Hartshorne Batcheler, "The Judge's Shack at Island Beach State Park" (unpublished 2006 manuscript on file with Island Beach State Park and the New Jersey State Historic Preservation Office in Trenton as well as online at The Friends of the Judge's Shack website), 25–31.
4. Theodore Roosevelt, *The Works of Theodore Roosevelt Volume 12 The Strenuous Life* (New York: P. F. Collier & Son, 1900), 3. Available on Project Gutenberg, https://www.gutenberg.org/files/58821/58821-h/58821-h.htm (accessed July 25, 2022).
5. Batcheler, "The Judge's Shack," details of the Hartshornes' life at the shack from 1942 on are found in the narrative section of the report, 11–24.
6. Linda Lear, *Rachel Carson: Witness for Nature* (New York: Henry Holt & Company 1997), chapter 8.
7. "An interview with Penelope Hartshorne Batcheler," *CRM Journal* (Summer 2005).
8. https://picclick.com/LL-Bean-Summer-1984-Catalog-263140129392.html
9. Sebastian Junger, *The Perfect Storm: A True Story of Men Against the Sea* (New York: W. W. Norton & Co, 1997).
10. Hesse, *Island Beach*, 128–31
11. Batcheler, *Island Beach*, 6, from letter to John F. Hartshorne, October 2, 1991.
12. Batcheler, "The Judge's Shack."
13. Henry Beston, *The Outermost House* (Garden City, NY: Doubleday and Doran, 1928), 3.
14. Ian McHarg, *Design with Nature* (New York City, NY: Natural History Press, 1969), 8.

No Wild Rivers in South Jersey: An Evironmental Biography

By Claude Epstein

Epstein's work, the culmination of a long career as professor of environmental studies at Stockton University, describes the impact that cultural adaption has wrought upon South Jersey's numerous waterways. *No Wild Rivers* describes the impact of indigenous peoples as well as the successive waves of European arrivals on the waterways they encountered.

453 pages, illustrated, hardcover.

ISBN: 978-1-947889-07-1. $24.95

Available from Second Time Books, the Stockton University Bookstore and Amazon.com

Red Knots & Horseshoe Crabs

Susan Allen

The busiest Jersey Shore buffet opens following full and new moon high tides in the spring. The menu is limited to what looks like cotton candy-flavored Dip'n'Dots spilled onto the sand, but in reality those multicolored dots are horseshoe crab eggs packed with enough protein to fuel shorebirds on the second leg of their migration to the Arctic.

Watching the hollow-shelled horseshoe crabs crawling ashore to spawn is as close as one can get to seeing dinosaurs. In fact, these crabs are older than dinosaurs and have earned the name living fossils.

Spawning Crabs and Feasting birds.

Sunset on Delaware Bay. In the spring, the Delaware Bay beaches transform after sunset into a sight not far from a prehistoric scene.

Storm Photo. When the shallow waters of the Delaware Bay warm up to around 60 degrees, horseshoe crabs that have been wintering on the continental shelf know that it is time to crawl ashore to spawn. They prefer the high tides of new and full moons, when the high tides are the highest, to bury their eggs in moist sand that won't get too saturated.

Hungry Bird Searching. Just as the crabs are spawning, Red knots and other shorebirds species that are migrating north to their Arctic breeding grounds arrive along the Delaware Bay beaches. They are exhausted and underweight. They refuel for the second leg of their migration by pecking the protein-rich horseshoe crab eggs out of the sand. The pit stop lasts for about a month.

Red Knots & Horseshoe Crabs

Red Knots and Other Shorebirds. The beaches are packed in May and June. However, the dwindling numbers of Red knots are startling to conservationists who survey the population through aerial counts and banding.

(Following two pages) Horseshoe Crab Eggs. The multicolored eggs become translucent as they age and just before they are ready to hatch, the crab embryo is visible. They hatch looking like a miniature version of the adult crab minus the telson, which they will gain after they begin molting.

Banded Ruddy Turnstone. A Ruddy turnstone takes off after being banded and assessed by a scientist. Shorebirds are weighed and banded, and blood and feather samples are collected. This data gives researchers a better picture of their survival and migration. Photographers and bird watchers who see a banded bird can help fill in details of the story by reporting their sightings at www.bandedbirds.org.

(Opposite page) Tagged Crab. The horseshoe crab's story is also monitored by scientists through tagging and survey efforts. The circular tag on the crab has contact information for observers to report their sightings.

Tracks. At low tide, the mass of spawning crabs has mostly disappeared, but tracks in the sand are clear evidence of their journey out and back into the bay. Crabs that don't make it back into the water, bury themselves in the sand to stay moist and protect themselves from the sun and predators.

Red Knots & Horseshoe Crabs

Wave of Eggs. Near the end of the spawning season, water close to the coastline can be thick with blue-green eggs washing in and out with the tide.

Eggs Wash Ashore. The green wrack line is full of horseshoe crab eggs.

Feeding on Eggs. A shorebird feeds on a cluster of horseshoe crab eggs as thousands of birds surrounding it do the same.

Red Knots & Horseshoe Crabs

Death Spiral. The circular pattern surrounding an overturned crab was drawn by its telson (tail) as it struggled continuously to right itself. The birds have taken flight.

(Opposite page) Knots. A flock of Red knots frantically takes flight as a Peregrine falcon, just out of frame, stoops from the sky.

Susan Allen, who works in University Relations and Marketing at Stockton University and is a local photographer, spends the month of May on the Delaware Bay to document the Red Knot Horseshoe Crab phenomenon.

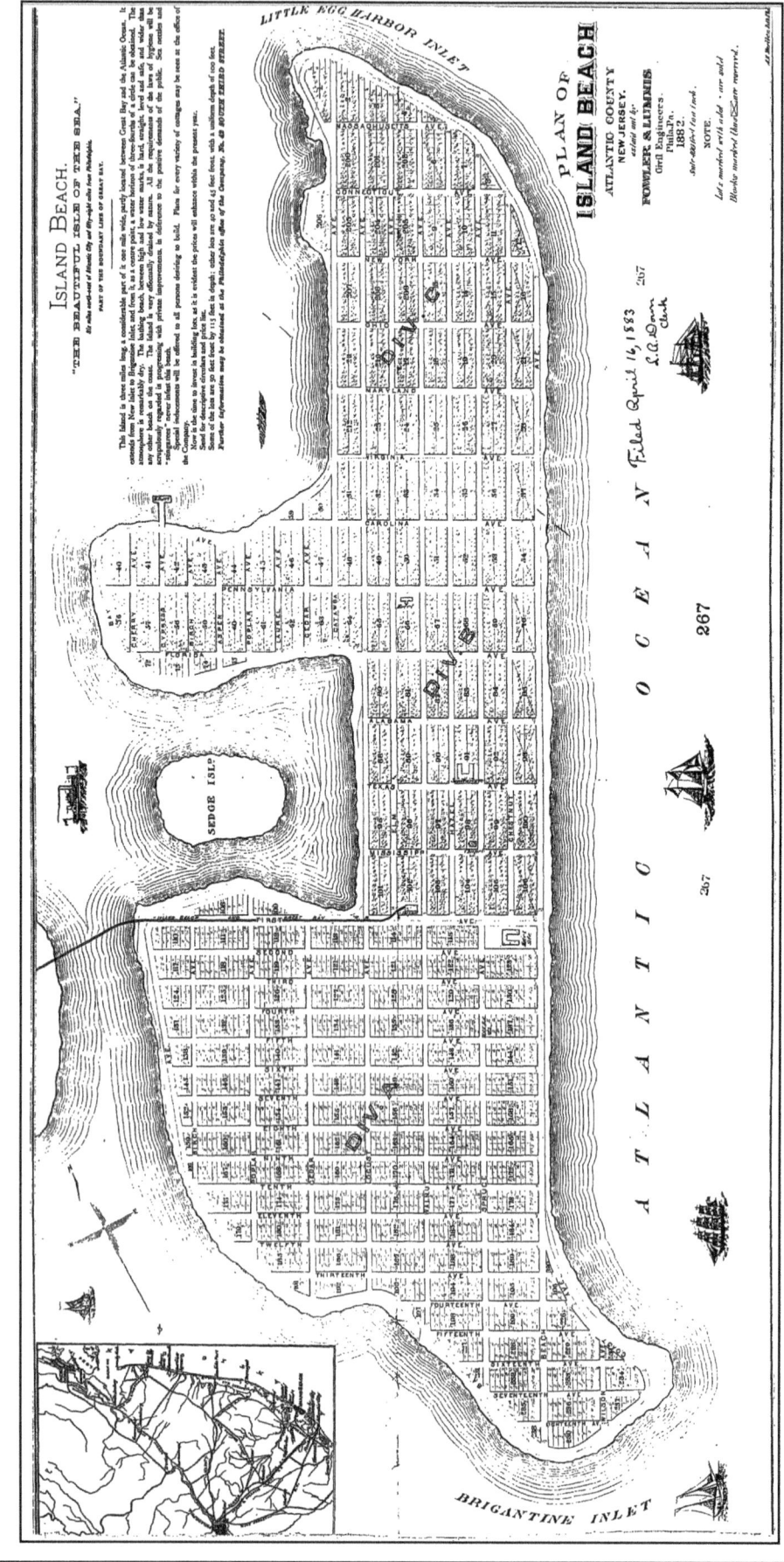

Figure 1. *Plan of Island Beach, Atlantic County New Jersey* (Fowler & Lummis, 1882). Marketing map for Brigantine Island, 1881. Courtesy of the Atlantic County Historical Society.

Rails to Brigantine

Norman Goos

Railroads Came First

Once upon a time ... it all began with an exciting idea to build a railroad and trolley line in Brigantine and a railroad bridge over the Absecon Inlet to connect with the Camden & Atlantic Railroad line (C&ARR) coming from Camden into Atlantic City to help transform the then empty Brigantine Island into a "2nd Atlantic City." This comprises Brigantine Railroad Dream #1. We know nothing of the preliminary planning and meetings, but an article in the Trenton *Daily State Gazette*, dated November 9, 1880, reports that the project officially began in 1880 when the projectors deposited $7,000.00 with the Secretary of State, State of New Jersey, to begin the approval process.[1] The Brigantine Improvement Company and its officers were the background investor-owners of this "experimental" railroad.[2] The same article listed the principals, who hailed from the Philadelphia and Haddonfield areas rather than local Atlantic City businessmen. The lease stated:

> The North Atlantic City Railway Company, agrees with the lessee, the Camden and Atlantic Railroad Company, to build and construct the said railway with one track laid, to furnish the right away for a second track, having seven feet width between said tracks, with room for sidings where requisite, the said width of the right away being 30 feet on each side of the center line of the said road, *and to put the part now built in good order and condition* [emphasis added], and ready for use and occupation as soon as it is conveniently can be done.[3]

The lease featured a 50-year lifespan with the rent set to not exceed $5000 per year to repay construction cost bonds. The lease required the C&ARR to supply the engine, cars, personnel, etc. The lease predicted an annual profit of about $50,000 for the lessees. The lessors, the North Atlantic City Railway Company, would profit from the land sales and development in Brigantine as the new city grew. The promoters planned to build a station where the numbered streets in Brigantine switch from North to South, now Roosevelt Boulevard. They also determined that a trolley would run the entire length of the island. Some old maps show that the island was to be wall-to-wall small houses with hotels along the beach; see the 1881 marketing map on the previous page (Figure 1). The project did not include the area at the far south, including Peter's Island and Quarter's Inlet, since storms and longshore currents had previously kept these areas from becoming permanent "above water" land. The project cost amounted to $2000 per mile for the 3½-mile section of the train line from the inlet to the station, plus the Absecon Inlet bridge cost.[4] No costs were given for the trolley system or the station.

Brigantine Railroad Dream #1 failed to come true. It appears a division existed among the Camden and Atlantic board members about the wisdom of leasing an experimental railroad project yet being responsible for the capital outlay. The directors noted that they based their fear on their failed experiment in buying the 1872–1880 Mays Landing to Egg Harbor City railroad line (see Figure 2 on the following page).[5]

On July 29, 1881, *The Philadelphia Inquirer* printed the full text of the C&ARR's "death knell" board meeting minutes, describing all the potential problems with the bridge building issue. The idea publicly died because

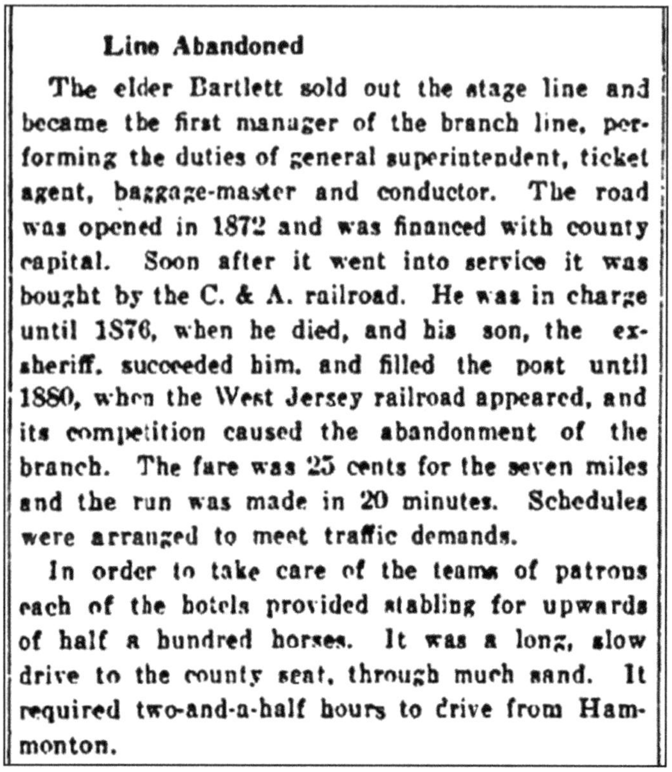

> **Line Abandoned**
>
> The elder Bartlett sold out the stage line and became the first manager of the branch line, performing the duties of general superintendent, ticket agent, baggage-master and conductor. The road was opened in 1872 and was financed with county capital. Soon after it went into service it was bought by the C. & A. railroad. He was in charge until 1876, when he died, and his son, the ex-sheriff, succeeded him, and filled the post until 1880, when the West Jersey railroad appeared, and its competition caused the abandonment of the branch. The fare was 25 cents for the seven miles and the run was made in 20 minutes. Schedules were arranged to meet traffic demands.
>
> In order to take care of the teams of patrons each of the hotels provided stabling for upwards of half a hundred horses. It was a long, slow drive to the county seat, through much sand. It required two-and-a-half hours to drive from Hammonton.

Figure 2. Brief description of the failed 1872–1880 Mays Landing to Egg Harbor City railroad line. "Line Abandoned," *The Atlantic City Gazette Review*, August 19, 1928, microform edition, 7.

some engineers felt a bridge could not be built for a reasonable cost over the fast-moving Absecon Inlet waters, although other engineers claimed it could be built.[6]

The argument "to build or not to build" revolved around management by ownership versus leasing the railroad to the C&ARR for their management. The lessors accomplished some work at the proposed station location because on Aug 19, 1881, the *Camden Morning Post* reported a fistfight among some workers on the project where "one African American man was seriously hurt, and several others injured."[7] The company dissolved when the C&ARR refused to sign a lease and underwrite the project, as reported in the *The Camden Post*.[8]

The official dates for dissolution are as follows: North Atlantic City Railroad Company, March 29, 1881; North Atlantic City Railway Company (trolley operation), November 2, 1881; Ocean Island and Brigantine Land and Improvement Company, June 7, 1892.[9] The developer received a refund of their state deposit. No maps or photos have been found to date showing more detail concerning the ill-fated project I have labeled Brigantine Railroad Dream #1. Although the project died, the idea remained very much alive in many entrepreneurial minds. It had too much profit-reaping potential to bury completely. The reader should note that no newspapers from Atlantic City, New Jersey, have survived from this 1879–1882 period to provide more information.

The Island Beach Company (a.k.a. The Ocean Island and Brigantine Land and Improvement Company) held their annual meeting in 1882 to elect new officers and to plan for the future.[10] They either owned or held options on almost all of Brigantine, also called North Atlantic City. It appears they had the same arrangement with all of what we call Little Beach today (see Figure 3). They planned to develop both islands end to end, from the ocean to the bay, by filling in the marshland.[11]

This long predated formation of the Environmental Protection Agency and the New Jersey Department of Environmental Protection, so virtually anything could be done construction-wise. The house lots comprised 4,000 square feet, starting at $150.00, and the company planned to build hotels, club houses, shops, and stores. The cottages would cost $800.00 to $2500.00, depending on size.[12] Outdoor life provided the biggest selling point—unpolluted, salubrious air, sunbathing, bird hunting, boating, fishing, etc. The company offered tours to see the land plots via a steam yacht from Leeds Point in Galloway Township every Thursday. The tour started at the waterfront ferry in Camden via the C&ARR to Absecon (then by carriage from Absecon to Leeds Point) and visitors returned later the same day. It sounds like it was a "high pressure land sales operation" at its best.[13] But how would these new homeowners and entrepreneurs easily get to their new ocean breeze paradise? The proposed answer was Brigantine Railroad Dream #2.

Sniffing possible profits, the Pennsylvania Railroad surveyed a route branching off their Camden to Atlantic City line. The branch would go from Absecon (or Pomona) to Leeds Point with boat travel to Sea Haven (a.k.a. Northern Brigantine or Little Beach), Beach Haven, and Barnegat City. It would connect not only with the Atlantic City bound Pennsylvania Railroad trains via Absecon, but it would connect to the New York trains in northern Ocean County.[14] The route to New York would be quite complicated. Figure 3 shows how the main line from Camden would branch at Pomona or Absecon to go to Leeds Point. A steam yacht would then take the passengers and freight to Beach Haven and Little Beach.

One early map shows a steamboat landing on Little Beach.[15] The *Plan of Island Beach* map (Figure 1) also shows that Little Beach's proposed streets would carry

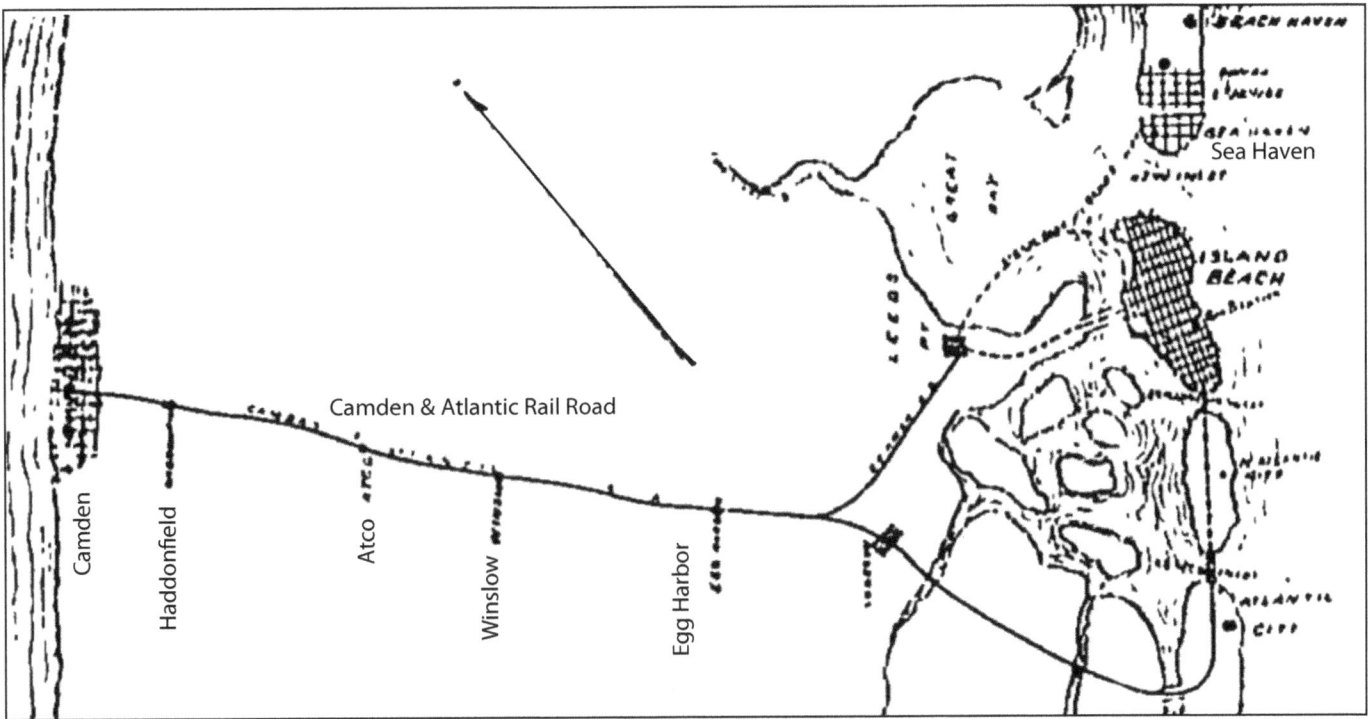

Figure 3. Plan for Railroad Dream #2. Courtesy of the Atlantic County Historical Society.

the names of larger American cities. It is assumed that a line would then go north via yacht to Long Beach Island and then connect via a bridge farther north above Tuckerton with the New York railroad lines.

By 1886, the Pennsylvania Railroad's Philadelphia & Beach Haven Railroad had completed a trestle and bridge across Barnegat Bay between Manahawkin and Ship Bottom, although likely too late for connectivity with passengers from Brigantine per the Dream #2 railroad proposal.[16] The frontispiece map actually shows a railroad and railroad trestle from Leeds Point to Island Beach.

Dream #2 was to be called The Island Beach and Great Bay Railroad (IB&GBRR). The route would include the usual spur off the main line going into Atlantic City, but the IB&GBRR would also connect via a bridge over Absecon Inlet and run the whole length of Brigantine and then cross another bridge onto Little Beach, forming a network of travel options. There are no records available to corroborate the correctness of this understanding of the overall grandiose plan, nor were there plans found for a trolley system. It also appears that some close connections existed with this group of entrepreneurs and the leaders from the failed Brigantine Railroad Dream #1.

Typical of this era's unregulated land sales, it is difficult to trace these types of financial connections. This dream, Brigantine Railroad Dream #2, never materialized. The core issues in this failure mirrored those in Brigantine Railroad Dream #1. The company apparently failed to raise the necessary construction funds and never attracted interest from the giant Pennsylvania Railroad to purchase or help finance this second experimental railroad idea. In the end, the promoters forfeited the steam yacht for non-payment as the court ordered it sold. The purchaser was none other than the principals of the Island Beach Company, the folks who failed with Brigantine Railroad Dream #1.[17] Hmm... could there be some funny business here? Two dreams went down in flames, but there was one more idea to try: Brigantine Railroad Dream #3. The third try is the charm and this one would come true, at least for a while.

The Brigantine Railroad dream scheme was originally resurrected in early 1887 as the Brigantine Beach Railroad along the same Absecon Inlet route, but wiser minds quickly prevailed about the bridge issue and the promoters dramatically changed the route to avoid the fast-moving inlet.[18] State and local politicians were quickly added to the Board of Directors to "grease the wheels" of the application and the loan processes.[19] This project would start in partnership with the C&ARR, with which company the promoters signed contracts in July 1887.[20] The Brigantine Land Company was again the principal owner of the railroad and plans called for it to connect with C&ARR at Pomona Junction on Swamp Siding, a couple hundred yards south of the present White Horse Pike and travel through Galloway Township via what is now Garfield Ave and Great Creek Road, out through today's Brigantine Wildlife Preserve, over Grassy Bay on a long trestle and into Brigantine through what is now the Brigantine golf course, and then along Roosevelt Boulevard to the same station earlier mentioned for the North Atlantic Railroad.[21] Plans called for two new hotels be built and Holcomb's older facility was to be remodeled. The plans also called for construction of an end-to-end trolley line on the island operated by a separate company, the Brigantine Transit Company (BTC); more about this later.

Look carefully at the wide 1890 centerline route map on the following page, filed with the New Jersey Secretary of State. Absecon-based city planner Rob Reid provided this copy from his private collection. The long, narrow map has been divided into three sections (top panel is west; bottom, east). Details are enlarged later in the article. You will note that "POMONA" is on the left side of the map (uppermost panel) and "BRIGANTINE" is on the right (lowermost). This is the railroad line we are discussing as Brigantine Railroad Dream #3, or the Brigantine Beach Railroad (BBRR).

Track and station work continued from 1887 until crews laid nine miles of track through late 1889.[22] The long trestle with its bridges over Grassy Bay was completed in early 1890. Unfortunately, no sooner did the crews complete the line than it was damaged by ice jams in a winter storm on February 23, 1890, and had to be repaired.[23] The winters seemed colder in the past. It appears construction crews completed most of the track laying and other work before the New Jersey Secretary of State granted final approval to the BBRR in 1890, but no one looked askance at what the railroad did. Historians have often humorously claimed that in the past, New Jersey had the best politicians that money could buy.

The 1890 centerline route depicts the construction route of the railroad, beginning at the Pomona or west end of the railroad line. Look at the enlarged portion of the Atlantic County Clerk's Office deed map #298 (Figure 4), which shows the early railroad from 1887 to early 1890 (Figure 5, the 1890 centerline map, shows it later in mid to late 1890 and thereafter). Now look carefully at Figure 4 and find the label "Mays Landing" on a vertical road on the right side of the map, a third of the way down from the top. This is Wrangleboro Road today going from Stockton University to Hamilton Mall. Certain northern portions of the road are still known as the May's Landing-Pomona Road and the Port Republic Road. Note that the map does not depict the White Horse Pike, even though it existed at that time. Now on this Mays Landing-Pomona Road, find the word "Atlantic City RR," which denotes the Camden and Atlantic Railroad (today's railroad—the C&ARR). The curved line that starts under the "P" in the name "Peter" represents a C&ARR Pomona Station siding called Swamp Siding. Swamp Siding derives its name from the land around it being the swampy source of Moss Mill Creek and Clark's Mill Creek (they both feed Lake Fred at Stockton and then become Nacote Creek after the Port Republic mill pond). Then, the next curved line coming off Swamp Siding, about 300' west of Pomona Road today is the beginning of the BBRR in 1887.

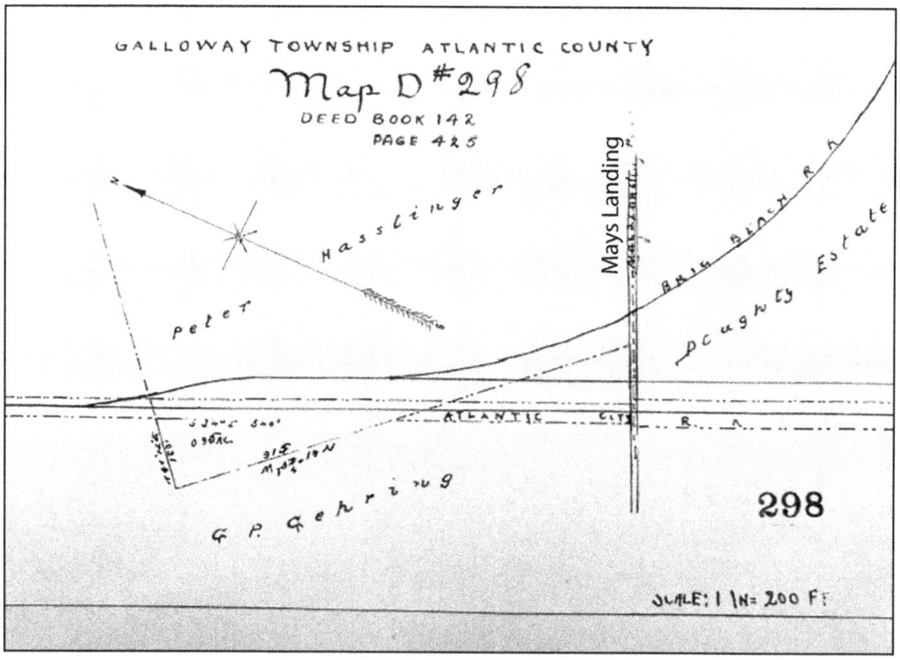

The C&ARR carried all the BBRR building material as the work crews built the track, switch connections, the five stations, the trestle and bridges, and the equipment used to cut the roadbed through almost six miles of virgin forest. The line crossed the White Horse Pike at the start of Great Creek Road (Apple Road today) just east of the Galloway Diner and proceded on a curve to today's Buchanan Ave through Pinehurst (see Franklin map, Figure 6).[24]

Figure 4. Atlantic County Clerk's Office deed map #298.

Rails to Brigantine

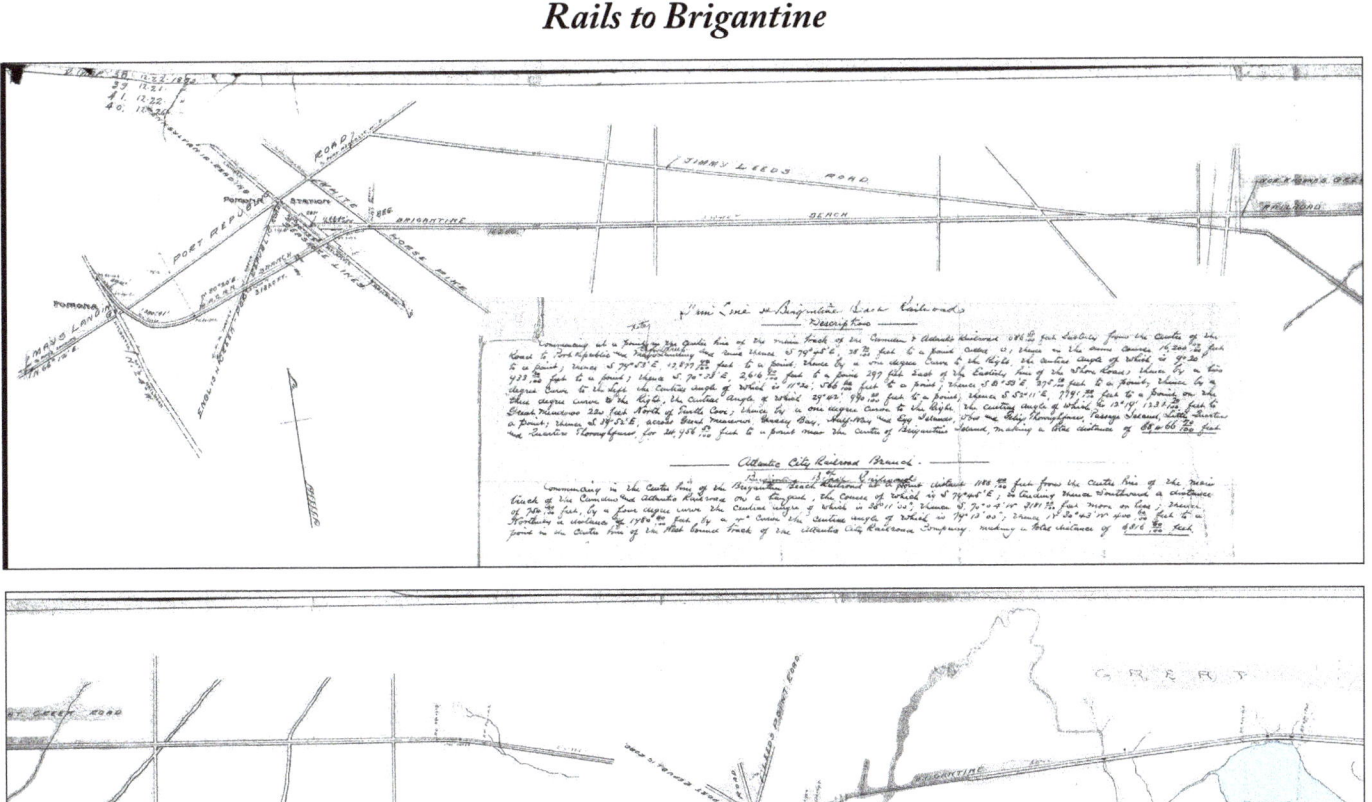

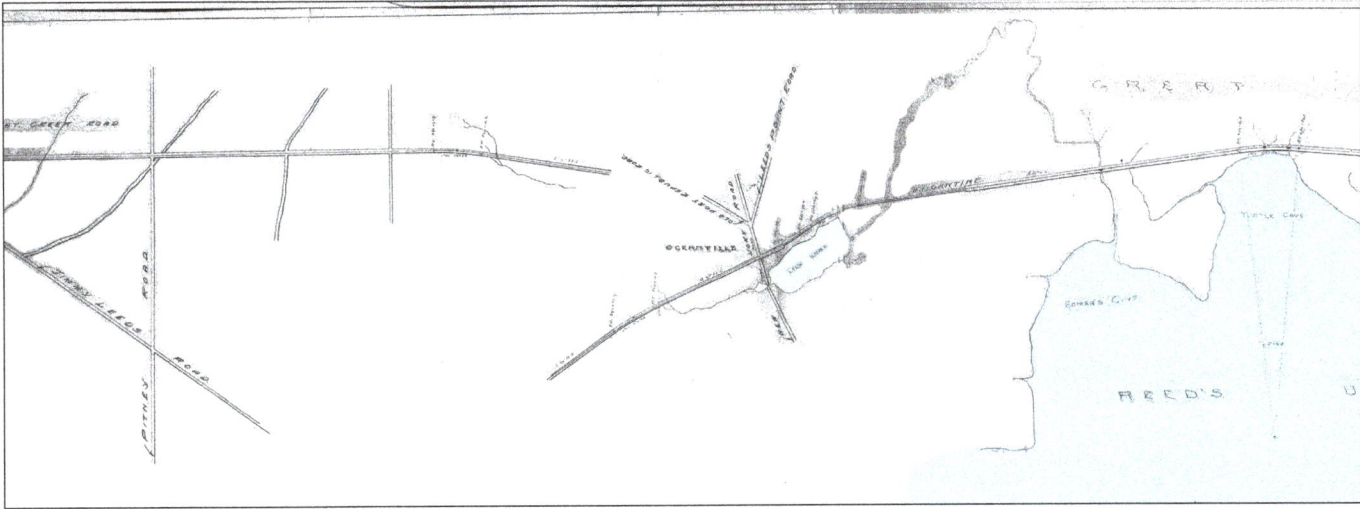

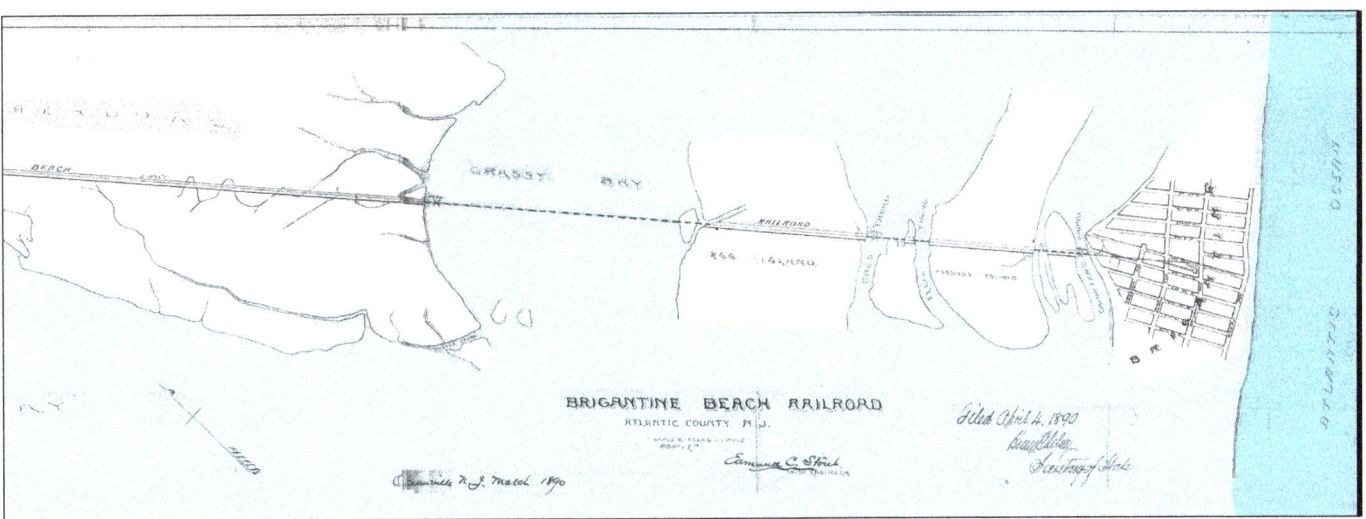

Figure 5. Centerline Route map (1890) showing the train line of Brigantine Beach Railroad: "Commencing at a point in the greater line of the main track of the Camden & Atlantic Railroad, 086 50/100 feet Easterly from the center of the Road to Port Republic . . . ." The original map is part of the New Jersey Secretary of State records, New Jersey State Archives, Trenton, NJ. Courtesy of Rob Reid.

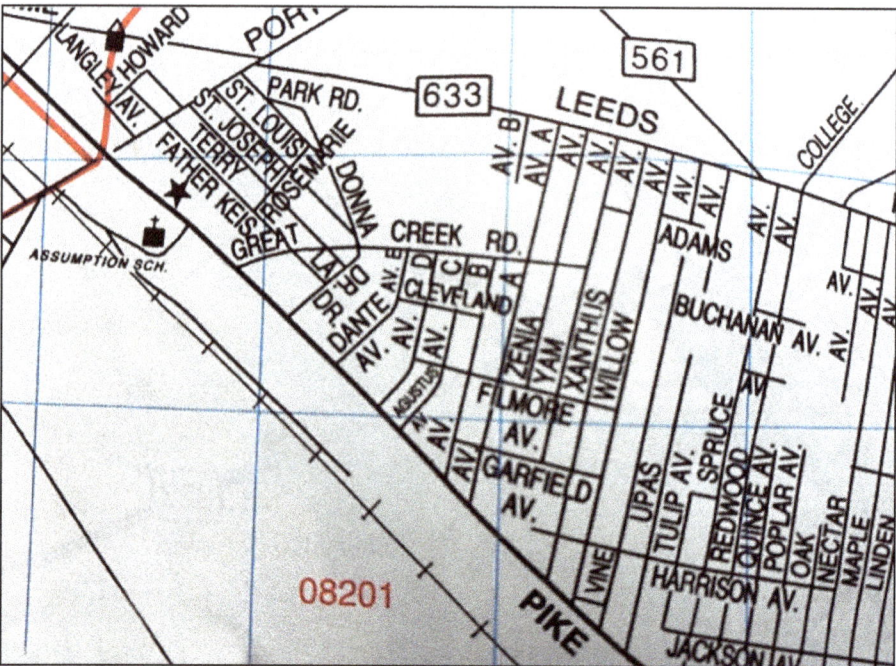
Figure 6. Detail from *Metro Street Map of Atlantic County, NJ*, Franklin Map, n.d.

From there, the BBRR crossed Jimmie Leeds Road east of today's Garden State Parkway overpasses and tracked farther eastward in almost a straight line to Oceanville and Shore Road.

The newly cut roadbed through the Galloway forest would later become Great Creek Road (see Figure 5). On its "Great Creek Road" section, it would be bridged over Mattix Creek and Doughty's Creek, both of which would flood out severely in heavy rainstorms. More about these floods later. The BBRR line would then continue through today's Brigantine Wildlife Preserve and across the bay to Brigantine on a long trestle with at least three drawbridges (gallows type bridges with bridge tender stations). Once on Brigantine Island, the railroad would traverse almost to the ocean, where a terminus station would be built (see Figure 7). There was at least one siding built on the mainland, located on the north side of Lily Lake for freight car storage. These cars were used for regular freight to Brigantine, plus shipments of oysters and clams for the ravenous Camden and Philadelphia epicurean markets. The siding and two inactive Philadelphia & Reading Railroad boxcars appear in the Atlantic County Historical Society photo dated to 1900 (Figure 8), taken across the lake looking northward at a section just east of Shore Road and the Oceanville Station.

Four interesting events occurred during construction. The first was a threat from area yachtsmen to demolish the trestle if the draw bridge did not feature 35-foot-wide openings. The BBRR acquiesced and avoided a threatened lawsuit and other more violent actions.[25] The second event was a strike by "Italian and Negro" workers who did not receive their pay on time.[26] When the workers began tearing up the track along today's Great Creek Road, and the story spread nationwide (from Dayton, Ohio, to as far away as California), the company found the money to make payroll. Incidentally, the company claimed to be financially stable at this point.[27] The third problem involved the shooting of a worker near the Pomona Station, a crime that remains unsolved.[28] The fourth problem involved the ongoing relationship with the C&ARR. The C&ARR trains carried and delivered all the building supplies for the BBRR from 1887–1890 at a great profit but decided in the spring of 1890 that the long-term financial prospects appeared bleak for the new railroad to Brigantine, so they backed out of the partnership and lease.[29] The Brigantine connection to Philadelphia's passengers and freight was temporarily severed.

Was Brigantine Railroad Dream #3 over? No! The Philadelphia & Reading Railroad's subsidiary, the Atlantic City Railroad (formerly the Philadelphia & Atlantic City Railway's narrow-gauge route) (P&R/ACRR) stepped in and became the new partner for the BBRR. Since the ACRR tracks ran west of the C&ARR tracks, a diamond crossing east of Pomona Road would have to be negotiated to allow the ACRR/BBRR to cross the C&ARR tracks. Both sides (C&ARR and the P&R/ACRR) lawyered up with politically connected attorneys. The C&ARR had obtained a restraining order, preventing the crossing until it received reimbursement for the damages it would incur.[30] A hearing was set before a judge, who appointed a committee to investigate and report on the potential damages. As of mid-July, the case was not completed and the BBRR planned to transfer the potential customers by horse-drawn coach over the 1300' between the P&R/ACRR's Pomona station and the beginning of the BBRR up on the same road. Then a new solution was proposed: build a short semi-independent railroad spur to connect the P&R/ACRR and BBRR. It was to be called

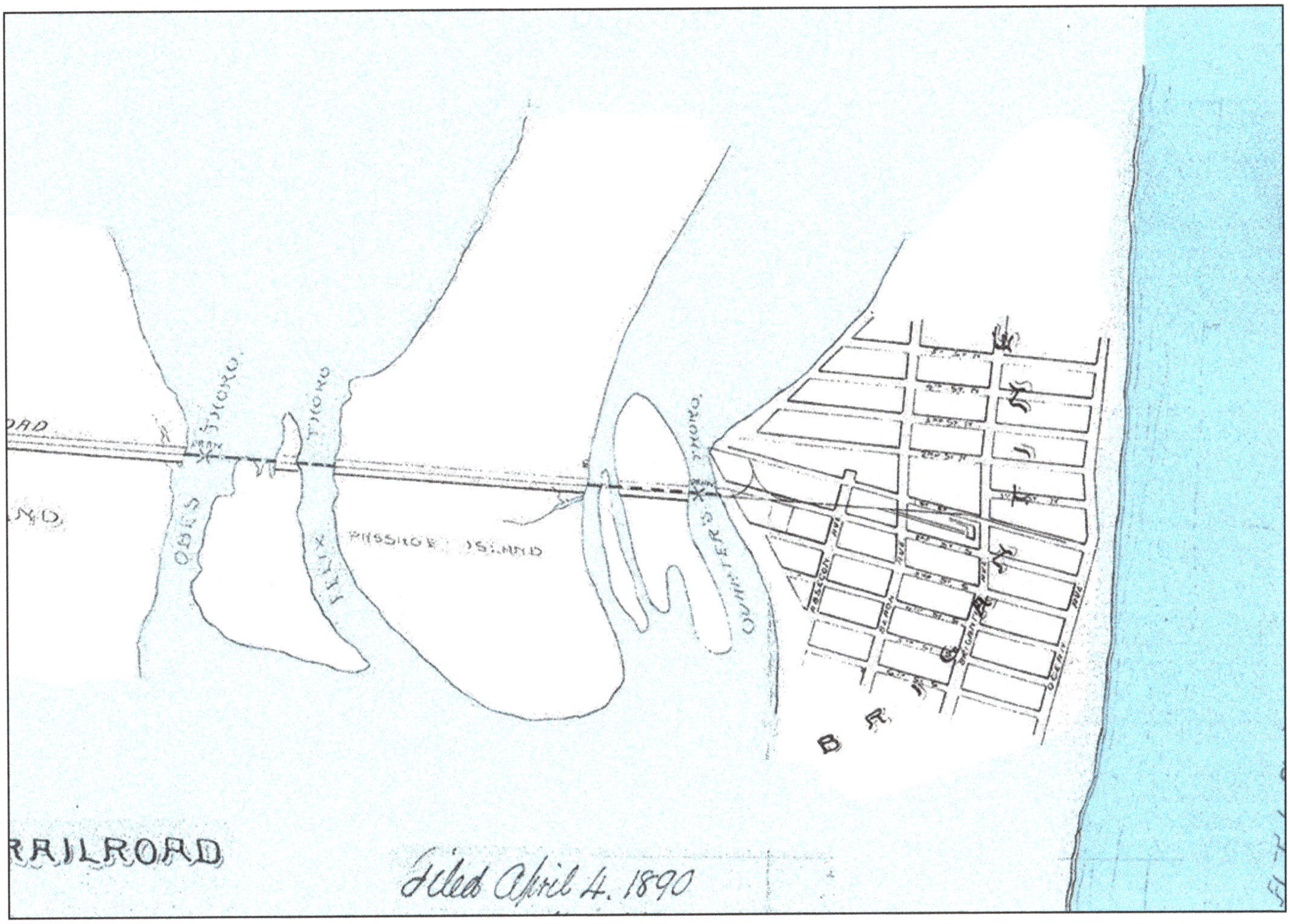

Figure 7. Detail from 1890 Centerline Route map showing Brigantine Island.

Figure 8. BBRR siding located on the north side of Lily Lake. The siding and two Philadelphia & Reading Railroad boxcars appear this 1900 photograph. Courtesy of the Atlantic County Historical Society.

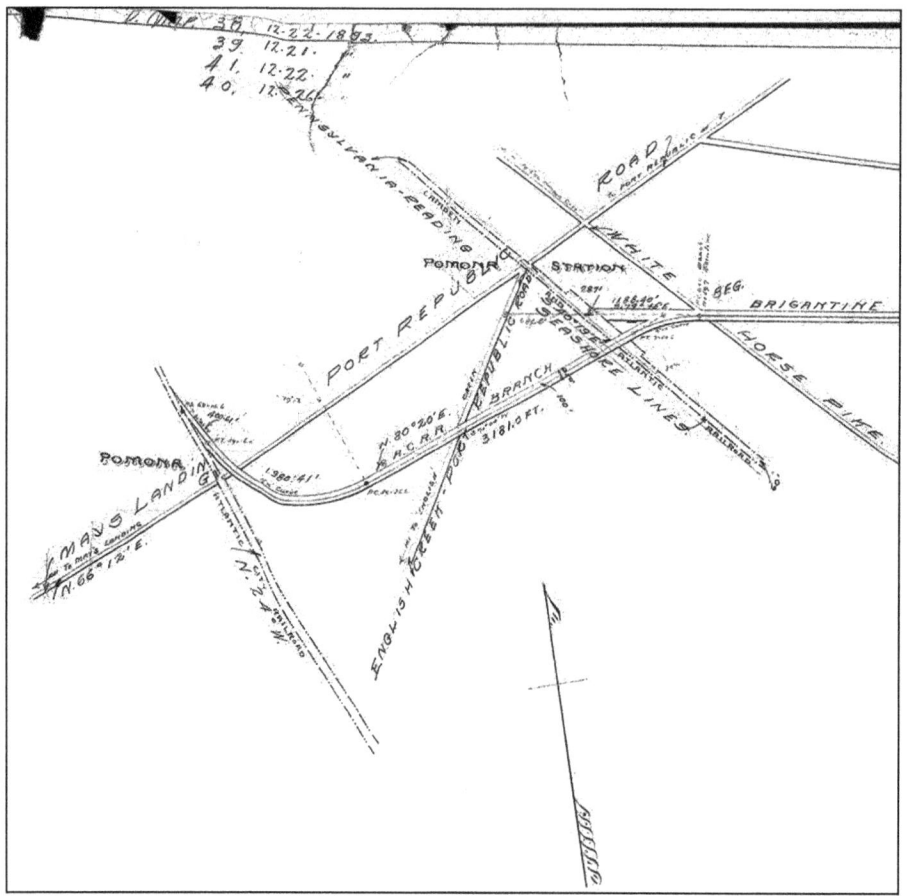

Figure 9. Detail from 1890 Centerline Route map showing the Pomona Branch Railroad.

the Pomona Branch Railroad, a.k.a., the Pomona-Atlantic City Railroad.[31] If you start at the lower left of the map diagram (Figure 9), you will note that the new connector railroad began at the "G" in the road label of "Mays Landing." It curved northward and crossed English Creek Road before crossing over the C&ARR tracks. The crossing included an interlocking tower to control the signals that guarded the diamond crossing from collisions. The C&ARR required the BBRR to man this tower 24/7 (see Figure 10).[32] The track then curved to the right to cross the White Horse Pike and headed to the ocean some 9 miles away. If you carefully study this right curve, you will see the old connector to the C&ARR, a connector that was never removed. In fact, many old timers say that there was a station at this point and the stop was called the Pomona Station. An excursion broadside verifies this (Figure 11).[33] The list of freight and passenger stops starting at Brigantine Junction (the connection with the P&R/ACRR, about where the Hindu Temple stands today—571 S Pomona Rd, with an Egg Harbor City address) were Pomona (the crossing with the C&ARR), Absecon Road (Great Creek and Wrangleboro Roads), Port Republic (Great Creek Road and Pitney Road), Oceanville (Great Creek Road and Shore Road).[34] To this point, it had crossed two creeks. It first crossed Mattix Creek in the area between today's 2nd and 4th avenues (Mattix Creek, a.k.a. Two-mile Branch eventually flows through Smithville into Nacote Creek) and then Doughty's Creek about 1/3 of a mile before reaching Shore Road (Doughty Creek eventually flows into Lily Lake). It then continued on to Brigantine to the Oceanside Station (Brigantine Ave and Roosevelt Blvd). The BBRR and its spur was slated to open for business on August 28, 1890.[35]

After crossing Shore Road, the BBRR continued on the current route of Great Creek Road, out through what is today the Brigantine Wildlife Preserve. It crossed the meadows and its smaller creeks via trestles (see Figure 12) to Grassy Bay, where the track entered the first hand-operated "gallows-type" or A-frame end-pivot swing span-bridge constructed on the western side of the bay.[36] Built on trestling, the line continued across the bay and back on the meadows to reach Obe's Thoroughfare behind Brigantine (see Figure 14 for a photograph of Obe's Thoroughfare trestle). The line's second drawbridge was on the western side on Obe's Thoroughfare. The BBRR's third drawbridge was on the western side on Quarter's Thoroughfare, later infilled to create the Brigantine Golf Course (see Figure 5 for the bridge locations). It then entered Brigantine in today's golf course area and ended at its own station, located at Roosevelt Boulevard and Brigantine Boulevard.[37] Additionally, the line featured at least one clam and oyster shipping station on the eastern side of Lily Lake, where a freshwater tank served to refresh the bay oysters awaiting shipment to Atlantic City and Philadelphia. There may have been other oyster stations along the trestling or close to the bay, such as near the Oceanville Station. In fact, the shellfish business was so good that some people referred to the railroad as "The Clam Road."[38] You now have the big picture, so let's look at some interesting details.

During the building process many things occurred on the sidelines of the construction action. Hotel build-

Figure 10. The BBRR interlocking tower where their road crossed the C&ARR tracks. The crossing controlled the signals that guarded the diamond crossing 24/7 from collisions. Courtesy of Theodore Xaras.

struggled with its dire financial situation.[45]

Times were always tough for the BBRR. It entered receivership for reorganization as soon as it opened for business.[46] The line never had enough paying customers. Failure to make interest payments on the bonds sold to the Holland Trust Company of New York provided the legal rationale for declaring bankruptcy. In reality, the company probably expended all its cash fighting the C&ARR for the diamond crossing at Pomona and repairing storm damage to its trestles. Attachments to its other assets for interest non-payment on its bonds continued into the next year.[47] In 1892, a spring storm washed out some track over the bay, which had to be rebuilt,[48] but ing boomed in Brigantine. Advertising drew buyers from near and far regarding the bird hunting, fishing, boating, and health benefits of the island. Building lot and house sales occurred in both Pomona and Brigantine.[39] The promoters of the line and the island's developers extravagantly wined and dined the local and state politicians.[40] And the plan itself was growing, with an electric trolley line proposed in Brigantine, which would run from a pier jutting into Absecon Inlet to the edge of Brigantine Inlet, a.k.a. Wreck Inlet. Another piece of news arose when boaters discovered the infilling of Quarter's inlet due to an increase in the north-to-south longshore current, and so Peter's Beach was becoming one with Brigantine.

Bad news tempered all the good news. On September 17, 1890, the railroad announced it was in financial trouble.[41] More bad news followed when an October nor'easter storm damaged the trestling.[42] By January 1891, the first fatality occurred when a train struck a horse and buggy while crossing the tracks at the Absecon station. A storm in May 1892 again washed out the trestling.[43] Hopes, however, still ran high. Philadelphia capitalists entertained interest in building an electric railroad from the Oceanville station north into Ocean County to connect with the New York trains.[44] This, however, would not come to fruition and in 1894 the BBRR entered receivership. The railroad clearly

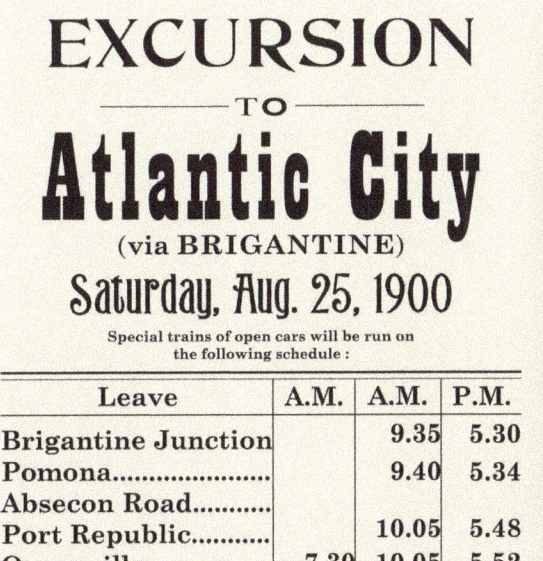

Figure 11. Facsimile of excursion broadside listing Pomona Station, among other stops on the BBRR.

Figure 12. Local resident Clarence Conover on an old piece of the trestle. Courtesy of Galloway Township Historical Society.

hopes for eventual success still ran high. After all, Atlantic City, just below Brigantine, was a boom town.

On November 13, 1893, Galloway Township received a petition to construct an electric trolley line connecting Absecon and Oceanville to Brigantine using the BBRR tracks, presumably to bring folks to the amusement park on Lily Lake. Figure 13 shows the BBRR crossing Shore Road at Oceanville. Try to find the RR crossing sign. This trolley link never materialized, and life remained a losing battle financially for the BBRR. A glance at the *Annual Statements of the Railroad and Canal Companies of New Jersey for the Year 1892* indicates its receipts included $2479.96 from passengers, $3927.98 from freight, and $399.97 from other sources, for a total yearly income of $6807.91, while its expenses for that year amounted to $13,522.61.[49] This created a loss of almost $7000, and a recurring problem for just about every year thereafter. Accidents occurred sporadically, including a few collisions with buggies and individuals along the route. The state courts appointed a receiver to run the railroad's finances in 1894.[50] A nor'easter washed out meadows railbed in October 1894.[51] In 1895, forest fires along Great Creek Road threatened the railroad. Snow and ice storms posed the threat of frozen switches, which could cause derailments. Railroad management planned a spur from Pomona to Egg

Figure 13. The BBRR crossing Shore Road at Oceanville. Courtesy of the Galloway Township Historical Society.

Harbor City to increase freight revenues, but this spur never materialized,[52] as the railroad slipped further into foreclosure.

While the BBRR physical traveled west to east, it finances traveled only in a southerly direction—that is, downhill. The railroad finally sold at a court-ordered auction to railroad director George H. Cooke of New York City for $50,000,[53] which paid off the existing mortgage and erased some of the bond debt. Mr. Cooke and partners also owned the Brigantine Transit Company, established to operate the trolley. Cooke and his new partners from New York City recapitalized the BBRR, but business remained low, unprofitably low. Ridership was so low that the P&R/ACRR applied to cancel its shared service agreement with the BBRR and to stop its subsidy payments. This action meant the loss of P&R/ACRR locomotives and other equipment, forcing the BBRR to purchase their own engine for $2750.00 from the Brooklyn Bridge Company.[54] A year later, the engine suffered damage in an accident and required costly repairs.[55]

Strangely enough, even with business down, or perhaps desperate for a new source of revenue, the BBRR entered into the first phase of a planned connection with the Tuckerton Railroad via twelve miles of trackage going northward and a Mullica River Bridge to open up Brigantine to the New York City market.[56] In February 1900, *The New York Tribune* reported:

> ... the new route will be over Jersey Central tracks from New York, by way of Red Bank, thence to Lakewood, and from there to Whiting Junction. From the latter point trains will be run over the Tuckerton Railway to Tuckerton, via Barnegat. From Tuckerton to Brigantine, a distance of 12 miles, there is no railway, but this short gap will be filled at once by the Brigantine Railroad Company.[57]

Year round, Brigantine's population amounted to only 100 people at this point, and it appears that this Tuckerton RR dream dissipated quickly.

In 1901, after a storm damaged the tops of the pilings upon which the trestling rested, work crews lowered the entire trestle a few feet, placing rail just above the high tide mark.[58] An eight-week cold spell that included a severe winter storm again damaged some trestling, requiring repair.[59] On October 12, 1903, a storm destroyed about 2000 feet of trestling by lifting it completely off the pilings and tossing it into the bay. This was the final death blow to the railroad's full operation. The date was erroneously reported as September 12, 1903, in the book *Atlantic City Railroad: Royal Route to the Sea*.

The same night that the trestle suffered destruction, the storm stranded an inebriated "trestle-walker" and the last locomotive to ever leave Brigantine struck him, killing the man, William Barney, and wedging his body under the engine.[60] Subsequent to the trestle's destruction across Grassy Bay, cartage of mail, freight and passengers occurred using a steamboat operating from the end of the trestle at the west side of Grassy Bay and then transported to Brigantine.[61]

In the summer of 1904, during a heavy rain one night, floodwaters lifted the bridge at Two-Mile Branch (Mattix Creek) and then destroyed it although the span dropped back down when the water subsided. An hour or so after this happened, the final train from Grassy Bay back to Pomona struck the collapsed bridge, destroying both the engine and passenger car and injuring several people.[62] The article describing the accident provides the names of both the train crew and the passengers.[63] This ended any vestige of life for the BBRR.

Workers summarily removed the rails in sections and sold them

Figure 14. Obe's Thoroughfare trestle. Courtesy of the Galloway Township Historical Society.

for scrap, starting in 1904 and finishing in 1913.[64] The railroad, however, retained the franchise of the right-of-way,[65] and plans surfaced from time to time to attempt rebuilding the line.[66] What remained of the railroad finally sold at auction as the *New York Times* reported on November 1, 1910,[67] and its assets sold for scrap. So ended the BBRR. Dreams to resurrect it persisted for a while, but never came to fruition. In 1955, Galloway Township approved paving the BBRR roadbed and calling it Brigantine Road.[68] When the name-change occurred to Great Creek Road is currently unknown.

But, what about the trolleys on the beach in Brigantine?

Electric Trolleys Came Second

Trolleys became the talk of the northeastern United States in the late 1800s, and thousands used them to commute to work and for recreational opportunities, whether a scenic ride or a trip to the local amusement park. But how and when did they begin? How did they become associated with the Brigantine Beach Railroad? And how did the profitable trolley company, the Brigantine Transit Company, finally meet its demise in 1903?

PRR electric trolley service in Atlantic City began on Atlantic Avenue on April 24, 1889, stretching from New Hampshire Avenue to Albany Avenue with a power plant at New York Avenue. The fare was only 10¢ and rider growth was exponential.[69] Steam engine service extended the line to Longport for 20¢, stimulating business along its route, causing the service to be expanded to year-round with electric heaters in the winter. The entrepreneurs with the BBRR saw this growth and decided to copy the trolley success story in Brigantine. The idea was being considered as early as July 1890 before the BBRR began service.[70]

The new trolley company carried the name of the Brigantine Transit Company (BTC). *The Philadelphia Inquirer* of April 18, 1893, reported that construction was ongoing, including building the engine house, the coal-fired boiler house to generate the electricity for the line, and the car storage and repair houses.[71] Coal would arrive via the P&R/ACRR to Pomona Junction and then would be transferred to Brigantine on the BBRR. A cottage constructed specifically for their use housed the construction employees, including being supplied with a cook to make their meals. The men

Figure 15. A double-decker trolley car of the Brigantine Transit Company. Courtesy of the Atlantic County Historical Society.

worked for contractor Burd P. Evans of Germantown, Pennsylvania. *The Philadelphia Inquirer* soon reported on May 1, 1893, that the newly built BTC steamer Brigantine had made its April 30, 1893, maiden voyage on the Delaware River,[72] and was almost finished. It would transport crowds of tourists and prospecting land passengers across Absecon Inlet from a new wharf at the foot of Rhode Island Avenue in Atlantic City to the newly built wharf in Brigantine. The shipyard of Neafie & Levy in the Kensington section of Philadelphia constructed the boat.

On May 7, 1893, *The Philadelphia Inquirer* reported that the work crews had almost finished the trolley rail line along with the first double-decker trolley cars.[73] The line of double-decker trolleys opened in the summer of 1893 and received revenue amounting to $2577.45 from passengers and $19.00 from freight for an aggregated income of $4835.92 with expenses of only $1548.68, making the operation a profitable venture at this point.

Despite the income, however, the company chose to pay no interest on its bonds or stock dividends that year. No accidents occurred along the route. J. Rush Ritter of Philadelphia served as president, George H. Cook fulfilled the position of secretary, and William Hacker performed in the role as treasurer. A Mr. Adams of Atlantic City was a board member and the company's Post Office address was located in Brigantine.[74] Some of these people also served as officers of the Brigantine Beach Railroad and the Island Development Company (Mr. Cook is a prime example). No hidden connection existed between the two companies and the Island Development Company. The BTC issued stock and borrowed approximately $176,000 via bonds. It spent $429,971 building the rail line, including erecting the necessary buildings and buying the equipment. The length of the rail line measured 6¼ miles along the beachfront. The line began on a pier at Rum Point at the south end of Brigantine Island, across Absecon Inlet from Atlantic City, and ran north on Brigantine Avenue to almost Brigantine Inlet, a.k.a. Wreck Inlet (see Figure 16—we'll come back to this map again).[75]

In order to further entertain its passengers, the BTC acquired the Atlantic City Gun Club property, located on the Maryland Avenue overlooking the meadows, for $1250. Ads touting the fishing and hunting opportunities abounded in the Philadelphia newspapers.[76] The June 19, 1893, edition of *The Camden Morning Post* claimed that the trolley line was almost finished, the boat trip would only take 10 minutes, and it would occur every 30 minutes in the summer.[77] The *Savannah Georgia Morning News* reported that the Coast Guard even put out several buoys for the line and the BTC was operating not just one ship, but "several steamers" by the end of the summer.[78]

A storm soon occurred on Sunday and Monday, Mar 25–26, 1894, that damaged sections of the trolley tracks. It also threatened to damage the new steamer Brigantine, but her captain stayed aboard at great risk to himself and saved the vessel. A large team of workers traveled to Brigantine on Wednesday, March 28, 1894, and repaired the damaged track in one day.[79] The line had shut down for the winter of 1893–94 and plans called for the line to reopen on May 30, 1894, for the new season. The line officially opened for the summer on Sunday, June 10, 1894.[80] No other information could be found for this season, and presumably the line shut down again in the late fall.

As the next year began, the BTC had two new steamers delivered in May 1895.[81] The information from 1896 suggests all did not go well in 1895. The same was true for the BBRR, which entered receivership in 1894 and then sold out of receivership in 1895 for $50,000 to stockholder George H. Cook to relieve a portion of the BBRR debt load.[82] Additionally, it lost its partnership and underwriting from the P&R/

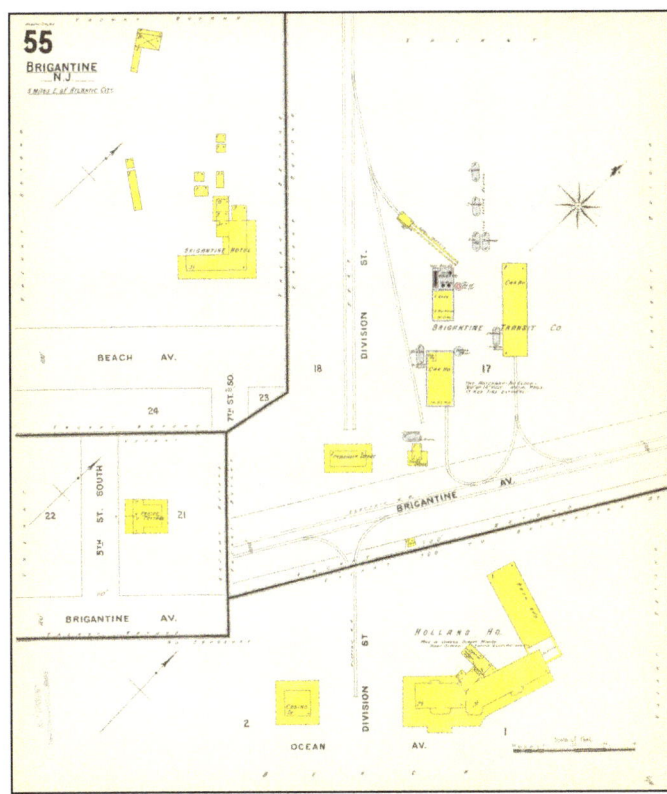

Figure 16. Brigantine, Plate 55, Sanborn-Perris Map Company. From *Insurance Maps of Atlantic City, New Jersey* (1896).

ACRR. Cook and his partners then decided that the BTC would take over managing the BBRR (August 7, 1895).[83] No other information has yet been found regarding 1895.

Much more information is available for the year 1896. The Charles Hillman Ship and Engine Building Company obtained a writ of attachment for $11,000 against BTC equipment, particularly the two new steamboats, the Catherine W and the Lorraine.[84] The next day saw claims filed against the BTC amounting to $400,000. These claims indicate that BTC president J. Rush Ritter caused the problems that brought the claims. Ritter served as the Real Estate Officer of the Solicitors Loan and Trust Company of Philadelphia. The court appointed Judge Thompson of Atlantic City as the Receiver for the struggling company, but creditors objected that the Judge also served as the attorney representing the company.[85] Hmmmm!

Creditors leveled scam accusations against the BTC and the Brigantine Land development Company, and claimed that Ritter created a financial bubble that had burst due to mismanagement.[86] The courts agreed on the potential for the appearance of a conflict of interest and removed Judge Thompson, replacing him with Charles Joline of Camden as the Receiver.[87] They did not comment on the scam idea. The court then authorized a bond extension of $5000 to pay the required operating insurance for the summer season. Receiver Joline confirmed the sale of the Brigantine Railroad and Steamboat Transit Company to Cooke for the $50,000,[88] and renamed it the Philadelphia and Brigantine Railroad Company.[89] Same owners, same railroads, but with much of the debt evaporated.

At this point, William F. Russell obtained a controlling interest in the BTC,[90] and things began looking upward. Co-owner George Cook sadly lost his adult son to a drowning accident that August.[91] The *Annual Statements of the Railroad and Canal Companies of New Jersey for the Year 1896* provided the following information: capital stock issued $250,000; bonded debts $250,000; floating debt $241,328.[92] The cost of equipment amounted to $328,302 over the 7-mile railroad. What happened to the other $410,000? Their report provided no listing of income versus expenses for the trolley line, but the railroad's revenue equaled virtually nothing: $1169 total with expenses of $2663.

One cannot imagine being able to service the interest on the approximately $750,000 debt load with a negative operating income. In 1897, some stockholders who shared the company's indebtedness bought the failing company for $50,000, comprising $19,000 for the steamers and $31,000 for the trolley line and electric plant.[93] The reorganization group, again led by George Cook, managed the company that year. The New Jersey State Report showed income of $5261 and expenses of $9085. In 1898, the State of New Jersey filing also showed income of $7737 and expenses of $13,143, not a good sign.[94] The 1899 *Poor's Manual of Railroads*, showing 1898 figures, provided an unusual picture of very large numbers of passengers carried on the trolleys, but very little profit—138,415 passengers carried at a net $4500 loss.[95]

Some historians and others have opined that this railroad and trolley system simply served as a vehicle to conduct a land sales operation in Brigantine in those early days. The same group had earlier purchased all of today's Little Beach, called it Island Beach, and attempted to sell it off in lots as well. They even promised a railroad going from Absecon through Leeds Point and over the marshes south of Great Bay, calling it the Great Bay Railroad. These companies went in and out of receivership often and then always sold to the same buyers operating under slightly different company names (read the copy from *Poor's* to draw your own conclusion). The same losses continued until 1903, when a storm destroyed the BBRR trestle over the bay.

Once the BBRR trains could no longer deliver hopper car loads of coal to the island, the electric plant ceased producing power and the electric trolleys ground to a halt. In 1905 some of the stockholders tried to reinvent the system. They reincorporated the original name for the first dream back in 1880, the North Atlantic City Railroad Company, and attempted to raise $210,000 to finance the re-start of both the BBRR and the BTC. The idea never got off the ground. Most of the tracks were removed during 1907 and the equipment sold for scrap in 1910.

So ended the Brigantine Transit Company and the Brigantine Beach Railroad, but not the dream! The 1914 Mueller map (Figure 17) shows that a Brigantine Railroad Dream #4 existed, but it was a short dream. As proposed, the line would operate purely as an electric railroad that the extant Atlantic City and Seashore Railroad would construct. At that time, Brigantine carried the moniker of East Atlantic City, probably yet another name change for marketing purposes. This railroad never left the drawing board nor have any records or plans come to light. The end of the dreams had finally arrived. From the permanent population figures for Brigantine that Dennis Niceler has found, it appears

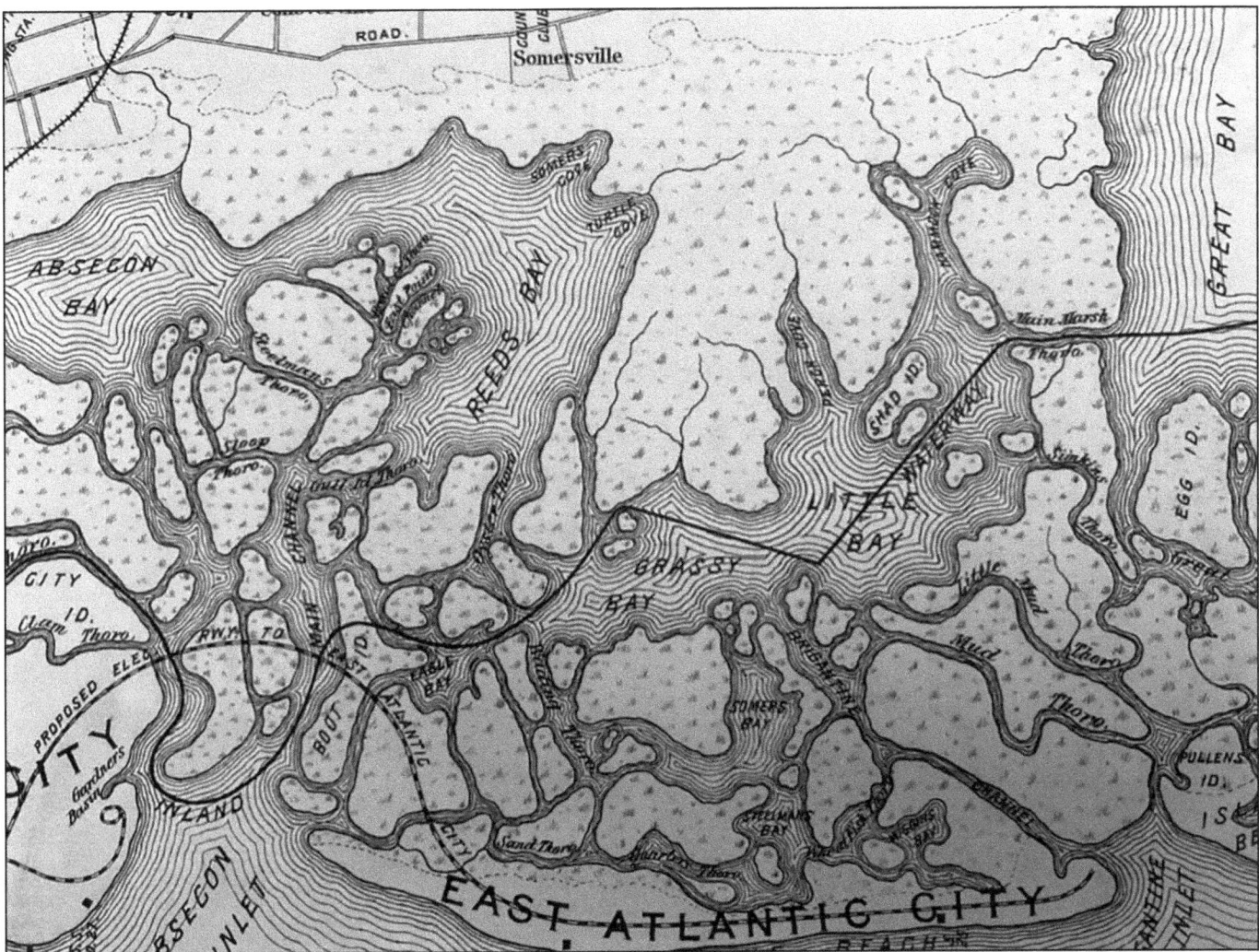

Figure 17. Detail, *Map of Absecon Island, Embracing Atlantic City, Ventnor City, Margate City, and Borough of Longport 1914*, "Index Map" (Philadelphia: A. H. Mueller, 1914).

that the land sales did not reach expectation: 1890 US census: not available; 1895 NJ census: 188; 1900 US census: 99; 1905 NJ census: 95. The city later contracted in population and then grew later, but without a railroad or trolley system: 1910 US census: 67; 1920 US census: "no info"; 1930 US census: 373.[96] This low population and slow growth removed the need for an expensive railroad connection. The first wooden automobile bridge into Brigantine dates to about 1924. Until then, people traveled via ferry.

A good summary statement would be that the BBRR (trains) and the BTC (trolleys) always had a close relationship, both intertwined and interdependent. One could not survive without the other. The Brigantine Trolley line operation beat out the Brigantine railroad for passenger numbers hands-down, but the trolley couldn't survive without the railroad.

About the Author

Rev. Norman Reeves Goos (normangoos@comcast.net) is a member and Past-President (2013–2015) of the New Jersey Society, Sons of the American Revolution; SAR Compatriot #169855. Norman is also a member of The New Jersey Sons of the Revolution (2014–#41604) and the Librarian and a Trustee of the Atlantic County Historical Society; he was also recently appointed by the County Freeholders as the Local Historian for Atlantic County. Norm is an ordained minister and retired Senior Pastor in the Wesleyan Church. He is the retired President of The Kairos Institute in Trinidad and Tobago, as well as Professor Emeritus of Ancient Greek in the Graduate School of that institution. Norm is married to Marilyn, a retired middle-school math and science teacher; they have two sons, six grandchildren and a growing quiver of great-grandchildren.

Endnotes

1. "Another New Jersey Railroad Chartered," *Daily State Gazette* (Trenton, NJ), November 9, 1880, microform edition, 3.
2. "The North Atlantic," *The Philadelphia Inquirer*, August 3, 1881, microform edition, 2.
3. "Brigantine Beach," *The Philadelphia Inquirer*, August 5, 1881, microform edition, 2.
4. Untitled comment, *The Trenton State Gazette*, April 27, 1881, microform edition, 4.
5. "Line Abandoned," *The Atlantic City Gazette Review*, August 19, 1928, microform edition, 7.
6. "The North Atlantic," *The Philadelphia Inquirer*, August 3, 1881, microform edition, 2.
7. "Atlantic City," *The Camden Morning Post*, August 19, 1881, microform edition, 1.
8. "The Brigantine Beach Co.," *The Camden Morning Post*, November 4, 1881, microform edition, 1.
9. New Jersey Secretary of State, *Corporations of New Jersey: List of Certificates to December 31, 1911* (Trenton, NJ: MacCrellish & Quigley, 1914), 831, 832.
10. "Local Gossip," *The Camden Morning Post*, November 25, 1882, microform edition, 1.
11. "Island Beach," *The Camden Morning Post*, March 30, 1883, microform edition, 4.
12. "Island Beach House," *The Camden Morning Post*, December 26, 1883, microform edition, 4.
13. "Island Beach House," *The Camden Morning Post*, January 2, 1884, microform edition, 4.
14. "A New Shore Railroad," *The Monmouth Democrat* (Freehold, NJ), August 14, 1884, microform edition, 3.
15. Unlabeled 3 Dec 1880 Atlantic County deed copy. See copy at Atlantic County Historical Society.
16. John Brinckmann, *The Tuckerton Railroad: A Chronicle of Transport to the New Jersey Seashore* (Edison, NJ: by the author, 1973), 61–66.
17. "A Yacht Sold," *The Camden Morning Post*, November 17, 1884, microform edition, 1.
18. "The Railroad to Brigantine Beach," *The Camden Morning Post*, April 22, 1887, microform edition, 1.
19. "Personals," *The Camden Morning Post*, May 19, 1887, microform edition, 1.
20. "The New Routes," *The Camden Morning Post*, July 29, 1887, microform edition, 1.
21. "Improvements in Brigantine," *The Camden Daily Telegram*, November 23, 1889, microform edition, 1.
22. Ibid.
23. "The Long Trestle Bridge," *The Camden Morning Post*, February 24, 1890, microform edition, 2.
24. *Franklin's Street and Zip Code Atlas of Atlantic, Cape May & Cumberland Counties, New Jersey* (King of Prussia, PA: Franklin Maps, 1990), 13–14.
25. "Yachtsmen Demanding a Bigger Draw," *The New York Tribune* (New York City, NY), February 25, 1890, microform edition, 3.
26. "Says the Story is Untrue," *The Harrisburg, PA Patriot*, July 29, 1890, microform edition, 3.
27. "Have Ample Funds," *New York Herald* (New York City, NY), July 30, 1890, microform edition, 2.
28. "An Egg Harbor Mystery," *The Philadelphia Inquirer*, July 6, 1890, microform edition, 1.
29. "Reading Wants to Cross," *The Camden Morning Post*, May 17, 1890, microform edition, 1.
30. Ibid, 9.
31. Ibid, 3 (plus see the map in this *SoJourn* article).
32. W. George Cook and William J. Coxey, *Atlantic City Railroad: The Royal Route to the Sea* (Oaklyn, NJ: West Jersey Chapter of the National Railway Historical Society, 1980), 60.
33. Ibid.
34. Ibid, 58.
35. "Brigantine Beach Railroad," *The Camden Morning Post*, August 27, 1890, microform edition, 4.
36. Cook and Coxey, *Atlantic City Railroad*, 72.
37. Ibid, 58–59.
38. "Brigantine R. R. Once 'Clam Road,'" *The Press of Atlantic City*, April 12, 1964, microform edition, 120.
39. "Seaside Lots," *The New York Herald* (New York City, NY), November 23, 1890, microform edition, 38.
40. "A Banquet to Atlantic's Mayor," *The Philadelphia Inquirer*, September 4, 1890, microform edition, 61.
41. "A Railroad Company's Troubles," *The Trenton Evening Times*, September 17, 1890, microform edition, 3.
42. "Damage on the Meadows," *The Pittsburgh Dispatch*, October 25, 1890, microform edition, 7.
43. "Railroad Troubles," *The Lancaster Semi-Weekly* (Lancaster, PA), May 5, 1892, microform edition, 2.
44. "May's Landing to New York," *The Camden Morning Post*, November 13, 1893, microform edition, 1.
45. Untitled comment, *The Camden Daily Courier*, June 13, 1894, microform edition, 1.
46. See note 40.
47. "Business Troubles," *New York Sun* (New York City, NY), March 17, 1891, microform edition, 7. See also "A Liveryman's Flight," *The Wilmington Daily* (Wilmington, DE), June 8, 1891, microform edition, 1.
48. "Trestle Washed Out," *The Lancaster Semi-Weekly* (Lancaster, PA), May 5, 1892. Photocopy of unpaginated article at Atlantic County Historical Society.
49. Wm. C. Heppenheimer, Comptroller of the Treasury, *Annual Statements of the Railroad and Canal Companies of New Jersey for the Year 1892* (Trenton, NJ: The John L. Murphy Publishing Company, 1893), 30.
50. "Official Action of the Chancellor," *The Camden Daily Courier*, June 13, 1894, microform edition, 1.
51. "High Sea Off the Jersey Coast," *The New York Tribune* (New York City, NY), October 19, 1894, microform edition, 1.
52. "Brigantine Railroad to be Operated," *The Camden Daily Courier*, August 13, 1895, microform edition, 1.

53 "Brigantine Railroad Sold," *The Lebanon Semi-Weekly* (Lebanon, PA), July 1, 1895, microform edition, 3.
54 "Bridge Engine Sold," *The Brooklyn Daily Eagle*, September 28, 1897, microform edition, 16.
55 "Miscellaneous," *The Monmouth Inquirer* (Toms River, NJ), January 27, 1898, microform edition, page unknown.
56 "Business News," *The Wall Street Journal*, February 24, 1900, microform edition, 5.
57 "The Most Important Announcement of the Week," *The New York Tribune* (New York City, NY), February 25, 1900, microform edition, 9.
58 "The Roving Reporter by Frank Butler," *The Press of Atlantic City*, 1937. This is an undated and unpaginated copy from the files of the Atlantic County Historical Society.
59 "Atlantic City's Storm Damage," *The Camden Morning Post*, February 24, 1902, microform edition, 6.
60 "Shore Storm Report," *The Philadelphia Inquirer*, October 13, 1903, microform edition, 1, 5. This was also reported In the *Atlantic City Daily Union*, *The Camden Morning Post*, and the *St. Louis Republic*.
61 Paul C. Burgess, *Annals of Brigantine* (Brigantine, NJ: Paul C. Burgess, 1997), unpaginated.
62 "Reading Still Fastest," *The West Schuylkill Press and Pine Grove Herald* (Tremont, PA), August 13, 1904, microform edition, 4.
63 "The Roving Reporter by Frank Butler," *The Press of Atlantic City*, 1937. This is an undated and unpaginated copy from the files of the Atlantic County Historical Society.
64 Frank Butler, *Book of the Boardwalk* (Atlantic City, NJ: Haines & Co., 1952), 98.
65 "Local News," *The Atlantic City Gazette Review*, January 4, 1910, microform edition, 8.
66 "Ambitions," *The Philadelphia Inquirer*, May 8, 1910, microform edition, 6.
67 "Auction Sales," *The New York Times*, November 1, 1910, microform edition, 11.
68 "Old Brigantine RR Bed Slated for Township Road," *The Press of Atlantic City*, October 19, 1955, microform edition, 1.
69 James N. J. Henwood, *Trolleys to the Boardwalk: A History of Atlantic City Trolleys, 1854–1955* (Chicago, IL: Central Electric Railfan's Association, 2021), 16.
70 "At Brigantine Beach," *The Camden Morning Post*, July 29, 1890, microform edition, 14.
71 "Germantown Artisans at Brigantine," *The Philadelphia Inquirer*, April 18, 1893, microform edition, 5.
72 "Busy on the Brigantine," *The Philadelphia Inquirer*, May 2, 1893, microform edition, 5.
73 "The Trolley Man," *The Philadelphia Inquirer*, May 7, 1893, microform edition, 2.
74 "Shore Storm Report," *The Philadelphia Inquirer*, October 13, 1903, microform edition, 2.
75 *Brigantine, NJ – Sheet #55*. The Sanborn Map Company. (New York NY: Sanborn Map and Publishing Company, 1896).
76 "Atlantic Gun Club," *The Pittsburgh Press*, June 18, 1893, microform edition, 9.
77 "A New Route," *The Camden Morning Post*, June 18, 1893, microform edition, 4.
78 "Briefs," *The Savannah Morning News* (Savannah, GA), August 16, 1892, microform edition, 5.
79 "The Opening of the Electric Railway," *The Philadelphia Times*, May 27, 1894, microform edition, 7.
80 "Atlantic City," *The Philadelphia Inquirer*, June 17, 1894, microform edition, 12.
81 "Special to the Inquirer," *The Philadelphia Inquirer*, June 26, 1895, microform edition, 2.
82 "Brigantine Beach Railroad Sold," *The Lebanon Daily News* (Lebanon, PA), June 28, 1895, microform edition, 3. This was also reported again in the February 20 edition of *The Philadelphia Times*.
83 "To Abandon the Brigantine Road," *The Philadelphia Inquirer*, August 7, 1895, microform edition, 2.
84 "Shipbuilders Want Their Money," *The Philadelphia Times*, January 7, 1896, microform edition, 8.
85 "Want a New Receiver," *The Philadelphia Inquirer*, January 9, 1896, microform edition, 4.
86 Ibid.
87 "In Chancery," *The Camden Morning Post*, January 20, 1896, microform edition, 2.
88 Brigantine Transit Line Sold," *Baltimore Sun* (Baltimore, MD), February 5, 1897, microform edition, 2.
89 "Brigantine Beach Railroad Sold," *The Lebanon Daily News* (Lebanon, PA), June 28, 1895, microform edition, 11.
90 "Becoming More Evident," *The Philadelphia Inquirer*, June 21, 1896, microform edition, 17.
91 "Drowned at Brigantine," *The Scranton Tribune* (Scranton, PA), August 24, 1896, microform edition, 2.
92 William S. Hancock, *Annual Statements of the Railroad and Canal Companies of New Jersey for the Year 1896* (Trenton, NJ: MacCrellish & Quigley, 1897), 33–34.
93 "Transit Company Sold Out," *The Philadelphia Inquirer*, February 5, 1897, microform edition, 8.
94 Wm. C. Heppenheimer, Comptroller of the Treasury, *Annual Statements of the Railroad and Canal Companies of New Jersey for the Year 1892* (Trenton, NJ: The John L. Murphy Publishing Company, 1893), 29.
95 Henry Varnum Poor, *Poor's Manual of the Railroads of the United States* (New York City, NY: H. V. & H. W. Poor, 1899), 1017.
96 Personal communication, Dennis Niceler, February 8, 2020, while walking the old roadbed of the BBRR at the area of its connection in Pomona with the other railroads.

Detail from *Road Map of New Jersey*, 1918. This map also shows railroads to the barrier islands. State of New Jersey, State Highway Commission.

Crossing the Salt Marshes in South Jersey:
Remembering the Railroads

Kenneth W. Able and Paul W. Schopp

The physical intermodal connections between the South Jersey mainland and the coastal barrier islands are numerous and varied. They include highway and railroad rights-of-way for human use, but often these manmade structures create unintended consequences as they sometimes form permanent barriers in the waterways and the productive salt marshes. The ecological impact from these barriers is still being assessed. These human connections developed as the seasonal and permanent population of the barrier islands grew. While waterborne vessels served to provide the earliest transportation services to and from the barrier islands, railroad development wrought the most prominent and permanent changes. Connectivity construction for railroads began in the 1850s and culminated in the early 1900s in response to the need for transport of seafood, other foodstuffs, and tourism. The difficulty of building across the salt marshes because of natural conditions (soft substrates, many waterways, storms, etc.) and human factors (railroad construction practices, mergers, economic failures, development of the automobile) influenced the route and methodology of construction. Here we provide brief histories of the railroads in South Jersey that crossed the salt marshes and their status and ecological effects for a subset of these former rail lines.

Brief Histories of the Railroads and their Construction across the Salt Marshes

Philadelphia & Long Branch Railroad

After a number of corporate mergers and restylings that occurred between 1870 and 1880, the Pennsylvania Railroad's (PRR) subsidiary, the Philadelphia & Long Branch Railroad, emerged and constructed the right-of-way through the Pines, over the salt marshes, and across the bay between Whitings and Seaside Park. The company completed the line in July 1881. In describing the right-of-way, a corporate history states, "The terrain along the coast is flat and marshy. The grading was largely sand and averaged about 13,000 cu. Yds. per mile."[1] Known as the "Back Road," this line provided the PRR with another route to New York City as it extended up to Bayhead, where it connected with the New York & Long Branch Railroad, a route that the PRR and the Central Railroad of New Jersey operated on a joint basis. Service to Seaside Park ended on December 1, 1946, when 300 feet in the middle of the 7000-foot trestle across Barnegat Bay suffered catastrophic damage from a bad fire. It was the longest timber railroad bridge on the Pennsylvania Railroad system.[2] Despite calls from local governmental officials and members of the business community for repairing the trestle and restoring rail service, the railroad filed for the discontinuance of all passenger train service requiring use of the bridge.[3] Today, Shore Boulevard, West Atlantic Avenue, East Atlantic Avenue in Ocean Gate all occupy portions of the former railroad right-of-way across the salt marsh.

Philadelphia & Beach Haven Railroad

In October 1883, interests associated with the PRR incorporated the Long Beach Railroad Company. Virtually no work on constructing the line began until developers began property improvements on Long Beach Island. By June 1885, survey crews were busy laying out the route for the new railroad. The company released construction contracts in July 1885, including building the trestle and movable bridge across Barnegat Bay and the gravel right-of-way on the marshes. By the end of August 1885, 50 men were engaged in grading the right-of-way on the mainland. They completed the route across the salt marshes during October. Workmen finally completed the trestle over Manahawkin/Barnegat Bay in May 1886. The line was never a great source of revenue and eventually the Long Beach Railroad dissolved from financial troubles. In January 1894, the PRR oversaw the formation of a new company, the Philadelphia & Beach Haven Railroad, to assume control of the assets and operations of the Long Beach Railroad.[4] Revenue continued to dwindle, particularly after completion of the first vehicular bridge to the island in June 1914, built with private funding.[5] Many summer revelers still preferred the train until arterial roads became more vehicle friendly with improved surfaces and proper grading. On November 16, 1935, a terrible nor'easter struck the area with 60 mph gale-force winds. The following day's tidal surge floated away almost 5,000 feet of trestling on Manahawkin Bay.[6]

That ended all rail service to Long Beach Island and the PRR could not have been happier to raze and salvage what remained of the line as maintenance had been a cash drain for some years. Today, East Bay Avenue in Manahawkin, Stafford Township, intermittently occupies the former railroad right-of-way, as does West 8th Street in Ship Bottom.

Philadelphia & Brigantine Railroad

The Brigantine Beach Railroad filed its incorporation papers with the state in August 1889 and then granted a franchise to build between Pomona, where the line would have a junction with the Camden & Atlantic Railroad, and Brigantine Island. In November 1889, the chief engineer for the new line surveyed the route and contractor Coffin & Company from New York City arrived to begin construction. The Camden & Atlantic profited from the new company because it delivered all of the construction materials to Pomona from Camden.[7] The centerline route map filed with the New Jersey Secretary of State (see page 39 in the

Figure 1. In October 1928, a sharp gust of wind caught the wing of an airplane as it approached the Atlantic City Airport, causing the plane to crash into the salt marshes outside the city. One occupant died and seven others suffered injuries. The plane evidently clipped communication wires as it went down. In the background is the right-of-way of the Pennsylvania Railroad's Camden & Atlantic route into Atlantic City. The berm stands high above the marsh floor, which appears to be fairly solid in this area, devoid of mud and water. Two water supply pipes cross the marsh in the foreground, carrying water to Absecon Island.

previous article) clearly delineates what portions of the right-of-way featured gravel fill and what portions traversed open water on trestling. As construction of the route continued into 1890, the Philadelphia & Reading Railroad's Atlantic City Railroad became quite interested in operating the Brigantine Beach Railroad and incorporated the Pomona Branch Railroad to build a connection between the two companies' tracks. During the summer of 1890, the contractor building the route to Brigantine Island constructed the right-of-way across the salt marshes and over the open water. The trestling totaled over 9,000 feet and featured three movable bridges located as follows:

1. Grassy Bay (at the eastern edge of the main salt marsh)
2. Obe's Thoroughfare (just east of Egg Island)
3. Quarter's Thoroughfare (adjacent to the west shore of Brigantine Island)

The trestling cut off transiting through Felix's Thoroughfare by watercraft.[8] The Atlantic City Railroad leased the Brigantine Beach Railroad for 10 years in August 1890, just as the line opened for service. Never a financial success, the company slipped into receivership in June 1894. Despite the route's precarious existence due to its economic conditions, the lease required the Atlantic City Railroad to continue maintaining the right-of-way, including the great expense of repairing the trestling and the filled route across the salt marshes damaged by frequent winter storms. In April 1896, the company emerged from bankruptcy as the Philadelphia & Brigantine Railroad. Despite no longer being bankrupt, the company's expenses continued to exceed its revenue. The final blow came in September 1903, when a severe storm destroyed about 2000 feet of trestling. Management determined it would not rebuild the route across the salt marshes and bay and this decision ended the Philadelphia & Brigantine Railroad.[9] Today, East Great Creek Road and Great Neck Road occupy portions of the former railroad right-of-way.

CAMDEN & ATLANTIC RAILROAD

Legislatively incorporated in March 1852, the Camden & Atlantic retained Richard B. Osborne as its chief engineer. Construction of the line proved relatively easy across the southern New Jersey landscape until the crews reached the salt marshes. A corporate history records, "On the Atlantic Coast there are many lagoons and inlets and much soft marshy ground.... The subsoil is almost entirely sand with a few pockets of gravel and light clay.... [T]he only difficulty experienced in constructing the roadbed was on the four miles of marsh across the salt marshes near Atlantic City where considerable lengths of pile trestle were at first necessary....The only large bridge was a pile trestle 581 [feet] long with two 40-foot draw spans across the Thoroughfare at Atlantic City." This railroad operated as an independent company until 1883, when the PRR acquired control of it.[10] The Camden & Atlantic Railroad's route survived the formation of the Pennsylvania-Reading Seashore Lines in May 1933, and it remains in use today in 2022 as New Jersey Transit's Atlantic City Rail Line.

PHILADELPHIA & ATLANTIC CITY RAILWAY

Incorporated during the apex of the so-called "narrow-gauge fever" in 1876, the Philadelphia & Atlantic City Railway directors chose to build their new rail line with three feet and six inches between the rails (42") instead of the more normal three feet (36") standard narrow guage to allow for larger locomotives and cars and to prevent another railroad from readily subsuming the route. Among the incorporators of the new company were disgruntled board members from the Camden & Atlantic Railroad. Construction began in April 1877 on the east end of the route and built westward. In constructing the right-of-way across the salt marshes, the workers initially laid the tracks on timbers that would later be filled with gravel to prevent storm tides from undermining the track structure. By May, the labor force totaled 900 men who worked day and night to complete the route in time for the 1877 summer season. The line was completed in just 97 days, although many shortcuts were taken, including minimal grading and excavation. Trestling across Beach Thoroughfare measured 1300 feet, including the 100-foot movable bridge for boat traffic. The inaugural passenger train operated on July 7, 1877, with scheduled service beginning three weeks later.

After a series of financial reversals and corporate maneuvering to lease the Philadelphia & Atlantic City Railway during the early 1880s, the Philadelphia & Reading Railroad succeeded in becoming the owner in September 1883 after purchasing the company and its physical plant and equipment at a Master's Sale held at the courthouse in Camden. During the ensuing year, the new owner reconstructed the route as a standard gauge railroad. By 1889, the Philadelphia & Reading had consolidated all of its South Jersey rail operations

Figure 2. In this rare image looking towards the coast, workmen restore the timber cribbing under the Atlantic City Railroad's tracks through the salt marsh adjacent to "Meadows" interlocking tower on September 12, 1889, the day after a hurricane struck the South Jersey coast with great fury.

under the new Atlantic City Railroad. During the ensuing 40-plus years, the Philadelphia & Reading rebuilt and maintained the Atlantic City Railroad mainline as a first-class rail line, which permitted operating high-speed trains between Camden and Absecon Island. When the merger occurred to form the Pennsylvania-Reading Seashore Lines in May 1933, part of the preceding negotiations required the Atlantic City Railroad to abandon 31 miles of trackage between Winslow Junction and Salt Marshes Tower, thus ending the mainline into Atlantic City. With the tracks removed, the right-of-way lay fallow until the State of New Jersey constructed the Atlantic City Expressway. As designed, the new highway would use the Atlantic City Railroad's last four miles or so of the right-of-way as its route into America's Playground, including the crossing of the salt marshes and over the Thoroughfare.[11]

West Jersey & Atlantic Rail Road

With the Camden & Atlantic Railroad and the Philadelphia & Atlantic City Railroad narrow gauge providing the only access to the resort community of Atlantic City as independent rail operations, the PRR and its subsidiary, the West Jersey Railroad, possessed no direct access route to Absecon Island to profit from the excursion trade. To overcome this deficiency, a new line, the West Jersey and Atlantic Rail Road Company, drafted its incorporation papers in September 1879. Construction commenced two months later with James W. Allen as contractor. A corporate history reports, "The purpose of the construction of this railroad was to open up a large section of New Jersey then without rail service, and to bring to the West Jersey Railroad a share of the passenger traffic to and from the Atlantic Shore. The only difficulty met with in construction was on about four miles across the salt marshes near Atlantic City and this section was placed on a gravel embankment above the highest water."[12] Construction of the route into Atlantic City included a movable bridge over The Thoroughfare. When the PRR acquired control of the Camden & Atlantic in 1883, the West Jersey & Atlantic became less important until 1906, when the PRR electrified this route, along with the West Jersey to Millville, and operated high-speed passenger service. The PRR discontinued this electrified route to Atlantic City in 1931. Easterly portions of this line on the mainland remain in use today for freight service, although the trestle connection to Atlantic City has been removed.

Pleasantville & Ocean City Railroad/ Shore Fast Line

Just two years after its formation, the Philadelphia & Atlantic City Railway was in financial distress. The courts ordered a foreclosure sale in March 1879, although railroad management succeeded in delaying the sale numerous times. Meanwhile, Philadelphia & Atlantic City Railway president William Massey, seeking additional sources of revenue, incorporated the Pleasantville and Ocean City Railroad in June 1880, and held most of the equity himself. Construction began in July and reached its completion in October 1880. By May 1882, Massey sold his interest in the Somers Point line to men associated with the West Jersey Railroad, who raised the funds necessary to standard-gauge the route. The West Jersey held a keen interest in the route because it had completed the West

Crossing the Salt Marshes in South Jersey

Figure 3. The West Jersey & Atlantic's movable bridge over The Thoroughfare as the line enters Atlantic City looking back towards Camden. The view postdates the inauguration of electric train service on the route. In late October 1906, this bridge was the scene of a bad wreck of an electric train, with cars in the water and many fatalities.

Jersey & Atlantic Rail Road in June 1880 and a connection was then constructed between the two lines. The West Jersey & Seashore Railroad completed an electric line in 1906 between Camden and Atlantic City using its West Jersey and Atlantic Railroad, which started in Newfield. The high-speed cars began operating between the two cities in September 1906.

Another company, the Atlantic City & Shore Railroad, began operations earlier in 1906 and struck an agreement to use the West Jersey's route to Somers Point. In Pleasantville, passengers riding on the West Jersey's electric trains could transfer to the AC&S interurbans for a ride to Somers Point, where boats would move those passengers to Ocean City. In December 1907, the West Jersey & Seashore and its parent company, the PRR, completed a two-mile long trestle and steel movable bridge over Great Egg Harbor Bay between Somers Point and Ocean City, allowing the trolleys to travel between the two resort towns. The West Jersey & Seashore built this bridge with the idea of operating its electric lines cars into Ocean City, which service began in 1910, but it was never a great success and it ended in 1918. The railroad began discussions of resuming the service and studied the possible increased revenue from such service, but the study's results precluded the railroad from resuming the service. The Atlantic City & Shore, known as the Shore Fast Line, continued operations until 1948, when a hurricane damaged the Great Egg Harbor Bridge and the repairs amounted to more than the transit company could afford.[13]

Ocean City Railroad (Philadelphia & Reading)

In June 1896, a group of Ocean City real estate developers incorporated the Ocean City Railroad Company, although work on the route had begun in March of the same year after awarding the construction contract to the Philadelphia firm of Edmunds & Miller. The ten-mile line would extend from Cedar Swamp Creek at Petersburg to Ocean City. Construction suffered delays due to the West Jersey & Seashore (PRR formed in 1896) purchasing parcels of land and filing injunctions to stop work. The West Jersey & Seashore viewed the new line as a competition and a direct threat to its revenue. By the end of 1896, the construction crews had only completed 3.40 miles, reaching the site

Figure 4. The Pennsylvania Railroad completed building a movable bridge and trestle approaches over Great Egg Harbor Bay between Somers Point and Ocean City in December 1907 with the idea of operating electric trains between Camden and Ocean City. This service operated between 1910 and 1918 but did not generate enough revenue to warrant continuing the service. Meanwhile the Pennsylvania Railroad allowed the Atlantic City and Shore, commonly known as the Shore Fast Line, to operate its trolleys between Atlantic City and Ocean City. This service continued until 1948, when a storm destroyed the bridge.

Figure 5. The Atlantic City Railroad's Crook Horn movable bridge. Note the railroad berm standing high above the marsh floor and featuring a riprap covering as a preventative maintenance measure to prevent flood tides and storm surges from washing away the berm. The marsh features grasses and standing pools of water in this view.

Crossing the Salt Marshes in South Jersey

of the first large trestle on the salt marshes. By spring 1897, work resumed, including on a section known as Bray Island. The rush to reach Ocean City often caused the crews to lay track directly upon the marsh grasses and the first train arrived in Ocean City in May 1897. Despite this train arrival, construction of the right-of-way was so poor, the South Jersey Railroad refused to continue train operations at the end of July. Workmen completed the reconstruction during September. A storm struck in October and exacted great damage to the Ocean City and the Sea Isle City rights-of-way through the salt marshes. The Philadelphia & Reading Railroad gained full control of the Ocean City Railroad in 1901 and began making improvements to the right-of-way, including a new swing span over Crook Horn Creek.[14] When the West Jersey & Seashore Railroad and the Atlantic City Railroad merged to form the Pennsylvania-Reading Seashore Lines as a singular operational entity in May 1933, most of the Atlantic City Railroad's route were retained and the West Jersey & Seashore's various lines were abandoned and torn up. Such was the case with the Atlantic City Railroad's Ocean City line, which continued to provide train service to Ocean City until October 1981, when the ring gear failed on the Crook Horn swing span. The Coast Guard ordered the Crook Horn movable bridge removed due to it being a hazard to navigation. The removal occurred in 1992. Today, the right-of-way can be viewed on aerial photographs as an empty grade extending from fast land just east of the Garden State Parkway at Milepost 23.

Figure 6. The long sweeping trestle the West Jersey & Seashore constructed to connect Sea Isle City with Avalon across Townsend's Inlet during the 1880s. Note the A-Frame swing bridge built into the trestle to provide ready transit for watercraft.

Sea Isle City Branch/Avalon Branch/Ocean City Railroad (Pennsylvania Railroad)

The West Jersey Railroad constructed a rail line across the salt marshes from its Sea Isle City Junction with its Cape May & Millville Railroad, just north of Seaville, to Sea Isle City. Philadelphia-based contractor P. McManus commenced building the Sea Isle City line in May 1881 and completed it in June 1882. In August 1883, the West Jersey Railroad extended the track on the island from Sea Isle City to Townsend's Inlet and then extended a bridge across the inlet to Avalon by June 1888, when the first excursion train operated to Avalon.[15,16] The Ocean City Railroad incorporated in February 1884 as a paper company under aegis of the West Jersey Railroad. In April 1884, the Ocean City Railroad and its contractor, P. McManus, began constructing a rail line down the island known as Peck's Beach (now Ocean City) and across Corson's Inlet to Ludlam's Beach and Sea Isle City. According to a corporate history, "The bridges were largely short trestles. There was one 165 [foot] drawbridge and one deck-plate-girder span over Crook Horn Creek, total length 192 [feet], and one wood and steel viaduct 4000 [feet] long with two steel draw spans built in 1891."[17] The West Jersey & Seashore, formed in 1896, continued to use this route for access to both resorts until 1933, when a merger of the two companies brought the Pennsylvania-Reading Seashore Lines into existence. Today, Bay Avenue occupies a portion of the abandoned right-of-way as does Ocean Drive.

Sea Isle City Railroad (Philadelphia & Reading)

Although the West Jersey Railroad's access to Cape May County began in the 1860s, the Philadelphia & Reading Railroad's Atlantic City Railroad entered the county by operating over the tracks of the South Jersey Railroad (née Philadelphia & Sea Shore Railway), formed in November 1889, and the Tuckahoe & Cape May, incorporated in February 1890. The original 1889 plans called for extending a line to Sea Isle City. Construction crews had cleared a right-of-way from Winslow to Sea Isle City and began laying ties and steel rails by February 1890. Any bridges required were built

Figure 7. The West Jersey & Seashore trestle across Corson's Inlet that connected Sea Isle City with Ocean City, built in the 1880s.

with wood as the line featured no steel bridges in the beginning. By the end of May 1890, the crews reached the edge of the salt marshes at Seaville. Financial setbacks and poor management delayed the completion of the Sea Isle City until July 1893. The line initially featured rather shabby construction and lightweight rail. The bridges could only support the lightest of locomotives. The Atlantic City Railroad did what it could to reconstruct the line, but the traffic and revenue did not warrant expending large sums of money to put the route in first-class condition. By the mid-1920s, the parent company, seeking to pare expenses, sought permission from the Interstate Commerce Commission (ICC) to abandon its Sea Isle City route. The ICC granted the requested permission in August 1925. The Atlantic City Railroad removed the rails and salvaged what they could from the bridges.[18] Today, the route consists of an empty grade composed of gravel stretching out across the salt marshes, visible on aerial photographs.

Stone Harbor Railroad

Seeking to increase property development on Seven Mile Beach, the South Jersey Realty Company chartered two railroad companies in May 1912 to bring rail service to Stone Harbor. The first company, the Stone Harbor Terminal Railroad, served to connect to the Atlantic City Railroad's Cape May route at Cape May Court House, including a wye for turning trains and to provide northbound and southbound traffic access to the Stone Harbor Railroad, the second company formed, which would extend from the wye out across the salt marshes to its namesake. The original plan called for the Atlantic City Railroad to operate the line, and a special train of dignitaries rode a train over the unfinished route in June 1912. The owners determined they would operate the route themselves and wired the line for trolley service. Despite enduring financial failures, Stone Harbor interests retained control of the Stone Harbor Railroad, eventually replacing the trolley operations with railbuses. The Philadelphia & Reading's Atlantic City Railroad obtained trackage rights into Stone Harbor in 1917 and finally gained full control of the operation in June 1930 by acquiring all outstanding stock and assuming a judgment debt against the company. The Atlantic City Railroad immediately replaced the Scotch Bonnet Creek trestle, badly damaged by

Crossing the Salt Marshes in South Jersey

Figure 8. The Philadelphia & Reading's Atlantic City Railroad's bridge into Stone Harbor, situated immediately adjacent to the highway bridge leading to the resort. In the background can be seen the salt marshes through which the right-of-way passed before reaching the bridge.

periodic storms that swept the coast. All train traffic to Seven Mile Beach ceased in 1934. Today, Stone Harbor Boulevard occupies the former railroad right-of-way or is proximate to it.

ANGLESEA RAIL ROAD

The Anglesea Rail Road incorporated in November 1882 as an independent railroad company but entered receivership by December 1884. In April 1888, the New Jersey Court of Chancery decreed that the Anglesea Rail Road be conveyed to the West Jersey Railroad. The successor corporation merged the Anglesea Rail Road into itself through filing a new right-of-way map with the New Jersey Secretary of State. According to a corporate history, this "... line traversed a flat, sandy terrain." Construction commenced "... about December 1882 and completed about July 1883 ..." to Anglesea from Anglesea Junction (and later extended down Five Mile Island to Holly Beach, now Wildwood).[19] Philadelphia contractor Peter F. Collins received the contract for building the line.[20] Anglesea Junction provided a connection with the West Jersey Railroad in Burleigh. The route required three fixed bridges or culverts as it crossed the salt marshes: Mill Race; Cut-Through; and Beach Creek. In addition, the route featured an A-frame, end-pivot swing bridge over Grassy Sound Channel to provide for the movement of vessels through the Grassy Sound salt marshes. Local historian W. Scott Jett notes, "This draw bridge would be the most difficult and time-consuming segment of the construction; Grassy Sound at the railroad's right-of-way was almost 600 feet wide with strong tidal currents."[21] With consummation of the merger to form the Pennsylvania-Reading Seashore Lines in May 1933, the Atlantic City Railroad's route into Wildwood was retained and the West Jersey & Seashore's Anglesea Rail Road was abandoned and trackage and bridges removed. Today, the Anglesea Rail Road right-of-way comprises an empty grade, an unnamed road on Grassy Sound Marsh, and then Ash Avenue and West Oak Avenue in Anglesea.

WILDWOOD & DELAWARE BAY SHORT LINE

In its attempt to compete with the PRR's West Jersey & Seashore Railroad's routes to the various South Jersey shore resorts, it irked the Philadelphia & Read-

Figure 9. A West Jersey & Seashore train leaves Grassy Sound Station and moves across the A-Frame swing bridge and the trestle that carries the Anglesea Rail Road tracks across Grassy Sound and over the marshes before reaching the mainland and Anglesea Junction in Burleigh.

ing's management that its Atlantic City Railroad had no service to Five Mile Beach and its popular vacation hotspot, Holly Beach or Wildwood. Real estate developers posited that rail competition would only serve to improve service and increase platting new residential areas on the island. The Wildwood & Delaware Bay Short Line incorporated in June 1910 and the line opened for revenue traffic in December 1912. Constructed to handle heavy traffic, the four-mile route branched off the route to Cape May at Wildwood junction and included transiting the salt marshes on an embankment and a "substantial drawbridge" fabricated by the Pennsylvania Steel Company of Steelton, Pennsylvania.[22] With consummation of the merger to form the Pennsylvania-Reading Seashore Lines in May 1933, the Atlantic City Railroad's route into Wildwood was retained and the West Jersey & Seashore's Anglesea Rail Road was abandoned and razed. Passenger service to Wildwood ended in December 1972 and freight traffic ceased in June 1974. The railroad sold the right-of-way to a private individual with the stipulation that all trackage and bridges be removed. The new owner stripped the right-of-way of ties and rails, but when they attempted to remove the draw span, the crane employed in the demolition was too light, so the movable span dropped into Grassy Sound, where it still remains, on the bottom. Today, small portions of the Wildwood & Delaware Bay Short Line can be found in West Wildwood and Oak Avenue, Wildwood. Remnants of the concrete piers for the approach spans and the movable bridge remain in situ.

Crossing the Salt Marshes in South Jersey

Table 1. Railroad lines, arranged north to south, crossing the coastal salt marsh and bays to reach South Jersey's barrier islands*

No.	Railroad Name	Parent	Location	County	Current Status
1	Philadelphia & Long Branch RR	PRR	Barnegat Bay	Ocean	Shore Boulevard; West Atlantic Avenue; East Atlantic Avenue; empty grade; trestling across bay burned 1944
2	Philadelphia & Beach Haven RR	PRR	Manahawkin to LBI	Ocean	East Bay Avenue intermittently; West 8th Street
3	Philadelphia & Brigantine RR	P&R	Reeds Bay/ Grassy Bay	Atlantic	East Great Creek Road; Great Neck Road; empty grade
4	Camden & Atlantic RR	PRR	Absecon Bay	Atlantic	Intact and in use
5	Philadelphia & Atlantic City Railway	P&R	Lakes Bay	Atlantic	Atlantic City Expressway
6	West Jersey & Atlantic RR	PRR	Lakes Bay	Atlantic	Intact and in use up to the ACE-Route 40 Interchange
7	Pleasantville and Ocean City Railroad/Shore Fast Line	PRR	Great Egg Harbor Bay	Atlantic/ Cape May	MacArthur Boulevard (NJ-52)
8	Ocean City Railroad	P&R	Corsons Sound	Cape May	Empty grade; Crook Horn movable bridge removed in 1992
9	Ocean City Railroad	PRR	Ludlams Bay/ Townsends Inlet	Cape May	Bay Avenue; R-O-W to Avalon, partially Ocean Drive
10	Sea Isle City RR	P&R	Corson's Inlet	Cape May	Empty grade across the salt marshes
11	Stone Harbor Railroad	P&R	Great Sound	Cape May	Stone Harbor Boulevard
12	Anglesea Rail Road	PRR	Grassy Sound	Cape May	Empty grade; unnamed road on Grassy Sound Marsh; Ash Avenue and West Oak Avenue in Anglesea
13	Wildwood & Delaware Bay RR	P&R	Grassy Sound	Cape May	Empty grade; an unnamed street at the south end of Q and P streets in West Wildwood; West Oak Avenue in Wildwood.

*It should be understood that virtually all of the above railroad rights-of-way comprise solid-fill berms through the salt marshes and timber trestling and movable bridges where warranted when crossing open water. Empty grade means the solid-fill right-of-way is intact across the salt marshes, but devoid of any track superstructure.

Key to parent company: PRR=Pennsylvania Railroad; P&R=Philadelphia & Reading Railroad

Status and Ecology Today of Representative Railroads

Roadbeds for railroads across the salt marshes share many ecological characteristics with automobile roadbeds,[23] but railroads have received much less attention especially when they cross marshes even though they may cause some of the same negative impacts as automobile roads. Six of these have been revisited to evaluate their status and ecological effects today (Figure 10). Of the railroad beds successfully constructed across the salt marshes in South Jersey (Table 1, Figure 10) only the line from Philadelphia to Atlantic City remains in operation (Figure 2). The remnants of the lines from the mainland near Palermo to Ocean City, from the mainland to Sea Isle City, and those from the mainland to North Wildwood and West Wildwood are still obvious from the air and from land if you are willing to do a little walking (Figure 10).

While the railroad beds are variable relative to location and local topography, they share a number of characteristics. They are often high, frequently 6–8 feet above the marsh, with the bed consisting of gravel and rock and other types of road fill (Figure 12). They are wide as well, ranging from 30–40 feet and appear to be impermeable to tidal waters. They are continuous over long distances with one of the longest (4.6 miles) reaching Atlantic City from the mainland with the shortest of 1.7 miles coming into Wildwood and Sea Isle City (Figure 10). As a result of their extensive length and width, the construction of these railroad beds accounted for the loss of extensive amounts of meadow grasses, amounting to an estimated 61 acres. This is important because these meadow grasses are one of the most productive habitats in the world.[24]

Over these distances the railroad beds are occasionally broken by bridges over small (Figure 13) and large waterways (Figures 14, 15) such as the Intracoastal Waterway (Figure 16). Despite these watery connections, the railroad beds often act as dams that prevent the typical sheetflow of water over the marshes on high tides,[25] thus they may be negatively influencing water circulation over broad areas, especially near the mainland where there are fewer bridges, thus they impede water flow in the same way that roads do.[26]

A visual characteristic, both from the air and the ground, of all the abandoned railroad beds is the presence of salt tolerant red cedar trees growing on the higher elevation of the railroad bed (Figures 13, 16, 17). An obvious influence of these long, linear dams is on connectivity within the marsh. This is most common as an alteration of water circulation because it is limited to the creeks and channels that comprise the waterways, except in case of extreme flooding, as has occurred in the past.[27] The damming effect of the railroad beds is compounded because they originate from the high elevation at the western end where they join the mainland (Figure 10). Thus, there is little circulation possible along the western edges. One also wonders how the railroad bed dams influence the hydrodynamics[28] and detrital transport, a key component of the many ecological services of the salt marshes.[29]

The effects of highwater during storms is evident by the accumulation of marsh grass or wrack, typically on the north side of the east-west roadbeds, from the most common nor'easters. If the wrack is not obvious, its effects *are* because of the lack of live vegetation as a shadow around the railroad bed (Figure 16) because the accumulated wrack kills the marsh grass[30] when it is deposited on a high tide. It may remain there until the next storm.

At the same time, the higher elevations of the roadbeds represent an extension of the mainland, with salt-tolerant trees (red cedar, holly, others), shrubs (groundsel tree, marsh elder), etc., into the marsh (Figure 17). A particular example of the extension of invasive Phragmites[31] is onto the margins of the railroad beds, yet it does not occur in the adjacent salt marshes. While Phragmites is believed to be deleterious to fishes and crabs,[32] it may provide variable habitat for birds.[33] At one extreme, the railroad beds also become disposal points in the salt marshes for the obvious dumping of mollusk shells (surf clams, channeled and knobbed whelks) from fishing and processing operations as is obvious on the railroad bed to West Wildwood. In other instances, the remnants of the railroads are treated as gardens (Figure 18).

Thus together, railroads through the salt marshes of South Jersey have had a variety of impacts on the flora and fauna of these habitats as well as the humans that constructed them.

Crossing the Salt Marshes in South Jersey

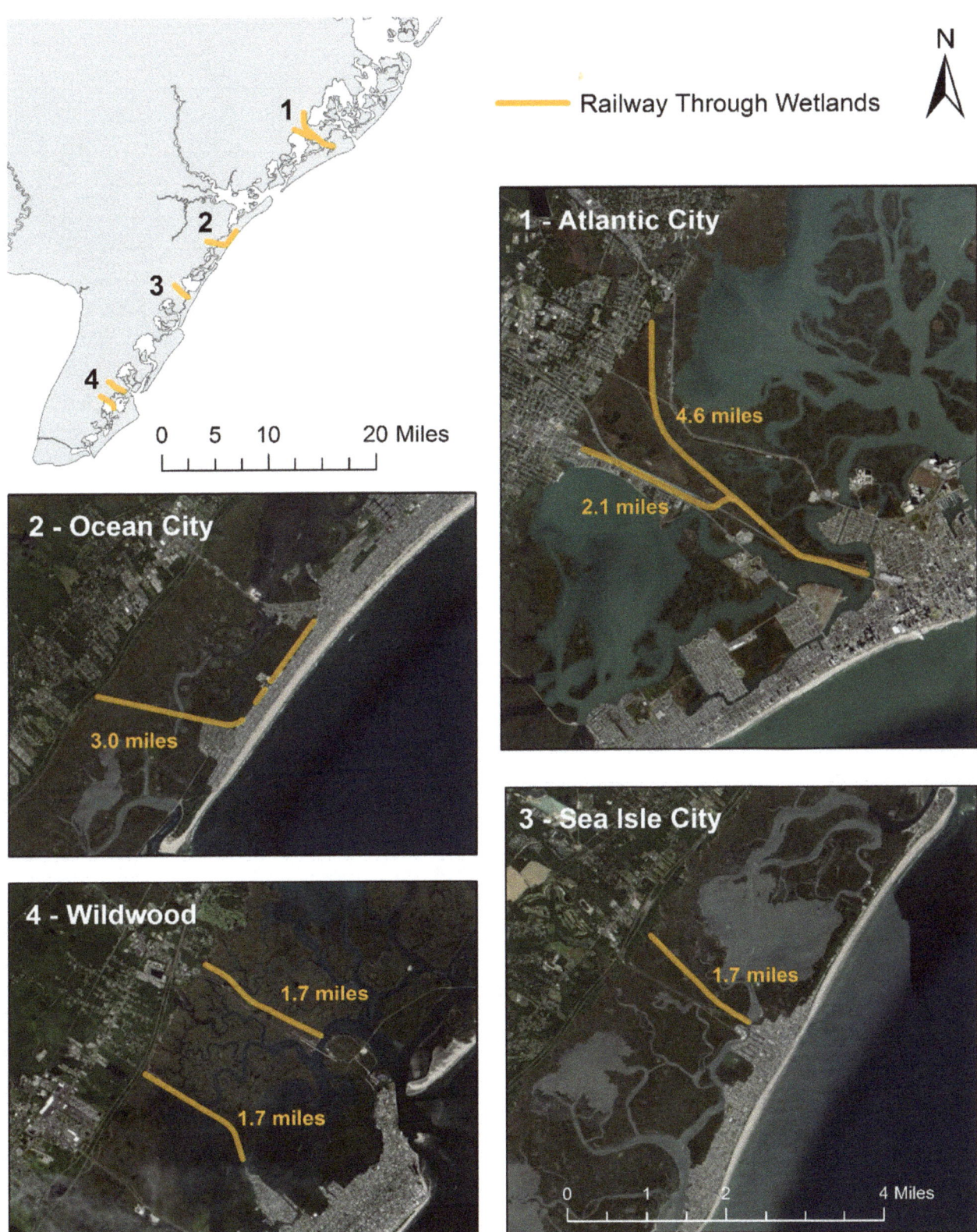

Figure 10. Locations of the railroads recently evaluated with distances across the coastal salt marshes from the mainland, across the Intracoastal Waterway to the associated coastal towns on the barrier islands in South Jersey (see inset). All aerial imagery is depicted at the same scale. We investigated two lines into Atlantic City from Absecon and Pleasantville (1), a single line from near Palermo into southern Ocean City (2), a line into Sea Isle City from near South Seaville (3), and two lines near Wildwood with one crossing the salt marshes into North Wildwood parallel to Rt. 147 and another into West Wildwood from near Whitesboro from Wildwood Junction (4).

(Top left) **Figure 11**. Photo of existing railroad line from Absecon to Atlantic City. (Top right) **Figure 12**. The railroad bed into Ocean City (on the horizon) from the mainland shares many characteristics with other railroad beds (note the former ties that supported the rails) across the salt marshes, including extensive gravel/rock bed high above the marsh. Also, the edge of the marsh is devoid of vegetation because it was previously covered by wrack (dead vegetation) from past storms. (Mid left) **Figure 13**. Photo of former railroad bridge, over unnamed creek, on its way to Ocean City from February 2020. Characteristic road fill is evident in the lower portion of the image. (Mid right) **Figure 14**. Former railroad line trestle between West Wildwood and Wildwood where it crosses Post Creek Basin in a photo from February 2020. (Bottom left) **Figure 15**. Photo of former railroad line concrete bridge crossing Old Turtle Thorofare on its way to West Wildwood, in upper right, from the mainland in a photo from March 2020. Between this site and West Wildwood is a line of trees that indicate the continuation of the old railroad bed.

(Next page) **Figure 16**. Aerial photo from May 2019 of former railroad line bed crossing the salt marshes on its way to Ocean City. The bridge in Figure 13 is evident in the lower portion of the photo. In the distance (upper center) the former roadbed crosses two waterways. The one closest to the barrier island and Ocean City is part of the Intracoastal Waterway.

Crossing the Salt Marshes in South Jersey

(Right) **Figure 17**. Photo from Garden State Parkway of former railroad bed to Ocean City from Garden State Parkway overpass from February 2020.

(Below) **Figure 18**. Remnant of former railroad line behind southern Ocean City now decorated as a backyard garden in a photo from October 2020.

Crossing the Salt Marshes in South Jersey

Acknowledgments

Several individuals from the Rutgers University Marine Field Station helped to gather images and information, including Miranda Rosen and Ryan Larum. Judy Redlawsk made the collection of aerial images possible by providing her helicopter and her piloting expertise. Pat Filardi, Peter Able and Sue Able assisted with groundtruthing aerial images and details of individual railroad beds.

About the Authors

Ken Able is a Distinguished Professor Emeritus in the Department of Marine and Coastal Sciences and the former director of the Rutgers University Marine Field Station where he is still located. His interests continue to be focused on estuarine ecology and especially salt marshes.

Paul W. Schopp is the assistant director of the South Jersey Culture & History Center and he has maintained a longstanding interest in transportation modalities in South Jersey among many other historical topics related to the eight lower counties of New Jersey.

Endnotes

1. Coverdale & Colpitts, *The Pennsylvania Railroad Company: The Corporate, Financial and Construction History of Lines Owned, Operated and Controlled to December 31, 1945, Volume IV Affiliated Lines, Miscellaneous Companies, and General Index* (Philadelphia, PA: Allen, Lane & Scott, 1946), 127–42.
2. "Flames Wreck Bridge Over Barnegat Bay," *The Philadelphia Inquirer*, December 2, 1946, 1, 14.
3. "Ocean Chamber Hits Rail Service Cut Plan," *Asbury Park Evening Press* (Asbury Park, NJ), December 24, 1947, 6.
4. John Brinckmann, *The Tuckerton Railroad: A Chronicle of Transport to the New Jersey Seashore* (Edison, NJ: by the author, 1973), 61–66.
5. George B. Somerville, *The Lure of Long Beach* ([Beach Haven?], NJ: The Long Beach Board of Trade, 1914), 76.
6. Brinckmann, *The Tuckerton Railroad*, 139–40.
7. George Cook and William Coxey, *The Atlantic City Railroad: Royal Route to the Sea* (Oaklyn, NJ: West Jersey Chapter, NRHS, Inc., 1980), 57.
8. Ibid., 58–59.
9. Ibid., 59–60.
10. Coverdale & Colpitts, *The Pennsylvania Railroad Company*, 188–92.
11. Cook and Coxey, *The Atlantic City Railroad*.
12. Coverdale & Colpitts, *The Pennsylvania Railroad Company*, 221–23.
13. Robert A. Stanton, "Electric Trains to Ocean City," *West Jersey Rails Quarterly* 14, no. 2, winter (Palmyra, NJ: West Jersey Chapter, NRHS, 2008).
14. Cook and Coxey, *The Atlantic City Railroad*, 68–75.
15. Coverdale & Colpitts, *The Pennsylvania Railroad Company*, 208–10.
16. Robert Matt, *The History of Avalon* (Avalon, NJ: Avalon Home and Land Owners Association, 1992), 7.
17. Coverdale & Colpitts, *The Pennsylvania Railroad Company*, 208–10.
18. Cook and Coxey, *The Atlantic City Railroad*, 60–72.
19. Coverdale & Colpitts, *The Pennsylvania Railroad Company*, 218–20.
20. W. Scott Jett, *Borough of Anglesea, 1885-1906*, vol. 1 (n.p., 2018), 19.
21. Ibid., 20.
22. Cook and Coxey, *The Atlantic City Railroad*, 93–95.
23. Forman, R. T. T., D. Sperling, J. A. Bissonette et al. *Road Ecology: Science and Solutions* (Washington: Island Press, 2002); Andrews, K. M., P. Nanjappa and S. P. D. Riley, eds., *Roads and Ecological Infrastructure: Concepts and Applications for Small Animals* (Baltimore, MD: Johns Hopkins University Press, 2003).
24. Gedan, K. B., B. R. Silliman and M. D. Bertness, "Centuries of Human-Driven Change in Salt Marsh Ecosystems," *Annual Review of Marine Science* 1 (2009): 117–41.
25. Leonard, L. A. and M. E. Luther, "Flow Dynamics in Tidal Marsh Canopies," *Limnology and Oceanography* 40, no. 8 (1995): 1474–84.
26. Forman et al., *Road Ecology*.
27. Stephenson Jr., E. T. and G. W. Ueckermann Jr., "A History of the Pleasantville Salt Marshes, Part II:1850–1969," *The Atlantic County Historical Society, Sixty-Fifth Yearbook* (Somers Point, NJ: Atlantic County Historical Society, 2013), 35–64.
28. Baker, R., B. Fry, L. P. Rozas and T. J. Minello, "Hydrodynamic Regulation of Salt Marsh Contributions to Aquatic Food Webs," *Marine Ecology Progress Series* 490 (2013): 37–52.
29. Peterson, C. H., K. W. Able, C. F. DeJong, M. F. Piehler, C. A. Simenstad and J.B. Zedler, "Chapter 4. Practical Proxies for Tidal Marsh Ecosystem Services: Application to Injury and Restoration," *Advances in Marine Biology* 54 (2008): 221–66; Barbier, E. B., S. D. Hacker, C. Kennedy, E. W. Koch, A. C. Stier, and B. R. Silliman, "The Value of Estuarine and Coastal Ecosystem Services," *Ecological Monographs* 81, no. 2 (2011): 169–93.
30. Hartman, J., H. Casewell and I. Valiela, "Effects of Wrack Accumulation on Salt Marsh Vegetation," *Oceanologica Acta. Proceedings 17th European Marine Biology Symposium, Brest, France. 27 September – 1 October 1982* (1983): 99–102; Hanley, T. C., D. L. Kimbro and A. R. Hughes, "Stress and Subsidy Effects of Seagrass Wrack Duration, Frequency, and Magnitude on Salt Marsh Community Structure," *Ecology* 98, no. 7 (2017):1884–95.
31. Weinstein, M. P. and J. H. Balletto, "Does the Common

Reed, Phragmites australis, Affect Essential Fish Habitat?" *Estuaries* 22, no. 3 (1999): 793–802; Chambers, R. M., L. A. Meyerson and K. Saltonstall, "Expansion of Phragmites australis into Tidal Wetlands of North America," *Aquatic Botany* 64 (1999): 261–73; Smith, J. A. M,, "The Role of Phragmites australis in Mediating Inland Salt Marsh Migration in a Mid-Atlantic Estuary," *PLoS ONE* 8, no. 5 (2013): e65091.

32 Hagan, S. M., S. A. Brown, and K. W. Able. "Production of Mummichog (Fundulus Heterocclitus): Response in Marshes Treated for Common Reed," *Wetlands* 27, no. 1 (March 2007): 54–67; Hunter, K. L., D. A. Fox, L. M. Brown, and K. W. Able. "Responses of Resident Marsh Fishes to Stages of Phragmites australis Invasion in Three Mid Atlantic Estuaries," *Estuaries and Coasts* 29, no. 3 (June 2006): 487–96.

33 Parsons, K. C., "Reproductive Success of Wading Birds Using Phragmites Marsh and Upland Nesting Habitats," *Estuaries* 26, no. 2B (2003): 596–601; Trocki, C. L. and Paton, P. W. C., "Assessing Habitat Selection by Foraging Egrets in Salt Marshes at Multiple Spatial Scales," *Wetlands* 26, no. 2 (2006): 307–12; Tonjes, D. J., "Impacts from Ditching Salt Marshes in the Mid-Atlantic and Northeastern United States," *Environ. Rev.* 21 (2013): 116–26.

A Delaware River scene. Man on horseback talking with a man carrying an oystering rake on the shore of the Delaware River; another man is standing on a sea wall and gesturing toward approaching dark clouds; and a fourth man is standing on a bluff just above the shoreline. Philadelphian James Fuller Queen (1820 or 1821–1886), who completed this watercolor, was a well-regarded artist, lithographer, and chromolithographer, known for his attention to detail and composition. From the Marion S. Carson Collection, Library of Congress. Although the location is not known, the hills in the background and oyster shovel suggest the Jersey side of the Delaware.

A Curious Case of Survival:
History of the Red Dragon Canoe Club

John Lawrence

Introduction

The Red Dragon Canoe Club (RDCC), reputably the second oldest, continuously operating boat club in the United States, formed 135 years ago in a late Victorian world that would hardly be recognizable to us today. Yet the RDCC not only persists but thrives today as an active and growing institution. This fact is a textbook example of what anthropologists of the Victorian period called a "cultural survival"—a social practice, belief, or custom that emerged at some point in the past for a specific purpose but survives long after the need for that function has ceased. For example, consider the case of saying "gesundheit" when someone sneezes. We don't think about it now, but the term originally served as an incantation to ward off an illness more severe than a sneeze. We now have antibiotics to fulfill that purpose, but we still say "gesundheit."

How the RDCC has survived the past 135 years is a fascinating story, weaving together national trends in popular culture and sport and different actors and groups of people at different times who took active steps that promoted the longevity of the institution, whether that was their direct intent or not. With the 20/20 vision that retrospect provides, we can discern what decisions were made, by whom, when, and under what circumstances that kept the RDCC alive, when it could have easily met the fate of so many similar clubs that only exist today in sepia-toned photographs of men with funny haircuts.

The Club's Origins

The origins of the RDCC lie at the intersection of two social trends in white, middle-class society of the late nineteenth century: the increasing popularity of social clubs and the emergence of organized sports competition for men. *Fin de siècle* and early twentieth century America witnessed the single largest growth in the number of clubs, associations, lodges, veteran's groups, etc., in its entire history. Sociologists speculate that this "crescendo" in growth—of which the RDCC is just one example—was a response to the disruptive effects of the rapid technological, economic, social, and political changes of that period.[1]

Although the origins of the canoe are lost to the mists of time, canoeing was not recognized as a "sport" until 1866 when a Scotsman, John MacGregor, founded the Canoe Club in England. A number of socially prominent men, including the Prince of Wales, later King Edward VII, were among its founding members.[2] Imitating one's betters being a common practice, the sport crossed the big pond when the New York Canoe Club was founded in 1871, the Keystone Canoe Club in 1883, and the RDCC in 1887. The Philadelphia Canoe Club was not chartered until 1905.

The early history of the RDCC is linked to that of the Keystone club. Under the leadership of W. J. Norgrave, the Keystone Canoe Club made its home at the foot of Monroe Street in the Tacony section of Philadelphia, while the RDCC established its headquarters on Second Street at Cooper's Point, Camden. Harry B. Kramer appears to have led the formation of the RDCC. According to the Keystone Club's meeting minutes, an informal meeting of the Keystone C. C. was held Friday evening January 4, 1889, and the following motion was carried.

To unite with the R.D.C.C. under the name of *R.D.C.C. of Philadelphia* and made certain conditions agreed upon by committee appointed to represent the respective clubs, thereupon a joint meeting of the clubs was called with Capt. Norgrave in the chair and the two clubs were formally united.[3]

C. B. Haag was Commodore of the Keystone at the time of the merger and retained that position in the new club; Harry Kramer was elected Vice-Commodore, cementing the leadership of the two former clubs.[4] The reasons for this merger were never explained, but a review of early membership rolls suggests an answer. It reveals that the number of members of either club was not very high at the time and, perhaps it was felt, not sustainable. In January of 1889 both clubs together only amounted to 35 persons, who resided on both sides of the Delaware River.[5] The RDCC's original club house on Cooper's Point was chosen for the amalgamated membership, despite the name being changed to the Red Dragon Canoe Club of Philadelphia.[6]

By all accounts, the RDCC prospered under the combined membership, beating some well-known English canoes in an 1886 competition, and capturing the American Canoe Association (ACA) Trophy in 1889.[7] Despite these victories, and the reported high spirits of the membership, disaster struck early and frequently in the first decade of the club's history. Within a year of the clubs' amalgamation and the stupendous victory at the ACA, the club's home at Cooper's Point and fleet of 20 canoes, "one war canoe, one yacht, one sloop, and one naptha [sic] launch" were destroyed by fire on the night of December 16, 1889.[8] The RDCC clubhouse sat proximate to the Quaker City Canoe Club and both structures perished. The clubs apparently wasted no time in building new boathouses on the site, but on November 25, 1890, these too suffered loss to flames that consumed not only the RDCC's boathouse, boats, and clubhouse, but those of several other clubs as well.[9]

Although a number of dispirited members subsequently left the club in the summer of 1891, about 15 stalwarts reconstituted the club in "a certain two story

Figure 1. The spacious 1799 riverside mansion belonging to the colonial-era Morris family. Following several disastrous fires, the Red Dragon Canoe Club moved to this location in 1892.

A Curious Case of Survival

frame house situated on the Delaware River and adjoining the wharf at Bridesburg."[10] Incredibly, the Bridesburg clubhouse also burned down within a year and the club quickly relocated upriver to the spacious 1799 riverside mansion belonging to the colonial-era Morris family.[11] The property contained many amenities: two and one-half acres of land at the confluence of the Delaware River and Wissinoming Creek, tennis courts, a shooting range, fifteen rooms and twelve fireplaces, a wharf and a spur from the nearby PRR mainline (Figure 1). The club also erected thirteen bungalows and cabins and a canoe house, which was built in 1903 and had a storage space for 27 canoes.[12]

The RDCC grew and thrived at Wissinoming for the next 30 years, despite yet *another* fire in 1899, which partially damaged the clubhouse; none of the boats, however, burned on this occasion.[13] Regardless of this mishap, the RDCC became *the* premier and best-known canoe club on the Delaware River. Active participation in the organization of the ACA and vigorous competition at their annual meets helped to cement the club's reputation, to which the numerous trophies the RDCC still hold attests. The RDCC hosted the only ACA annual meet ever held on the lower Delaware River, at Delanco in 1902.[14]

Within the orbit of local canoe clubs, the RDCC hosted annual regattas in the fall, attended by many if not all canoe clubs along the lower Delaware (below Trenton). These were more than mere sporting events, but gala social events with dinners and dancing, as reported in the local news.[15] The club itself was socially active, both on the water and off. A friendly competi-

Figures 2 (top) and **3**. Historic photographs of members of the Red Dragon Canoe Club.

tion occurred between members for how many miles they logged in their boats annually, and a trophy given to the winner.[16] Races for different classes of canoes (single bladed and double-bladed paddling, sailing) took place periodically within the club (Figure 2). The club organized canoe/camping trips throughout the area, but also going as far north as Canada, on a regular basis (Figure 3). Monthly dinners were held at the clubhouse, as was an elaborate Annual Mess, a tradition still strong at the RDCC (Figures 4 and 5).

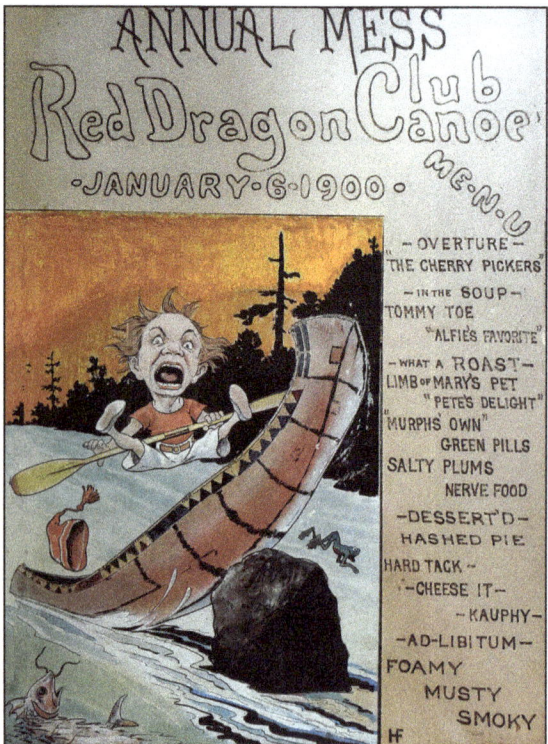

Figure 4 (top). Bart Keen's wild goose dinner at the club. Figure 5 (left). Advertisement for RDCC Annual Mess, January 6, 1900.

A New Challenge Confronted

The success of the RDCC in meeting and surviving the disastrous clubhouse fires and its peregrination across the river was not an accident. Not only did the social cohesion of the club undoubtedly play a role, but the strong organizational structure and financial stability of the club did as well. Two club histories commented independently on this fact. As early as 1895, a newspaper report credited the "unceasing efforts" and "persistent and untiring energy" of club members and their "management" in surmounting problems.[17] In 1917, Commodore W. H. Logan restated this quality in slightly different tones: "A unity of spirit and a tendency to conservative action have marked the club since its inception."[18]

By "conservative action" we suppose that Commodore Logan referred to the fact that for all the fun and games, the RDCC was well and strictly organized and financially stable. Members who conducted themselves in a manner unbecoming of a gentleman faced being expelled. The club obtained its formal incorporation through the Commonwealth of Pennsylvania in 1895. Monthly meeting agendas included discussion of club business, the annual election of officers, and collecting dues, with the Purser providing the annual financial status of the club to the membership at the beginning of each year. In addition, ad hoc committees formed as needed to address specific issues, and their reports and recommendations presented to the club, whose members then frequently voted on the recommendations of the committee. A Sinking Fund was established at an early date for use as needed to cover club expenses.[19]

By the end of the First World War, the organizational strength of the club would be put to the test. However delightful the Wissinoming home for the club had been in 1892, 25 years later, it was very different. Crime was an issue and encroaching pollution from industry on the river befouled the local waters and the boats and made swimming impossible. One club history states that with the opening of the Tacony-Palmyra ferry "the privacy of former days was lost," prompting the desire to move upriver.[20] Although this was certainly the case once the ferry began operations, the first mention of the club seeking a new home is found in the club's meeting minutes for March 1917—the Tacony-Palmyra Ferry service did not begin until 1922.[21] The same meeting minutes for 1922 suggest the real need for the move: the two-and-a-half acres the club occupied underwent subdivision between two or more owners and securing leases from all of them proved difficult. The Tacony-Palmyra Ferry Company owned one of the subdivided lots and the company had drawn plans for building a bridge to replace the ferry.[22] The old Morris mansion ironically suffered demolition in 1928/29 for construction of the Tacony-Palmyra Bridge.

To confront the question of moving, the RDCC, true to form, established the "upriver site committee." Between 1917 and 1922 the committee reported to the club the results of their search, culminating with selection of the Shipman property in Edgewater Park (Figure 6). An agreement of sale for $10,000 was executed in the fall of 1922.[23] The five-acre Shipman property, site of a *circa* 1870 Second Empire, three-story mansion overlooking the Delaware River in suburban Edgewater Park, fulfilled all the club's needs. The only impediments were location and financing. While idyllic, Edgewater Park was quite a distance from Philadelphia and Camden where club members lived. The search committee adroitly addressed this issue in their final report by presenting to the membership all the transportation options available to reach Edgewater Park.

Financing the $10,000 purchase price required more maneuvering.[24] The "All Hands" call went out to assist in financing the purchase, relying on club solidarity to meet this challenge. This did not require, however, use of club members' personal funds. Two thousand dollars of the $4,000 available in the sinking fund would be used and the club formed a new corporation, the Red Dragon Colony, to finance the remaining costs. The plan stated:

> We now ask your subscription to shares of the cumulative non-participating 4% preferred capital stock of the RED DRAGON COLONY, to be incorporated in New Jersey with an authorized capital stock of $12,000.00 consisting of 240 shares of preferred stock at $50 per share, of which preferred stock 160 shares of the par value of $50.00 each will now be issued and sold at $50 per share to club members only, and transferable only to club members, with the option to the colony to call and redeem one or more shares thereof at any time after the expiration of three years, at $50.00 per share.[25]

Figure 6. The Shipman property, purchased by RDCC in 1922.

This plan was put into effect and the property sold to club member J. E. ("Judge") Murray on December 30, 1922, who subsequently sold it to the Red Dragon Colony for $1.00.[26] Various repairs were carried out before the RDCC occupied the new clubhouse the following spring. It would be inaccurate to say that the planning, decisions, and actions taken at the time "saved" the RDCC, but there is no doubt that the history of the club, even if it survived, would be very different if it had not moved to Edgewater Park.

New Blood and New Boats

In fact, the move to Edgewater Park set the stage for perhaps the greatest transformation of the club in its 135-year history and is an example of the law of unintended consequences at work. Commodore Frank T. Wilson, whose time with the RDCC spanned the move from Wissinoming to Edgewater Park, was eyewitness to and our best source of information on this transformation.[27] He noted a number of changes to the club concomitant with the move upstream. Directly related to the move was an initial loss of membership, and it appears that it was principally the older members who resigned, ostensibly due to the distance to the new club. Intriguingly, Wilson refers several times to club members' increased use of the automobile, not only to get to the club from Philadelphia, but to engage in various social events. No longer was it necessary to paddle to your destination as it became socially acceptable by club members to arrive by other means. Not mentioned by Wilson, but one can read between the lines of his history, was a decline in the popularity of canoeing as a sport in America by the 1920s.[28]

Club membership began to climb again after the Great Depression, now consisting primarily of men living in the vicinity of Edgewater Park, not Philadelphia or Camden.[29] Another difference became apparent: the new membership were sailors, not paddlers. This transformation can be positively dated to the spring of 1940, when a group of Comet racers from the Beverly Yacht Club moved en masse to the RDCC. According to Camden's *Courier-Post*, Beverly Yacht Club did not possess a club house per se, and the group of Comet racers wanted a place where they could host and entertain visiting clubs during their competitions. In a telling sidebar, the article further stated that:

> the comet racers have joined the Edgewater Park club and the new influx of such active members into the Red Dragon organization, *which has had a placid, non-athletic air about it for years*, will stimulate the Dragons greatly [emphasis added].[30]

One of the Comet sailors who joined at this time told Mr. Jack Perkins, former Commodore of the RDCC, that the RDCC obligated all those from the Beverly Y. C. to join as individuals, which they did, and the RDCC accepted all into the RDCC.[31] Whatever its original motivation, this prerequisite undoubtedly helped to retain the institutional integrity of the RDCC. Thus began a new and invigorated chapter in the history of the RDCC. The club went on for the next two decades to not only double in membership, but to become a major player in local as well as national competitive sailing (Figure 7). At its height as primarily a sailing club, there were 31 sail boats moored on the Delaware River in front of the RDCC club house.[32] Mr. Rod Merrill, a teenager in the late 1950s–1960s and son of former RDCC Commodore Rodman Merrill, recalls that at that time the club dedicated itself to competitive sailing almost to the exclusion of paddling or purely social events; in his words: "competitive sailing was what the club was about."[33] He fondly recalls the degree of camaraderie and equality amongst the club's sailors, which ranged from mere teenagers like himself to champion seamen in the international sail racing scene.

Regarding unintended consequences, if not for the move to Edgewater Park, the RDCC may have faded to a loose footnote in the history of the canoeing craze at the turn of the last century. The opportunity to renew itself as an active sports club via the Beverly Y. C. proved fortuitous, but the RDCC did not have to take it. In so doing, however, the sailors probably saved the club. They may not have recognized the implications of their actions, but all indications are that if they had not made the move, the club would probably not have survived to mid-century.

Changing Times and New Challenges

The advent of sailing and a larger, more localized membership may have brought new life to the club, but it also had consequences. By the 1980s, the young blood of the 1940s had aged and the penchant for racing had flagged. The small Comet and Lighting-class racing boats were traded in for larger cruising boats. With that aging process came a shift in the social life of the club, where social events became as important, if not more important, than sporting events. In the memory of one of the members of that period, it was

A Curious Case of Survival

Figure 7. The Red Dragon Canoe Club in its sailing days.

the camaraderie of the club, the natural beauty and the history of the property that brought in new members. In fact, according to this same former member, one of the Commodores of the time, Frank Keenan, didn't even own a boat.[34]

By the mid-1980s the expanded membership of the club, number of boats on the waterfront, purchase of an adjoining vacant lot in 1971 and above all, the boisterousness of its social events forced a break with the RDCC's Edgewater Park neighbors. Legal proceedings ensued and over a two-year period and many legal bills, a number of agreements were hammered out that constricted the club's behavior but allowed it to survive in its Shipman Mansion home. According to various members, this process had a painful but ultimately salutary effect on the club. The leadership recognized that changes were needed and took positive steps to revitalize the club. The club initially had a desperate need for promotion, as its location on a cul-de-sac in a sleepy neighborhood did not foster awareness of the club's existence outside of its membership.[35]

To assist with that promotion, and to be a contributing member of the general community, a sailing school opened at the club in 1996 and ran for ten years. Organized and overseen by three club members, William Van Keuren, Robert Medeiros and Doug Campbell, the school focused on teaching sailing on the Delaware River to school-aged children. To place this effort on firm financial footing, the club formed a 501(c)3 non-profit organization capable of obtaining grant monies. About 1998, the Campbell Soup Company of Camden awarded a grant to teach sailing to 50 or 60 inner-city youths from Camden.[36]

The experience of creating a non-profit corporation for the sailing school set the stage for the club to tackle another major problem. Not only had the membership aged, but by the year 2000, the 130-year-old clubhouse was a faded lady and in dire need of a new roof. This was not a new problem; the roof was an issue when the RDCC purchased the property in the 1920s and had undergone some repairs again in the 1980s.[37] Regardless, by the twenty-first century the slate mansard roof was leaking so badly that action could no longer be delayed. The author recalls that when he joined the club around 2015, guarded talk of selling the property if the roof could not be fixed could be heard among members.

To finance the restoration and address other financial needs, another non-profit corporation, the Shipman Mansion Foundation, was formed in 2013. Club members Norma Carter and Doug Campbell, both with previous experience setting up and running non-profit corporations, spearheaded the effort. It proved to be the salvation of, if not the club itself, at least its continued home in Edgewater Park. The RDCC membership fortunately had the mansion clubhouse placed in the National Register and the State Register of Historic Places in 2000 and 2001 respectively. This made the property eligible for monies directed to the restoration and preservation of historic sites. So, beginning in 2014, the Foundation began a successful run of grant writing that secured five separate grants from federal and state preservation and planning organizations. Those monies enabled the Foundation to completely restore the Shipman Mansion roof (Figure 8) as well as restore interior spaces, the 1870s privy (Figure 9), catalog its extensive collection of historical documents and photographs, and plan for the future.

Not only has the Shipman Mansion Foundation succeeded in bringing the physical clubhouse back from the brink, but it has also simultaneously given value back to the community while promoting the RDCC to new prospective members. Since 2014, the RDCC clubhouse has hosted both an annual spring and fall lecture series, as well as a summer concert series and house tours, all of which the local community supports and attends, resulting in adding substantially to the club's membership roster. Efforts have also been made to expand RDCC membership beyond its traditional white base to reflect more accurately the wider community of which it is a part. While perhaps essentially a social club, ongoing efforts to revive sailing and paddling at the club have ushered in slow growth over the past several years.

Conclusion

The RDCC has survived because it has adapted to the times in which it found itself. That change has not always been easy and has sometime been resisted, but it has prevailed. The one constant, which has been remarked upon by many observers since almost the beginning of the club, is the sense of community and camaraderie that has always existed, despite the disputes

Figure 8. The club house of the Red Dragon Canoe Club, the Shipman mansion, with restored roof.

A Curious Case of Survival

that will naturally occur. This characteristic of the club, noted as early as the 1895 *Public Ledger-Philadelphia* article,[38] features prominently in the most recent oral interviews with present and past club members: "the community is really very gratifying to be part of, that is my greatest memory of this place."[39] It is doubtful whether the RDCC would have survived the vicissitudes of the past 135 years without it.

Figure 9. The recently restored privy, which dates to the 1870s.

Acknowledgements

This history is dedicated to the memory of Peter Clayton Carter 1946–2022.

First and foremost, I would like to extend my thanks to the entire membership of the Red Dragon Canoe Club, past and present, from whom I absorbed and gained great affection for the club and much of the lore and mystique surrounding its history. Discerning the actual history from the lore provided the motivation for this work, and a number of current members assisted greatly in that effort. Foremost amongst them was Mr. Doug Campbell, who not only gave much of his personal time to interview, but tracked down former members, who were invaluable sources to the club's past: Ken Shuttleworth, Jack Perkins, and Rod Merrill. Mr. Willian VanKeuren contributed not only information on the club's history, but on the broader historical context of canoeing as a sport in the early twentieth century. Finally, I would like to thank Ms. Norma Carter for her undying enthusiasm and perseverance in digging through the club's archives for the documents so necessary for straightening the crooked road of oral tradition.

About the Author

Mr. John Lawrence is a continuing member of the RDCC who now resides in Hartford, NY. Formerly, he filled the roles of Quartermaster and (briefly) Commodore for the club. Professionally, Mr. Lawrence is an archaeologist employed by the Federal Emergency Management Agency (FEMA) and in that role has traveled throughout the United States and its commonwealth territories.

Endnotes

1. Robert D. Putnam, *Bowling Alone: The Collapse and Revival of American Community* (New York: Simon & Schuster, 2000), 384.
2. This club was later christened the Royal Canoe Club under the patronage of Queen Victoria, in 1877.
3. *Keystone Canoe Club and RDCC 1883–1889–90*. RDCC archives, Edgewater Park, New Jersey, 14.
4. *Keystone Canoe Club and RDCC 1883–1889–90*, 14.
5. *Keystone Canoe Club and RDCC 1883–1889–90*, 17–18.
6. "Description and History of the Red Dragon Canoe Club," *Public Ledger-Philadelphia* (Philadelphia, PA), September 9, 1895, 19. The discrepancy between name and location may have been a compromise: keep the clubhouse in Camden but name the club for Philadelphia, where most of the membership lived.
7. Ibid.
8. Ibid.
9. "Doomed to Fire. Second Street Boat Houses Again Burned," *The Morning Post* (Camden, New Jersey), Tuesday, November 25, 1890, 1.
10. *The Red Dragon Canoe Club. A Brief History*. Compiled by W. H. Logan Jr., written by T. M. Hill. Unpublished mss., RDCC archives, Edgewater Park, NJ, 1917, 2.
11. Logan, *Red Dragon Canoe Club*, 2.
12. Logan, *Red Dragon Canoe Club*, 2. Frank Wilson, *Old Red Dragon*, unpublished mss., RDCC archives, Edgewater Park, New Jersey, 1953, 2-3.
13. "Canoe Club Burned Down," *Trenton Evening Times* (Trenton, New Jersey) Thursday, March 23, 1899, 6.
14. Wilson, *Old Red Dragon*, 5.
15. "Red Dragon Contest," *The Times Philadelphia* (Philadelphia, PA) Sunday, October 9, 1892, 15. "Canoe Club to Spend Memorial Day Paddling," *The Evening Journal* (Wilmington, Delaware), Thursday, May 26, 1910, 6.

"Cupid in a Canoe Race," *York Daily* (York, Pennsylvania), Tuesday, September 12, 1911, 3. "Alfred Hopkins Wins District Canoe Title," *The Philadelphia Inquirer* (Philadelphia, Pennsylvania), September 5, 1921, 6.
16 Logan, *Red Dragon Canoe Club*, 1917, 4; *RDCC Log Book*. RDCC archives, Edgewater Park, New Jersey
17 "Description and History of the Red Dragon Canoe Club," *Public Ledger-Philadelphia* (Philadelphia, PA), September 9, 1895, 19.
18 Logan, *Red Dragon Canoe Club*, 1917, 2.
19 Wilson, *Old Red Dragon*, 9.
20 Wilson, *Old Red Dragon*, 12.
21 *RDCC Minute Book 1917–1924*, RDCC archives, Edgewater Park, New Jersey, 37. "Tacony and Palmyra Ferry Opened," *The Philadelphia Inquirer*, Sunday, May 7, 1922, 2.
22 *RDCC Minute Book 1917–1924*, 151.
23 Ibid., 163.
24 To the purchase price should be added the cost of numerous repairs to the property, which had not been occupied since 1917, when Paul and Alice Shipman had passed away.
25 *RDCC Minute Book 1917–1924*, attached document.
26 Burlington County Deed Book 620:212 and 645:158.
27 Wilson, *Old Red Dragon*, 13.
28 K. Monroe, "Comeback of the Canoe" www.wcha.org/tidbits/scouting_comeback.
29 Wilson, *Old Red Dragon*, 14.
30 "Beverly Y. C. Plans Bigger Program," *Courier-Post* (Camden, New Jersey) May 13, 1940, 22.
31 Beverly Yacht Club (perksites.com).
32 Doug Campbell, personal communication, January 21, 2022.
33 Rod Merrill, personal communication, July 2, 2022.
34 Ken Shuttleworth, personal communication, January 22, 2022.
35 Shuttleworth, personal communication, January 22, 2022; Campbell, personal communication, January 21, 2022.
36 Campbell, personal communication, January 21, 2022.
37 *RDCC Minute Book 1917–1924*, 86. Shuttleworth, personal communication, January 22, 2022.
38 "Description and History of the Red Dragon Canoe Club," *Public Ledger-Philadelphia* (Philadelphia, PA), September 9, 1895, 19.
39 Shuttleworth, personal communication, January 22, 2022.

This flight of humor was featured above the fold, top right, in the Saturday issue of The West Jersey Pioneer *(Bridgeton, New Jersey), January 10, 1857.*

HOW TO OPEN OYSTERS.

"Talk of opening oysters," said old Hurricane, "Why, nothing easier, if you only know how."

"And how's how?" inquired Starlight.

"Scotch snuff," answered old Hurricane, very sententiously. "Scotch snuff. Bring it ever so near their noses, and they'll sneeze their lids off."

"I know a genius," observed Meister Kark, "Who has a better plan. He spreads the bivalves in a circle, seats himself in the centre, and begins spinning a yarn. Sometimes its an adventure in Mexico—sometimes a legend of his loves—sometimes a marvellous stock operation in Wall Street. As he proceeds, the "natives" get interested—one by one they gap with astonishment at the tremendous and direful whoppers which are poured forth, and as they gap, my friend wipes them out, peppers 'em and swallows them."

"That'll do," said Starlight, with a long sigh. "I wish we had a bushel of the bivalves here now—they'd open easy."

The Fabled Settlement of Fish House and the Tammany Pea Shore Fishing Company

Paul W. Schopp

Early History

In a corner of present-day Pennsauken Township, Camden County, lies a place that time has forgotten. At the foot of a colonial road called Cove (Landing) Road, where it once ended on the shore of the Delaware River, the small community of Fish House developed during the nineteenth century along a stretch of riverbank known as "Pea Shore."

When the first settlers sailed up the Delaware River to the area that comprises today's Philadelphia, they found a large island situated midstream with a long sweeping cove behind it. The island became known as Petty's Island. The cove behind it originally carried the name "Steele's Bay," named for William Steele, a merchant of Cork, Ireland, and proprietor of a large tract of land in West Jersey fronting on the Delaware River in this area.[1] It appears that Steele never sailed from Ireland to view his land holdings; rather, he named his brother-in-law, John Ithel, a Philadelphia victualer, as his land agent.[2] It was Ithel who sold the land associated with Steele's Bay to Richard Basnet and others.[3]

Farms soon developed along the shoreline of the Delaware after Ithel divided and sold Steele's land. Farmers in the Steele's Bay area include the Wood, Burrough, Fish, Browning, and Stone families.[4] Deeds from the late eighteenth century indicate that local farmers carried on some banked-meadow farming along the shoreline.[5] By 1809, Steele's Bay was renamed Stone's Cove for John Stone, owner of an adjacent large farm.[6] The shoreline along the cove became known as "Pea Shore." This name stems from the farming activity ringing the cove. J. S. Lippincott, author of "Market Products of West New Jersey," published in the *1865 Annual Report of the U.S. Commissioner of Agriculture*, noted in this article:

> The peculiar advantages, local and general, enjoyed by the eastern bank of the Delaware river to furnish to the epicurean tables of the adjoining city those delicate, early vegetables, unsurpassed in quality in any other region, as well as those heavy supplies of more common produce indispensable to the health and comfort of the masses, render this district peculiarly worthy of notice. The more favored portion of this region is located immediately upon the river bank, extending northeast to Pensaukin creek, about five miles beyond the city of Camden. From the very early opening of spring in this locality, and the success which attends the early pea culture, it is known as "Pea-Shore." On this narrow strip, vegetables have been raised, with almost uniform success, several days or a week earlier than on adjoining lands more remote from the river, and larger sums have been realized from their sale than have been made by the growers located at Norfolk, Virginia, noted for its extremely early products.

...The protecting agency of moisture appears to extend from one-half to three-quarters of a mile from the river, and to be modified by the wind prevailing at the time. When the wind is from the west, the later frosts of spring do not affect the river farms, while those a half mile distant may have their early vegetables seriously injured. Again in autumn it has been observed that as long as the winds prevail from the west, passing over the river, the late crops of tomatoes do not suffer, while the entire crop half a mile distant, beyond the low hills, may be entirely destroyed.[7]

John Hills' *A Plan of the City of Philadelphia and Environs Surveyed by John Hills in the Summers of 1801, 2, 3, 4, 5, 6, & 7*, published in 1809, is the first commercially produced map that identifies "Pea Shore" (Patch) as a toponym[8] (Figure 1).

Surveyors did not officially lay out the first road to the cove out until 1802.[9] However, evidence suggests that Cove Landing Road, leading from the Mount Holly Road over to the cove, served as a thoroughfare much earlier.[10] At the foot of this Cove or Landing Road was Gibson's Landing, the terminus of an early ferry, which operated from Gibson's Wharf in the Richmond section of Philadelphia.[11] This landing was later known as Holmes Landing, named for Joseph Holmes, a local farmer, who used the landing for moving produce to market in Philadelphia. In an 1865 deed, the landing is described as a wood landing, i.e., a place where wood was shipped to market.

Construction of the Hood house

In 1772, Parr Willard inherited land adjacent to the Cove Road and the Delaware River from his mother, Mary.[12] In 1792, Willard sold a lot of land fronting on the Delaware shoreline to Thomas Hood, a Doctor of Divinity. The deed for this transaction reserved the right for Willard and his assignees to enter upon the land and remove sand and gravel from the hillside for maintaining his banked meadowlands. He also reserved the use of an old burial ground for his family and heirs forever.[13]

Hood proceeded to erect a dwelling that faced Cove Road at the foot of the road on this three-plus acre lot of ground. The structure was a very plain four-bay house without any adornment or embellishment. It featured a center door and two shed-roofed dormers. Hood completed the house sometime between 1792 and 1795. It was certainly already standing in 1799, when Hood and two other parties sold the house and lot to Thomas Bowne, a Philadelphia ship joiner, in a tripartite deed.[14] The deed of title still included the exceptions Parr Willard inserted in 1792.

The Tammany Pea Shore Fishing Company

In 1813, Bowne sold the house and three-plus acres to a group of Philadelphians associated together as the Tammany Pea Shore Fishing Company.[15] Isaac Mickle, writing in his 1845 history of Old Gloucester County, stated, "The club had its origin in that old English social feeling which so strongly marked the generation of our grandfathers."[16]

The Tammany Pea Shore Fishing Company members either constructed a clubhouse and separate kitchen building or adapted one or both from existing structures. This two-building complex stood on the riverbank adjacent to the Hood house. This men's social and sporting club reportedly dates to 1809, formed by a group of artisan-class Philadelphians in the best tradition of the State in Schuylkill Fishing Company, although the latter association comprised wealthy gentry and included dinner guests like George Washington.[17] The members used the pier and shoreline for recreational fishing and held frequent banquets at the clubhouse.[18]

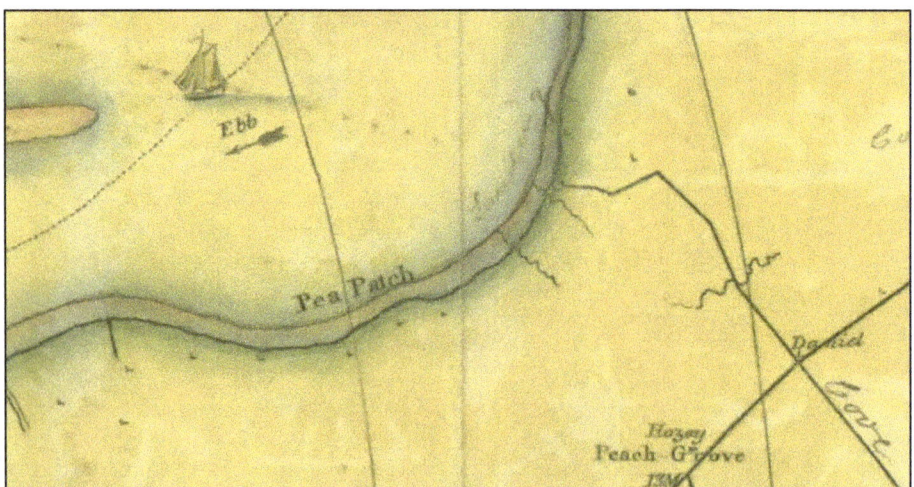

Figure 1. Cartographer John Hills served as an engineer in the British Army during the Revolutionary War. He remained behind in America at war's end and worked as a surveyor and mapmaker. Many consider Hills' published circular map of Philadelphia and its surrounding environs his finest work. This map is the first to identify "Pea Shore" (Patch) as a toponym. Courtesy of the Camden County Historical Society.

Tammany Pea Shore Fishing Company

The club sponsored informal sailing regattas in the cove and out into the river. Stone's Cove gradually became known as Fish House Cove due to the buildings of the Tammany Pea Shore Company (Figure 2).

The presence of the fishing company brought a festive air to the cove area and an increased level of activity. The clubhouse pier became the preferred place for sailing races to end. Spring, summer, and fall became the seasons for unending dinners, dances, and picnics for Tammany Pea Shore club members and guests. To cool off during hot weather, bathing occurred along the gentle sloping gravel beach. Under the sponsorship of a club member, banquets and functions of many other groups and organization could be held at the fish house.[19] And events were held—in abundance!

The Camden & Amboy Railroad and Transportation Company purchased a portion of their right-of-way from the Tammany Pea Shore company in August 1834.[20] The railroad's Camden Branch, operating between Bordentown and Camden, became fully operational by the end of 1834 and "Fish House" soon operated as a flag stop along the line so club members from Philadelphia could cross on the Philadelphia-Camden ferry and take the train to the fish house.[21] The single-track branch line crossed Cove Road just short of where the thoroughfare ended on the beach. The rail line then ran behind the fish house, but in front of the Hood house, on its route between Camden and Bordentown.

By December 1830, the number of surviving members from the original club organization had greatly diminished. With the original company membership dwindling, the officers decided to reorganize the club and admit new members. The remaining incorporators vested their interest in the fish house, Hood house, and grounds in the Tammany Pea Shore company's president, Jacob Fisler, by deed. Issuance of the deed to Fisler completed the reorganization of 1833–34.[22] The clubhouse underwent a full reconstruction during 1834[23] (Figures 3 and 4).

In March 1835, Fisler, acting in his official capacity as president, sold the Hood house and 2.39 acres of land to Robert Hoare of Philadelphia.[24] Hoare, a member of the fishing company, purchased the dwelling and moved in, apparently serving as a de facto caretaker for the fish house and premises. The increased activity at the club's property required Hoare's presence to maintain order. Dinners and many other events continued to be held at the Tammany Pea Shore Fishing Company headquarters (Tammany Pea Shore Fishing Company Guest Book).[25]

Figure 2. Artist and member William Roderfield executed this fine illustration of the original Tammany Pea Shore Fishing Company headquarters for the top of the association's new charter, drawn up in 1834. Courtesy of the Historical Society of Pennsylvania.

Figure 3. Tammany Pea Shore Fishing Company member William Rank prepared this drawing of the second clubhouse and kitchen building as he recalled it in 1850. Based on this primitive artwork, it appears the membership lengthened the main clubhouse between 1834 and 1850. Courtesy of the Joseph Felcone Collection.

Figure 4. How the final form of the clubhouse appeared as taken from the end of Cove Road, marked by the higher white wall alongside the roadway. The white seawall is all that remains of the club. Down the beach are some houseboats set up on stocks to keep them from floating away with high tide. The beach looks inviting in this summer scene. Courtesy of the Camden County Historical Society.

Figure 5. A hand-colored lithograph from circa 1852 shows visitors enjoying the public grounds of the Tamany Pe Shore Fishing Company. The club house and dining hall is to the left; the smaller building to the right is the cook house

Tammany Pea Shore Fishing Company

hiladelphia artist Thomas M. Scott completed the drawing for this print. He often, as in this case, worked with printer ter S. Duval, one of the most prominent lithographers and printers of his day. Courtesy of Joseph J. Felcone.

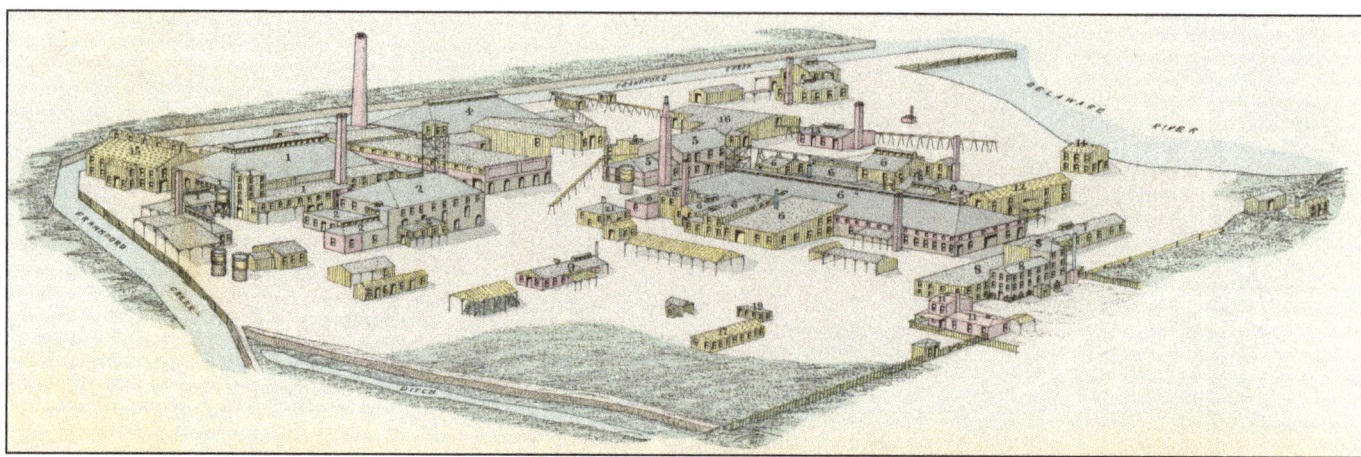

Figure 6. A birds-eye view of Charles Lennig's Tacony Chemical Works. Detail, *Hexamer General Surveys*. Courtesy of the Free Library of Philadelphia.

Industrial Activity

As in many other areas, industrial activity arrived on the shores of Fish House Cove. At some point in time, probably during the 1840s, a brickyard and clay pipe manufactory appears to have been established on the riverbank with the clay extracted from the pit Parr Willard formerly used to obtain sand and gravel for his banked meadow. In 1856, the American Aluminum Fire Brick and Water Pipe Manufacturing Company, incorporated in 1849 as a New Jersey company, assumed control of this older brick and pipe manufactory.[26] However, the new firm suffered financial reverses and lost its plant through Sheriff's Sale. The clay uncovered in the former gravel and sand pit proved to be quite valuable, and in 1863, Charles Lennig of Bridesburg, Pennsylvania, had purchased it.[27] He used the clay in his Tacony Chemical Works on Frankford Creek, possibly to make retorts or storage containers for the strong acids produced there[28] (Figure 6). The Lennig Estate continued ownership of this land into the twentieth century as recorded in various Camden County Deeds.

Other brick manufactories developed along Pea Shore. Joseph Wharton, a Philadelphia Quaker industrialist and the namesake of New Jersey's Wharton State Forest, purchased an existing brickyard and employed the recently invented Culbertson Brickmaking Machine. He operated at this location with two different partners and finally withdrew from the business at the end of 1853 when it proved to be less than profitable.[29] In 1866, Augustus Reeve of Salem County purchased an existing brickyard, where he served as superintendent, and expanded it to form the Pea Shore Brick and Terra Cotta Works[30] (Figure 7). Nearby, the Hatch brothers operated their Fairview Brick Works, which they began in 1869 after the Camden Brick Company gave up its lease of the Hatch clay pits[31] (Figure 8).

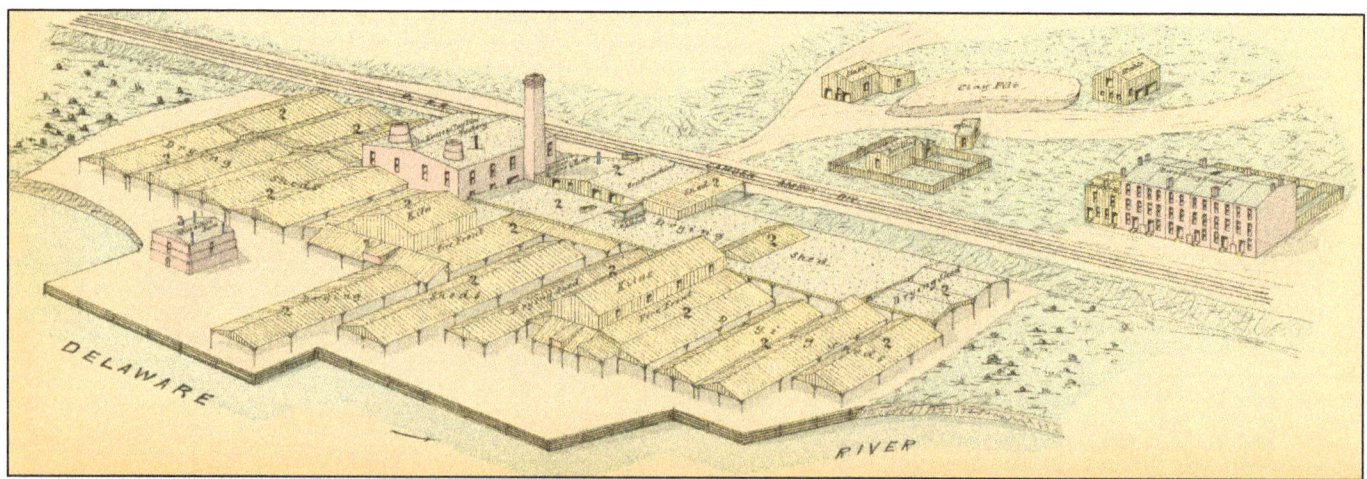

Figure 7. Birds-eye view of Augustus Reeve's Pea Shore Brick & Terra Cotta Works. Detail, *Hexamer General Surveys*. Courtesy of the Free Library of Philadelphia.

Tammany Pea Shore Fishing Company

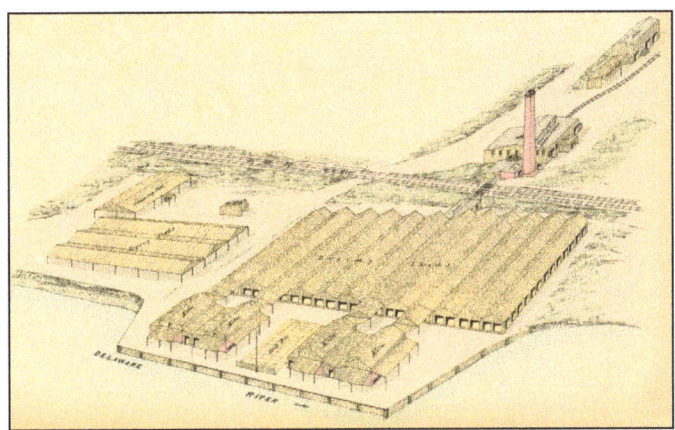

Figure 8. Birds-eye view of Hatch's Fairview Brick Works. Detail, *Hexamer General Surveys*. Courtesy of the Free Library of Philadelphia.

Recreational Uses

Robert Hoare continued to live in the Hood house until sometime in the late 1840s. By 1850, the Hoare family resided in North Camden and probably leased their Fish House dwelling.[32] Robert Hoare died in 1854 and his wife eventually remarried and in 1867 sold the homestead to Emily G. Vennell, wife of Isaac K. Vennell.[33] The Vennells soon opened a general store to serve the many people who frequented the fish house and bathing beach in Fish House cove.[34] In January 1890, Isaac obtained a liquor license and established a hotel and bar in the former Hood house[35] (Figure 9).

Other hotels and taprooms sprang up in Fish House. These included Schiller Heights, later the property of the Tippin family (Figure 10), and the Hastings-Sutton Hotel, owned by two half-brothers. The former stood on the opposite side of Lennig's clay pit, while the latter establishment stood diagonally behind the Vennell Tavern House.[36] Mention is made of residents from the Kensington and Fishtown section swimming or sailing over to Pea Shore, drinking a few rounds at one of the hotels, most notably Shiller Heights, and then returning to their native soil or to Petty's Island for a fish bake.[37]

Both Philadelphia and Camden residents flocked here. The Good Gray Poet, Walt Whitman, was a regular visitor to Pea Shore in his later years:

> Warrie driving up and Anne arriving about the same time. W. [Walt] ready to come downstairs. Said to me as he buttoned his vest, "Things proper if not pretty here must be mended before a fellow goes on the streets." ... Anne sat back with him—I in front with Warrie. ... Uptown to State Street bridge and Pea Shore. We had asked him where to go. By his own word it was Pea Shore. He spoke of "the beautiful openness of things up here." Of one of the factories, "I don't know but the factories are the most beautiful buildings in Camden." ... Look at the river, lying off there—flowing—and the city across—and the mist. It is a misty day, Horace! And off here—look how the road runs, curves, passes away into the horizon. And—pointing to the curious rims of deep water-grass running all through the flats—"Leaves of Grass! The largest leaves of grass known! Calamus! Yes, that is

Figure 9. Isaac K. Vennell's Fish House Hotel, offering lager beer and liquor as libations for thirsty customers. This photo shows the hotel in its original location overlooking the railroad. Mr. Vennell is the man with the mustache. Around him are his wife, children and visitors imbibing in his offerings. Author's collection.

Figure 10. Andrew Tippin's Schiller Heights Hotel, located on a salient on the south side of present-day Tippins Pond. The previous name for Schiller Heights was Cedar Grove when industrialist Samuel Ross owned the property. Author's Collection.

Figure 11. Walt Whitman and Warrie (Warren) Stafford on the docks in Camden, New Jersey. Courtesy of the Library of Congress.

Tammany Pea Shore Fishing Company

Calamus! Profuse, rich, noble—upright, emotional!" ...He dwelt on clouds, sky, fences, trees—read signs, saw distant steeples, chimneys of factories, curls of smoke. ... W. much admired a wooden schoolhouse—"A prime success." Asked me, "Do you know the crossroads [Westfield Avenue and Cove Road]?" And by and by we turned to the left and to the river. The road we were on [Cove Road] seemed to lead into the water. I jumped out and went ahead—found that we could get down there, though log and debris would prevent following the shore. So W. said, "Drive right close to the water, Warrie"—and there we were—Pea Shore at last. W. even elated—seemed to sniff the air. "This is very beautiful, very—and its beauty is much like Doctor Johnston's style, which is the best style because it is no style at all." Then, "Oh! The great quiet here—not a sound but the curling up of the waters! After Mickle Street this is heaven! ... Yes, this is peace, peace!"

"It has been long since I was here—it is a grand memory! How would it do to get a house up there on the hill, Warrie? Here is air, water, freedom! See the stretch of the city—above there clouds. Oh! The clouds! And the line of the shore, here! See, Anne—see the boats—the white sails. And you think, Horace, we can't get along the shore here? Well, we can't risk anything—I can't. So, Warrie, I would turn the horse—we must go back the same road."[38]

A row of seven two-story attached frame dwellings once stood on a tract of land across Cove Road from the modern-day parking lot for Tippins Pond (Figure 12). These houses not only served as temporary living quarters for vacationers and revelers, but also as rental dwellings to transient brickyard workers. Joseph Lonton constructed these tenements in the late 1840s or early 1850s with the facades facing the Delaware River. Each unit had a front porch for sitting and viewing the river. This structure remained extant, although derelict, until c. 2000, with commercial offices served as the last occupants in the early 1990s.

By 1886, quite a little settlement had developed at Fish House. The railroad had provided both a small passenger and freight station for the convenience of residents and visitors alike ten years earlier (Figure 13). The Federal Government established an official Post Office in Fish House during 1886, the first post office

Figure 12. Joseph and Hannah Vennell Molloy's boys in front of the row houses in Fish House. This photograph predates 1915, when the lean-to shed was attached to the rear of the first row house to house the relocated post office. Author's Collection.

Figure 13. The Pennsylvania Railroad's 1876 Fish House passenger station, which also housed the Fish House Post Office until the station closed in 1915. Courtesy of the Interstate Commerce Commission Record Group, National Archives.

Figure 14. A postal card featuring a Fish House circular date stamp indicating the local post office had received the card from the sender and it awaited the recipient to pick it up. Author's Collection.

in today's Pennsauken Township[39] (Figure 14). Harry Vennell's wife, Annie, served as the first Postmaster for this office. Harry worked as the railroad station agent in Fish House, and it was logical that a portion of the station served as the post office.[40] Later, in 1915, when the Pennsylvania Railroad closed its Fish House station as an agency and converted the building to an open shelter, the post office was relocated to a lean-to shed constructed behind the southernmost end row house across from the Vennell Tavern House[41] (Figures 15 and 16).

Figure 17. The Delair Railroad Bridge, completed in 1896. The first bridge constructed over the Delaware River below Trenton. Construction of this bridge required an expansion of the trackage passing through Fish House, causing the Pennsylvania Railroad to acquire land from the Hatch and the Vennell families. The bridge remains in use today for New Jersey Transit's Atlantic City route and for freight service. Author's Collection.

Figure 15. After the Fish House passenger station closed as an agency station, the building was converted to an open shelter. In this view, the diminutive freight station remains in situ, and the open passenger shelter is tucked behind it. Notice Cove Road's rise to the railroad crossing before dropping down to the beach. Author's Collection.

The Pennsylvania Railroad erected a large steel bridge across the Delaware River just north of Fish House during 1895–96 to provide better access to the agricultural center of South Jersey[42] (Figure 17). This was the first bridge to span the river south of Trenton. With its construction came attendant junctions and multiple trackage. The railroad company determined that it needed the land upon where the Vennell Tavern House stood.[43] The railroad and the Vennell family consummated the sale of the property in 1896 after the railroad informally agreed to relocate the hotel building farther up Cove Road, constructing a new foundation in the process. The former tavern house remains in this new location today (Figure 18). It is the last remnant of a once vibrant settlement.

The End Begins

As the twentieth century dawned, recreational activity at Fish House was waning. Summer revelers still sought the beach for bathing and the cove for boating, but its extensive use by Philadelphians slowly died out. Other clubs along the Pennsauken shoreline appeared more attractive. Such notable organizations as the Sparks Club (1884), the Mozart Club (1869), the Mohican Club, the Red Mill, and the Beidemann Club (1878) all vied for Philadelphia members and visitors.[44] The Vennell family reconfigured the former Vennell Tavern House back into a private dwelling. The Fish House Post Office closed permanently in 1924.[45] Eventually, both Shiller Heights and the Hastings-Sutton Hotel disappeared, the former burning down in the 1970s.[46]

Figure 16. The lean-to shed attached to the rear of the first row house served as the second location for the Fish House Post Office. The row houses and this closed postal facility disappeared about 2000. Walter Vennell Photograph, Author's Collection.

Tammany Pea Shore Fishing Company

Figure 18. The Hood/Vennell house after the Pennsylvania Railroad moved the dwelling up Cove Road to its present site. The building to the right is the Hastings-Sutton Hotel. The Hood/Vennell house remains standing today, although it windows are overlain with plywood and it is currently unoccupied. Author's Collection.

The Tammany Pea Shore Fishing Company slowly devolved with aging membership. The last event of note held at the clubhouse was the 25th anniversary dinner of the Railroad Association of Philadelphia in May 1913.[47] Four years later, the Tammany Pea Shore membership had already disbanded. A May 1917 edition of *The Philadelphia Inquirer* carried a classified notice: "A RARE CHANCE for party of young men to acquire the old Tammany Pea Shore fishhouse, located at Fishhouse Station on the Amboy and Camden Division. . . ."[48] The advertising changed by June of the same year: "AT FISH HOUSE STATION, Tammany Pea Shore Fish House, Two brick houses; lot; riparian right; has been used as a club since 1809."[49] No buyer came forward, so advertising began anew in a June 1925 edition of the *Camden Courier*: "Old Tammany Pea Shore Fishing Co. property at Fish House Station for sale; $4000; immediate possession. . . ."[50] Again it appears no sale occurred. The following nebulous discourse is based on snippets of uncitable information the author has gleaned over the years. A group of Alsatian immigrants reputedly took over the club house and an Italian club also supposedly used it. These groups finally moved out and squatters took over the building. The end was not far away. Reportedly, the fish house and kitchen underwent demolition in March 1939, leaving no trace of its existence except a few documentary records, the white seawall, and a lithograph of the fish house and kitchen that artist Thomas M. Scott executed in c. 1852 (Figure 5).[51]

Another industrial enterprise, albeit a much later one, was the starch works of the Atlas Cereal Manufacturing Co. This plant opened in 1900 and, based on photographic evidence, was constructed entirely on pilings along the shallow shoreline of the river with a ramp or gangplank leading from the fast land. (Figure 19) This plant operated until about 1915 and then closed, although it remained standing in 1923.[52] Augustus Reeve's brick and terra cotta works closed in the first decade of this century, having consumed all of its local clay. He relocated operations to Maple Shade, Burlington County. The Hatch family's Fairview Brick Company's yard was a victim of the Great Depression, closing down in 1930.[53]

With the Tammany fish house closed and in a state of disrepair, recreational activity on the decline, and the industries and brickyards closed, watercraft no longer required access to the wharves and piers along the northern part of Fish House Cove. In 1931, the United States Army Corps of Engineers oversaw the deposition of almost 220,000 cubic yards of dredging spoil behind the Fisher Point Dike, essentially completely in-filling all of the cove north of Cove Road, obliterating the riverside remains of the brickyards and the starch works. The Army Corps derived the dredge spoils from work being done to create a 28-foot-deep channel between Allegheny Avenue, Philadelphia, and the Pennsylvania Railroad Bridge at Delair.[54] The south end of the cove previously received other dredge spoils with industrial development occurring, leaving only the central section of the cove unspoiled and providing a glimpse of how this area once appeared.

Conclusion

Today, the little settlement of Fish House is almost just a memory. The only surviving reminder of its past glories is the former Vennell Tavern House (Hood

Figure 19. Another view of the Fish House Freight Station with the Atlas Cereal Company starch works in the background. Author's Collection.

Figure 20. A postcard view of the Tammany Pea Shore Fishing Company clubhouse as it appeared up to the time of its demolition. Author's Collection.

House). In 1988, Pennsauken Township recreated the former sand/gravel/clay pit that Charles Lennig last used into a scenic area called Tippin's Pond. The township used Green Acres funding to accomplish this work. A parking lot now occupies the site of the Hastings-Sutton Hotel and the former location of the Vennell Tavern House (Hood House). Cove Road no longer ends on the beach at water's edge but continues out onto the dredge fill to a former Paragon/Texaco bulk oil terminal. No visible remnants can be found of the Tammany Pea Shore Fishing Company clubhouse (Figure 20), save the white seawall that protected it from the river. The Burrough/Willard burial ground disappeared in the mist of time, and bathers would be hard-pressed to find the gentle sloping beach for their recreational activities (Figure 19).

Figure 21. The beach along Pea Shore or Fish House Cove. You would be hard pressed to find the same gentle sloping beach today except for a very small segment of it. Courtesy of the Camden County Historical Society.

About the Author

Paul W. Schopp is the assistant director of the South Jersey Culture & History Center and has maintained a longstanding interest in Delaware River social and industrial development among many other historical topics related to the eight lower counties of New Jersey.

Endnotes

1. Liber B, Colonial Deeds and Conveyances for West New Jersey, New Jersey Secretary of State Record Group, microform edition (Trenton, NJ: New Jersey State Archives, 1688), 217 ff.
2. Ibid., 115 ff.
3. Ibid., 217 ff., 231 ff.
4. Various Colonial Deeds and Conveyances for West New Jersey and Gloucester County Deeds, microform edition (Trenton, NJ: New Jersey State Archives).
5. Liber C, Gloucester County Deeds, Gloucester County Clerk's Office, microform edition (Trenton, NJ: New Jersey State Archives, 1792), 90 ff.
6. John Hills, *A Plan of the City of Philadelphia and Environs* (Philadelphia, PA: John Hills, 1808).
7. James S. Lippincott, "Market Products of West New Jersey," *Report of the Commissioner of Agriculture for the Year 1865* (Washington, D.C.: Government Printing Office, 1866), 249 ff.
8. Hills, *A Plan of the City of Philadelphia and Environs*.
9. Book A, Gloucester County Road Returns, Gloucester County Clerk's Office, microform edition (Trenton, NJ: New Jersey State Archives, 1802), 255 ff.
10. Book A, Gloucester County Road Returns, Gloucester County Clerk's Office, microform edition (Trenton, NJ: New Jersey State Archives, 1771, 1783), 48 ff., 76 ff.
11. Hills, *A Plan of the City of Philadelphia and Environs*.
12. Will 0831H, Wills, New Jersey Secretary of State Record Group, microform edition (Trenton, NJ: New Jersey State Archives, 1772); Survey Book T. Surveyor General's Office, Council of West New Jersey Proprietors, microform edition (Trenton, NJ: New Jersey State Archives, 1783), 294 ff.
13. Liber C, Gloucester County Deeds, op. cit.
14. Liber R, Gloucester County Deeds, Gloucester County Clerk's office, microform edition (Trenton, NJ: New Jersey State Archives, 1799), 335 ff.
15. Liber R, Gloucester County Deeds, op. cit., 336 ff.
16. Isaac Mickle, *Reminiscences of Old Gloucester County* (Philadelphia, PA: Townsend Ward, 1845), 46.
17. William Milnor, *A History of the Schuylkill Fishing Company of the State in Schuylkill, 1732–1888* (Philadelphia, PA: The Members of the State in Schuylkill, 1889).
18. Nicholas B. Wainwright, *Philadelphia in the Romantic Age of Lithography* (Philadelphia, PA: The Historical Society of Pennsylvania, 1958), 43; Tammany Pea Shore Fishing Company Guest Book, manuscript volume (Philadelphia, PA: Samuel L. Paley Library, Temple University).
19. Tammany Pea Shore Fishing Company Guest Book, op. cit.
20. Liber L3, Gloucester County Deeds, Gloucester County Clerk's Office, microform edition (Trenton, NJ: New Jersey State Archives, 1834), 350 ff.
21. Edward Vernon, *Travelers Official Railway Guide of the United States and Canada* (New York City, NY: J. W. Pratt & Company, 1868), 90.
22. Liber O3, Gloucester County Deeds, Gloucester County Clerk's Office, microform edition (Trenton, NJ: New Jersey State Archives, 1830), 153 ff.
23. Tammany Pea Shore Fishing Company Charter. Manuscript document (Philadelphia, PA: Historical Society of Pennsylvania, 1834).
24. Liber O3, Gloucester County Deeds, Gloucester County

Clerk's Office, microform edition (Trenton, NJ: New Jersey State Archives, 1830), 156 ff.

25 Tammany Pea Shore Fishing Company Guest Book, op. cit.

26 Liber 27, Camden County Deeds, Camden County Clerk's Office, microform edition (Trenton, NJ: New Jersey State Archives, 1856), 463 ff.

27 Liber 41, Camden County Deeds, Camden County Clerk's Office, microform edition (Trenton, NJ: New Jersey State Archives, 1863), 4 ff.

28 Ernest Hexamer, *Hexamer General Surveys*, Collections of the Free Library of Philadelphia, Map Division (Philadelphia, PA: Ernest Hexamer, 1880, 1884, 1889), 1515, 1894, 2267.

29 W. Ross Yates, *Joseph Wharton, Quaker Industrial Pioneer.* (Bethlehem, PA: Lehigh University Press, 1987), 54–69.

30 Camden County Miscellaneous Record Book 1 (Camden, NJ: Camden County Clerk's Office, 1866), 307 ff.; George R. Prowell, *A History of Camden County New Jersey* (Philadelphia, PA: L. J. Richards & Co., 1886), 761–62.

31 Ibid., 762; Thomas Account Book, manuscript volume, collections of Paul W. Schopp Research Library; *By-Laws of the Camden Brick Company Located at Pea Shore, Camden Co., N.J.* (Camden, NJ: J. H. Jones & Company, 1855).

32 Sixth Decennial Census for Camden City, Camden County, New Jersey, Bureau of the Census, Record Group 29, microform edition, series M432, roll 445 (Washington, D.C.: National Archives and Records Administration, 1850), 66.

33 Will 0368D, Wills, New Jersey Secretary of State Record Group, microform edition (Trenton, NJ: New Jersey State Archives, 1854); Liber 53. Camden County Deeds, Camden County Clerk's Office, microform edition (Trenton, NJ: New Jersey State Archives, 1867), 546 ff.

34 Ninth Decennial Census for Stockton Township, Camden County, New Jersey, Bureau of Census, Record Group 29, microform edition, series M593, roll 856 (Washington, D.C.: National Archives and Records Administration, 1870), 53; Tenth Decennial Census for Stockton Township, Camden County, New Jersey, Bureau of the Census, Record Group 29, microform edition (Washington, D.C.: National Archives and Records Administration, 1880), 578B.

35 "Local Jottings," *Camden Daily Telegram* (Camden, NJ), January 11, 1890 (microform edition), 1; C. E. Howe. *Camden City Directory* (Camden, NJ: C. E. Howe Company, 1891), 839.

36 John Molloy, personal communication, The Evergreens, Moorestown, NJ, November 10, 1996.

37 Rudolph J. Walther, *Happenings in Ye Olde Philadelphia: 1680–1900* (Philadelphia, PA: Walther Printing House, 1925), 167–70, 214–16.

38 Horace Traubel, *With Walt Whitman in Camden: February 11, 1891–September 30, 1891*, vol. 8 (Oregon House, CA: W. L. Bentley, 1996), 360–63. Online edition found at: https://whitmanarchive.org/criticism/disciples/traubel/WWWiC/8/whole.html (accessed August 13, 2022).

39 United States Post Office Department Reports of Site Locations, 1837–1950, United States Post Office Department, Record Group 28, microform edition, series M1126, roll 376 (Washington, D.C.: National Archives and Records Administration).

40 Tenth Decennial Census for Stockton Township, Camden County, New Jersey, Bureau of the Census, Record Group 29, microform edition, series T9, roll 774 (Washington, D.C.: National Archives and Records Administration, 1880), 578b.

41 United States Post Office Department, op. cit.

42 William Judson Coxey, "The Delair Bridge," *West Jersey Rails II* (Haddonfield, NJ: West Jersey Chapter, National Railway Historical Society, 1985), 85 ff.

43 Liber 212, Camden County Deeds. Camden County Clerk's Office, microform edition (Trenton, NJ: New Jersey State Library, 1896), 323 ff.

44 Prowell, *A History of Camden County New Jersey* , 754; Walther, *Happenings in Ye Olde Philadelphia*, 197–98; Ben Calloway, "Sanctuary at Fish House Cove is Another Smart Step," *The Philadelphia Inquirer*, January 26, 1984 (microform edition), 10-E.

45 United States Post Office Department, op. cit.

46 Individual Property Record Cards, Pennsauken Township Assessors Office.

47 "Railroad Men to Dine," *The Philadelphia Inquirer*, May 10, 1913 (microform edition), 10.

48 "A Rare Chance . . .," *The Philadelphia Inquirer*, May 23, 1917 (microform edition), 18.

49 "At Fish House Station," *Evening Ledger* (Philadelphia, PA), June 17, 1917 (microform edition), 17.

50 "Old Tammany Pea Shore Fishing Co.," *Camden Courier* (Camden, NJ), June 25, 1925 (microform edition), 29.

51 Anonymous, "Farmline Map of Stockton Township, Camden Co., N.J.," Kimble Collection (Camden, NJ: Camden County Historical Society, c.1885); Nicholas B. Wainwright, *Philadelphia in the Romantic Age of Lithography* (Philadelphia, PA: The Historical Society of Pennsylvania, 1958), 43.

52 George C. Low, *The Industrial Directory of New Jersey* (Trenton, NJ: Bureau of Industrial Statistics of New Jersey, 1915), 174–75; Leon I. Watson. *Specific Applications of Schedules and Rating Systems as Filed* (n.p., 1923), 236.

53 Heinrich Ries and Henry B. Kümmel, *The Clays and Clay Industry of New Jersey. Volume VI of the Final Report of the State Geologist* (Trenton, NJ: Geological Survey of New Jersey, 1904).

54 Chief of Engineers, *Report of the Chief of Engineers, U.S. Army, 72d Congress, 1ˢᵗ Session.* House Document No. 9, Part 1 (Washington, D.C.: Government Printing office, 1931), 344 ff.

Ocean City's Oldest Surviving Church Structure

Except the LORD build the house, they labour in vain that build it.

(Psalm 127:1)

Loretta Thompson Harris

A Divine Purpose

Four Methodist ministers founded Ocean City, New Jersey as a Christian resort in 1879, modelling the new community after other towns that followed the religious camp meeting movement of the nineteenth century. Camp meetings were outdoor revival meetings where attendees came prepared to pitch a tent and worship together for days at a time. The earliest meetings ran from three or four days up to seven or eight days and included preaching, prayer meetings, hymn singing, weddings, and baptisms.[1] Religious services and associated events often ran continuously throughout most of each day.

An exact date for the origins of camp meetings is not clear. Historians have credited Presbyterian James McGready (c. 1760–1817) with inaugurating the first typical camp meetings between 1799 and 1801 in Logan County, Kentucky.[2]

On the East Coast in 1835, Jeremiah Pease and six men from the Edgartown Methodist Church secured a half-acre of land at Oak Bluffs on the island of Martha's Vineyard, south of Cape Cod in Massachusetts, to hold a religious camp meeting. This site became known as Wesleyan Grove. Preachers delivered their sermons from a shed constructed out of driftwood with a pulpit constructed on the front. Beyond the worship area, a semi-circle of society tents provided housing for attendees. Today, Wesleyan Grove has grown to a 34-acre National Historic Landmark District. Also known as the Martha's Vineyard Camp Meeting Association (MVCMA) or the Campgrounds, MVCMA declares itself the first summer religious camp established in the United States.[3,4]

Camp meetings grew in popularity following the Civil War. Various associations founded similar camps in Ocean Park, a village in Old Orchard Beach, Maine, a Free Will Baptist community, and at Merrick, a hamlet in Hempstead, New York, on Long Island.[5] New Jersey camps included those in Atlantic Highlands, Island Heights, Seaside Park, Cape May Point, Seaville, Malaga, Delanco, and Ocean Grove in Monmouth County. Ocean Grove, New Jersey's bastion of Methodism, was founded in 1869 and soon received the title of "Queen of the Victorian Methodist Camp Meetings." Rev. William B. Wood and Rev. Simon Wesley Lake visited Ocean Grove where the camp meeting movement inspired the two men.[6]

> In the providence of God, this magnificent section of land, on the seashore, has been obtained for Christian occupancy....
>
> We believe that God had it in reserve, like some other favored spots, for an inheritance of His people, and for real salvation purposes.[7]

Imbued With the Spirit

In 1879, brothers Ezra Blake Lake, Simon Wesley Lake Jr., James Edward Lake, and associate William

Burrell, all clergymen imbued with the spirit that Rev. Wood and Rev. Lake found in Ocean Grove, embarked upon a project to hold camp meetings at the South Jersey shore. With backing from their father, farmer Simon Lake Sr., who borrowed $10,000 and loaned it to his sons for working capital, the brothers incorporated under the name Ocean City Association and sold $100,000 worth of stock. Income from the sale of stock provided the funds to purchase much of Peck's Beach, Ocean City's original name. To insure the intended Christian character of the planned community, the association sold deed-restricted lots prohibiting the sale or manufacture of liquor and severely limiting activities allowed on the Sabbath. The founders dedicated lands between 5th Street and 6th Street from ocean to bay (the Strand) as open space.

The Ocean City Association constructed an open-air pavilion known as the Tabernacle, surrounded by a campground and tents on the Strand for worship services.[8] In 1881, the association built an enclosed frame construction auditorium at the pavilion. The Association held summer meetings in the auditorium and winter meetings in an educational building.[9] A non-denominational masonry building known as the Ocean City Tabernacle later replaced the frame auditorium.[10] The temporary camp meeting tents of the 1880s quickly yielded to permanent church structures and cottages.

In His Hands

In 1880, followers of the movement came together to form St. Peter's Methodist Episcopal Church. Rev. Ezra Lake was a member of the newly organized church and served as unofficial pastor during 1880. In 1881, the New Jersey Conference bishop stationed Rev. William E. Boyle in Ocean City as the first regularly appointed pastor of St. Peter's.[11]

On May 23, 1890, the official board of St. Peter's reached an agreement with the Ocean City Association to purchase three lots at a cost of $1,200 for a church at 8th Street and Central Avenue. The association conveyed a deed for the lots to St. Peter's after receiving full payment. In 1890, St. Peter's Methodist Episcopal Church changed its name to First Methodist Episcopal Church.[12] The first church on the island was a frame structure built in 1890 as First Methodist Episcopal Church.[13] Church officials laid the cornerstone for the new church with great ceremony on August 20, 1890. A newspaper account indicated the edifice would be completed in the fall at a cost of $8,000, one-half of which had already been subscribed. Despite the optimism

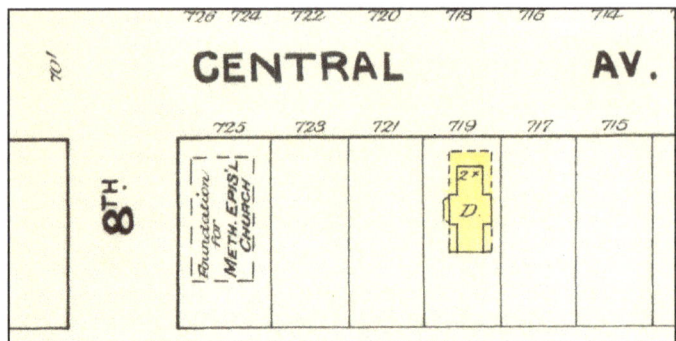

Figure 1. Detail, Sanborn-Perris Map Company, Plate 35, October 1890.

expressed in the newspaper, the Sanborn Map Company fire insurance map for Ocean City dated October 1890 shows just the foundation for the church.[14,15] The contractor finally completed the church, but after the target date, and the congregants dedicated the edifice on August 8, 1891.[16]

Figure 2. Original edifice, First Methodist Episcopal Church, Eighth and Central.

Grounded in Faith

Today, Tabernacle Baptist Church has the distinction of serving the community from a 130-year-old sanctuary, having purchased the structure from First Methodist Episcopal Church in 1906 and then relocated it to a new site.

Union Tabernacle Baptist Church began as a summer mission in 1897 when the growing camp meeting movement in Ocean City caught the attention of John Sheppard Trower, a devout Christian layman and wealthy businessman from the Germantown section of Philadelphia. John Trower, Rev. William Creditt, and

Ocean City's Oldest Surviving Church Structure

Rev. Samuel J. Comfort, all Germantown residents and members of First African Baptist Church in Philadelphia, led the effort to establish a mission in Ocean City.

> A colored people's mission has been organized, and is now holding services in the K. of P. hall, lately used by First Baptist Church. There is no morning service, but Rev. Samuel J. Comfort, the minister in charge, preaches every Sunday evening at 8:30 ... This mission is undenominational, and all colored persons are invited to identify themselves with it. There will be prayer meeting every Thursday night, and Sunday school every Sunday at 3:30 p.m. Tomorrow night there will be a concert and entertainment in the auditorium, for the benefit of the Colored mission of Ocean City. Rev. J. D. Jenkins, of Charleston, S. C., will produce twenty-six colored boys and girls from the Jenkins Orphan asylum in that city, and they will sing, play musical instruments and otherwise entertain the audience.[17]

The mission drew respectable sized congregations at each service. Jacob and Mary Still, Ocean City's first Black residents, supported Trower's vision of a Baptist church for people of color and worked with Trower to establish the mission.[18]

> The Colored People's Mission is quite largely attended each Sunday. Rev. Samuel J. Comfort was the speaker of last Sunday. These services are held at the K. of P. Hall.[19]

Figure 3. The Ocean City Knights of Pythias (K. of P.) Hall, c.1897.

Union Tabernacle Baptist Church became a full-fledged church in 1901 but continued to worship at the Knights of Pythias Hall while considering an offer from First Baptist Church to purchase a building they owned on Asbury Avenue below 8th Street.[20] Local churches customarily held evening "surf meetings" at piers along the beach. Tabernacle's mission held its evening services at Myer's Ocean Pier, 8th Street and the boardwalk.

Another New Church

> The second Baptist church recently opened here is now organized permanently under the name of the Union Tabernacle Baptist Church of Ocean City.
>
> The new church is the result of the earnest work of the pastor, Rev. William T. Amiger. The way for organization was opened at the union meeting held two weeks ago. Dr. William A. Creditt, of Philadelphia, addressed this meeting and made an earnest appeal to the audience, setting forth the importance of a permanent church organization. They will continue to hold their services in the Knights of Pythias hall for the present.[21]

Union Tabernacle Baptist Church was one of three churches in Ocean City's African American community known locally as the "Westside." The congregation convened in various meeting halls in town until 1903, when board member and benefactor John Trower arranged for regular services to move to Trower Hall, a property he owned. Services continued at Trower Hall from 1903 until 1906, leaving the congregation still in need of a permanent place of worship. Members of color from Macedonia Methodist Episcopal Mission had split from First Methodist Episcopal in 1893, purchased a lot from the Ocean City Association, and converted an old bakery into a church. St. James African Methodist Episcopal Mission, founded in 1900, had rented a lot and accepted the donation of a church building from First Presbyterian Church. They relocated the building to the rented lot in 1906.

After reconsidering and rejecting a 1901 plan still on the table to purchase a building on Asbury Avenue from First Baptist Church, John Trower ultimately negotiated an agreement in 1906 wherein Tabernacle Baptist Church would buy the church building and classroom that the First Methodist Episcopal Church would be vacating.[22] During the same year, members shortened

Figure 4. Trower Hall, Eighth and West, south side, c.1902.

the name to Tabernacle Baptist Church, dropping the word "Union." In 1907, the New Jersey Baptist Missionary Convention reached an Agreement of Sale with Henry and Mary Moore for two lots at 8th Street and West Avenue to place the buildings being purchased from First Methodist Episcopal Church.[23] In late November 1907, work commenced moving the church from 8th Street and Central Avenue to 8th Street and West Avenue, a distance of two blocks crossing the West Jersey Railroad. The move took three weeks and was completed without incident.[24] The contractor relocated the classroom building to the new site on December 12, 1907.[25] Several months later, the Moores executed the deed which actually conveyed the land to The New Jersey Baptist Missionary Convention.[26] The land remained in the name of the New Jersey Baptist Missionary Convention until June of 1946, when the convention conveyed the parcel to Tabernacle Baptist Church. Church leaders from Tabernacle Baptist finally recorded the deed five years later.[27] Thus, through a lengthy and complex real estate transaction, the new congregation gave the old Methodist edifice new life as a Baptist church.

Figure 5. Tabernacle Baptist, 1908.

Ocean City's Oldest Surviving Church Structure

Stepping Out on Faith

Tabernacle's benefactor, John Sheppard Trower, came from humble beginnings. Born in Eastville, Northampton County, Virginia, in 1849, John was a young man of 21 years when his father died. He worked as a farm laborer, soon saving enough money to present his mother with a deed to the farm. With just a few dollars in his pocket, Trower set out for Baltimore, where he worked as an oyster shucker before moving to Atlantic City, where he worked in local restaurants. After reaching Philadelphia, he and George Brown formed a catering partnership. Within a few years, Trower had opened a restaurant and developed a thriving catering business. He was also a confectioner, real estate investor, and philanthropist. John Trower served on the Board of Trustees at First African Baptist Church under Rev. Creditt. His business success led to others calling him "the best known and probably wealthiest Negro in the country."[28]

Figure 6. John Sheppard Trower.

Rev. Dr. William Abraham Creditt often preached at the newly founded Baptist mission in Ocean City and at First Methodist Episcopal Church, the church of Ocean City's founders. From 1897 through 1915, Baltimore native and Lincoln University graduate Rev. Creditt served as pastor of the First African Baptist Church (FAB or Cherry Memorial), Philadelphia's oldest African American Church and oldest Baptist church in Pennsylvania. He was former Chairman of the Educational Board of the National Convention and served on the Editorial Staff of the National Baptist Publishing Board before being appointed President of the Convention. By 1899, Creditt's congregation had outgrown its Cherry Street building. Rev. Creditt and Trower oversaw the purchase of land at 16th and Christian Street for the construction of a new church. They commissioned the Philadelphia-based architectural firm of Watson & Huckel to design a church and school. The new church was completed in 1906 at a construction cost of $100,000 (in excess of $3 million in 2022 dollars). Watson & Huckel also designed the Cumberland County Courthouse in Bridgeton, New Jersey.[29] Creditt and Trower worked on the new Philadelphia church concurrent with negotiations for an Ocean City church.

Figure 7. William Abraham Creditt.

Figure 8. Samuel James Comfort Jr.

Samuel James Comfort Jr. was a native of Charlotte County, Virginia, who became an orphan at age five. He was sent to Philadelphia, where he attended public schools and graduated from the Institute for Colored Youth. He worked as a tailor, caterer, and clerk, as well as a teacher and school principal, before attaining his degree in Theology from Lincoln University in 1887.[30]

Rev. Comfort pastored the 1898 and 1899 summer sessions at the Ocean City mission and remained until the mission obtained Rev. William T. Amiger as regular pastor in 1901. Rev. Comfort took no salary from the mission but supported himself through employment at the Brighton Hotel, Ocean City's first hotel, during the summer months. Rev. Comfort also pastored at Rev. Creditt's Cherry Street Baptist Church in Philadelphia. John Trower died in 1911 from heart disease at the early age of 61. In 1913, Rev. Comfort came out of retirement and returned to Ocean City from Boston to pastor at Tabernacle Baptist Church. Comfort's pastorate fulfilled the unexpired term of Lincoln University graduate Rev. William Kemp and assured the continuation of Trower's religious work. Kemp accepted a position in Massachusetts and went on to become a missionary and President of the State University of Kentucky. Again, Rev. Comfort did not accept a salary from the church.

In its heyday, Tabernacle Baptist Church served as a center for religious, educational, and cultural enrichment. It was known for its evangelical preaching and music ministry. Nationally known speakers and choirs frequented the church bringing spiritual and financial support.

In 1914, Rev. Samuel J. Comfort arranged for friend and colleague Booker T. Washington to visit Ocean City. The official greeting committee at his arrival included Commissioners Robert Fisher (representing an ailing Mayor Harry Headley) and R. Howard Thorn, Rev. S. Wesley Lake, Rev. Samuel J. Comfort, Rev. William K. Fisher, Rev. J. B. Haines, Otis M. Townsend, and Postmaster B. Frank Smith. The day included a sightseeing tour of the city, including a stop at Tabernacle Baptist Church, and ending with a walk on the boardwalk. Rev. Comfort hosted a luncheon at Hotel Comfort, where representatives from the business community, clergy, Mrs. Comfort, and Mr. Washington delivered prepared remarks. A large audience gathered at the First Methodist Episcopal Church later in the day to hear Mr. Washington speak. Informed by life experiences, education, politics, and activism, the speech Washington delivered on education and entrepreneurship was well accepted. Washington's tour of New Jersey also included visits to Morristown, Montclair, Paterson, Newark, Princeton, Burlington, Bridgeton, Gouldtown, and Cape May.[31]

In 1922, the John S. Trower Memorial Literary Society invited professor, orator, and linguist Dr. William Pickens to speak on the formation of the National Association for the Advancement of Colored People (NAACP) and encourage membership in that group. Dr. Pickens was a Yale Graduate and former Dean of Morgan State College, professor, and NAACP Field Secretary. His speech focused on NAACP membership and the Dyer anti-lynching bill then before Congress.[32, 33] Several years apart in their activism, Washington and Pickens advocated for differing views on how people of color should address the issue of racism. Pickens' book *Bursting Bonds, The Autobiography of a "New Negro"* is widely considered the beginning of the transition of Black autobiographies from the deferential

Ocean City's Oldest Surviving Church Structure

tone of Booker T. Washington's *Up From Slavery* toward the confrontational stance represented in books such as Richard Wright's *Black Boy*.[34]

Providence

W. A. Massey's original architectural design for the First Methodist Episcopal Church structure featured clustered, Gothic design, arched stained-glass windows. The windows of the restored Tabernacle Baptist Church replicate the original windows that the Methodists installed. The two rose windows set up in the gable of the façade along West Avenue and in the south elevation, looking toward 8th Street feature a Star of David/ Solomon Seal type design. The stars in these upper windows often lead people to mistake the church for a Jewish synagogue. Many questions and much speculation about the windows have produced no definitive answer as to the architect's choice of design.

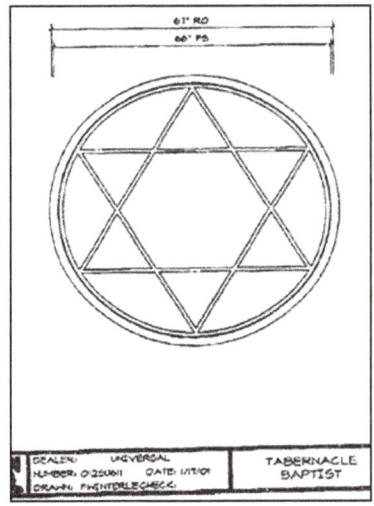

Figure 9. Star of David rose window design drawing.

The bell tower and steeple are unique to the building. Today, the finished height of the reconstructed steeple, excluding the cross, is 59 feet 7 inches.[35] A local lumber yard fabricated the wooden cross that tops off the steeple and local craftswoman and artisan Betsy King covered the cross with copper as a preservative measure.

Tabernacle Baptist Church underwent many physical changes as its members worked to save the building from the ravages of time and tide. From the removal and reassembly of the classroom for the short trip down 8th Street, to the elevation of the structure to create a

Figures 10, 11. (Top) Steeple under restoration and construction. (Bottom) Tabernacle Baptist Steeple and Bell Tower.

Figure 12. View of steeple top with copper enrobed cross.

Figure 13. Tabernacle Baptist in the 1920s.

Figure 14. Tabernacle Baptist in 1945.

Figure 15. Tabernacle Baptist 1963.

second floor, to the change from exterior to interior stairs, to the removal and replacement of the steeple and stained-glass windows, Tabernacle Baptist Church has endured. Photographs taken through the years serve to chronicle the changes to the edifice.

Ocean City's Oldest Surviving Church Structure

Figure 16. Tabernacle Baptist 1981.

Figure 17. Tabernacle Baptist 1996.

Figure 18. Tabernacle Baptist 2003.

This series of photographs serves to illustrate the changes wrought in Tabernacle Baptist's edifice in its 115 years of existence at 8th and West.

- In 1907, preparatory for moving the church two blocks, workmen separated the classroom building from the main edifice.
- After relocation, the contractor elevated the building to create a new first floor.
- The contractor relocated the exterior stairs to the interior and removed the steeple finials.
- Between 1965 and 1996, several major renovation projects at the church resulted in the removal of the belfry and steeple, stained-glass windows, and baptismal pool.
- In 1996, the community rallied to make repairs to preserve the building from condemnation. The Ocean City Historical Museum and Historic Preservation Commission lent their support. The commission then designated the Tabernacle Baptist Church site as a Local Historic Site, providing more credence for preserving the building.
- Tabernacle Baptist underwent complete restoration to near original condition in a four-year, $430,000 project spearheaded by retired realtor and builder Daniel Murray. Murray gained his inspiration from the memories of the choir music that emanated from the church and fell on his youthful ears as he stood listening on the sidewalk below.

Figure 19. Daniel Murray.

The project included replication of the original stained-glass windows which disappeared during an earlier construction project and replacing the steeple and belfry. Several of the original windows have found their way back to the church and will be used in a historic display of the windows, furniture, original Bibles, and personal songbooks.

- During the restoration, Mr. Murray recovered the 1887 Riday family Bible found enclosed within the church walls. The Bible had been presented to Rev. John R. Cherry in 1931 by Mrs. Paul Spiecker, whose husband owned the Fleetwood and Strand hotels.

SoJourn

Figure 20. The Riday Family Bible.

in light of repeated floods and storms. In 2019, the church's elderly and misguided pastor sought to sell the property, a violation of the terms contained within the church's original organizational document, causing local real estate taxes to accrue. A few faithful members carried the church financially while they invoked deed covenants and restrictions through the courts to prevent the sale. Again, the entire community rallied with love, labor, moral, and financial support as the faithful few fought to preserve this historic church. With a successful outcome in this latest battle, Ocean City's oldest surviving church structure now has a new lease on life and will continue to serve the spiritual needs of the community.

The history of Tabernacle Baptist Church is one of dedication, salvation, restoration, and continuing rebirths. The church languished in recent years as membership declined and it became increasingly more difficult to maintain such a grand structure, especially

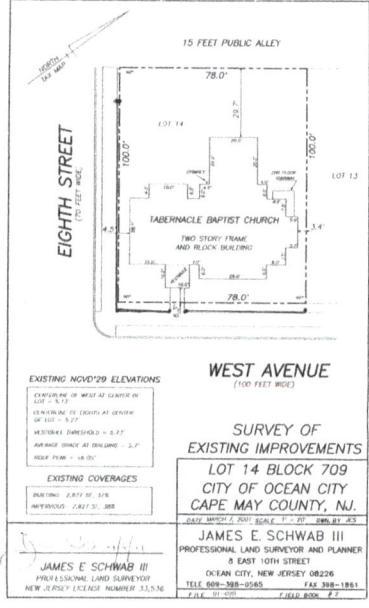

Figure 21. (Top left) View of the Tabernacle Baptist Church Sanctuary. **Figure 22.** (Bottom left) Tabernacle Baptist stained-glass windows restored. **Figure 23.** (Above) Survey map of church property dated March 2001.

About the Author

Loretta Thompson Harris is a fourth generation Ocean City native and retired corporate executive who served on numerous boards and headed several charitable organizations during her working years. Loretta currently serves as a volunteer researcher for the Ocean City Historical Museum. For more than thirty years, she has been researching her family history and documenting the untold story of Ocean City's African American and Native American history culminating in a book on Ocean City's Westside.

Endnotes

1. "Camp Meeting," published in the online version of the *Encyclopedia Britannica*. Found at https://www.britannica.com/topic/camp-meeting (accessed August 19, 2022).
2. Ibid.
3. "History of the Campground," Martha's Vineyard Camp Meeting Association. Found at https://www.mvcma.org/history-narrative.html (accessed August 20, 2022).
4. "Wesleyan Grove," Martha's Vineyard Camp Meeting Association. Found at https://en.wikipedia.org/wiki/Wesleyan_Grove (accessed August 20, 2022).
5. "Chautauqua-by-the-Sea," Ocean Park Association, Maine. Found at http://oceanpark.org (Accessed August 20, 2022).
6. William K. Pehlert, Ph.D., Loretta Thompson Harris, "Under This Tree," Church Exhibit, part of the permanent Ocean City timeline exhibit, (Ocean City, NJ: Ocean City Historical Museum).
7. William B. Wood, President, *First Annual Report of the Ocean City Association*, issued October 28, 1880.
8. "Ocean City Residential Historic District." Found at https://www.livingplaces.com/NJ/Cape_May_County/Ocean_City/Ocean_City_Residential_Historic_District.html (accessed August 20, 2022).
9. "The Cornerstone . . .," *The Bridgeton Pioneer* (Bridgeton, NJ), August 28, 1890, microform edition, 4.
10. "Ocean City Residential Historic District," op. cit.
11. Homer Gerken, Historian St. Peter's United Methodist Church, "Letter to the Editor: Corrections to Tabernacle Baptist Business Brief." Published in an unknown edition of the *Ocean City Gazette* (undated and unpaginated clipping).
12. Name change, "Under This Tree" Exhibit, op. cit.
13. William K. Pehlert, Ph.D., "St. Peter's M.E. Church," Manuscript research paper.
14. "Ocean City . . .," published in the August 6, 1890, edition of *The Philadelphia Real Estate Record and Builder's Guide*. Found at http://www. http://philageohistory.org/rdic-images/view-book-uv.cfm/PhilaBuildersGuide_v5 (accessed August 20, 2022).
15. Sanborn Map Company, *New Jersey Coast Map, Ocean City*, October (Sanborn-Perris Map Co., Ltd., 1890), 35.
16. Homer Gerken, op. cit.
17. "Colored Mission," *Ocean City Daily Reporter* (Ocean City, NJ), July 25, 1898.
18. "Jacob Still's Death," *Ocean City Sentinel* (Ocean City, NJ), June 13, 1901.
19. "The Colored People's Mission . . .," *The Ocean City Ledger* (Ocean City, NJ), August 20, 1898.
20. "New Church in Prospect," *Ocean City Daily Reporter* (Ocean City, NJ), July 8, 1901.
21. "Another New Church," *Ocean City Daily Reporter* (Ocean City, NJ), July 17, 1901.
22. "May Buy Church," *Ocean City Sentinel Ledger* (Ocean City, NJ), August 8, 1907.
23. "Church People Buy Two Lots. Colored Congregation Will Have Site for Building Near Railroad," *Ocean City Sentinel* (Ocean City, NJ), August 29, 1907.
24. "Work of Moving Old M.E. Church Building Begun," *Ocean City Sentinel Ledger* (Ocean City, NJ), October 31, 1907.
25. "Class Room Moved," *Ocean City Sentinel Ledger* (Ocean City, NJ), December 12, 1907.
26. Deed Book 222, Henry and Mary Moore to the New Jersey Baptist Missionary Convention. Drawn March 10, 1908, recorded April 23, 1908 (Cape May Court House, NJ: Cape May County Clerk's office, 1908), 214.
27. Deed Book 771, New Jersey Baptist Missionary Convention to Tabernacle Baptist Church. Drawn June 6, 1946, recorded Tabernacle Baptist finally recorded the deed five years December 4, 1951 (Cape May Court House, NJ: Cape May County Clerk's office, 1951), 389.
28. "John S. Trower," *The Washington Bee* (Washington, DC), April 29, 1911, microform edition, 6.
29. National Register nomination for the First African Baptist Church in Philadelphia, Pennsylvania. Found at *http://keepingphiladelphia.org/wp-content/uploads/2019/06/1600.06.Christian.FirstAfricanBaptist.Final-with-form.pdf* (accessed July 24, 2022).
30. "To Install Pastor. Ceremonies at Tabernacle Baptist Church Next Sunday," *Ocean City Sentinel Ledger* (Ocean City, NJ), May 15, 1913).
31. "Booker T. Washington Speaks in Ocean City," *Ocean City Sentinel Ledger* (Ocean City, NJ), September 1914.
32. Anti-Lynching Bill Forceful Exhibition by Ex-Dean Pickens.
33. "Hold a Successful Mass Meeting at Ocean City," *Atlantic City Daily Press*, June 3, 1922, microform edition, 20.
34. Harris Henderson, "William Pickens, 1881–1954, *The Heir of Slaves: An Autobiography*," Summary. Found at https://docsouth.unc.edu/fpn/pickens/summary.html (accessed August 22, 2022).
35. Construction documents, Tabernacle Baptist Church (Ocean City, NJ: City of Ocean City Code Construction Department, 2018).

Frank Astemborski at his workbench busy with decoy carving and assembly. Courtesy of the Astemborski family.

Scullers, Decoy Carvers, and River Rats on the Delaware River:

The Watermen of Delanco, New Jersey

Alice M. Smith

Zack Taylor (1927–2009), a boat and travel editor for *Sports Afield Magazine* and waterfowler, devotes an entire chapter on sculling for migratory birds on the Delaware River in his book, *Successful Waterfowling*. He explains sculling as the "perfect solution" for duck hunting on the Delaware River in this amalgamated quote: hunting a "Waterfowl ... raft[1] in open water far from the shoreline ... [makes] sculling ... the perfect solution; to propel the boat by a paddle, oars, or pole, while concealing all signs of man" [or men in the scullboat].[2] The Delaware River in Delanco, Burlington County, New Jersey, with its high shorelines along Delaware Avenue and its Mud Island and sandbar in the river, made sculling a deadly dance involving a specialized small craft (boat), long slender oars, rigs of detailed decoys, and watermen in pursuit of their raft of waterfowl.

Sculling boats can trace its origins back to the 1800s. Waterman, decoy carver, and boatbuilder Jess Heisler (1891–1944), from upriver in Beverly and Burlington, modeled his Delaware River sculling boat after the Barnegat Bay sneakbox. "The sneakbox originated about 1836 in West Creek, Ocean County, New Jersey."[3] Hazelton Seaman's sneakbox designs influenced Heisler's custom-made sculling boats. Known not only for his boat building skills and cabinetmaking skills, Jess also carved and painted three-piece Delaware River decoys. Heisler died on May 5, 1944, after carving nearly 2000 decoys during his lifetime. A pair of his sleeping mallard duck decoys sold for $28,800 in 2021.[4] Four years earlier in 2017, one of Heisler's prized pintail decoys sold for $36,000.

Figure 1. Jess Heisler in his hunting garb. Courtesy of the Astemborski Family.

Figure 2. A Jess Heisler sculling boat. Courtesy of Bob White.

The word *decoy*, according to Merriam & Webster, first appeared in print in 1630, believed to be derived from the Dutch word *de kooi*, or "the cage," one of the first forms of trapping prey. In 1624, the Dutch settled a group of Walloons on Burlington Island in the Delaware River, which waterway the Dutch named Zuydt Kille or South River.[5] The colony remained there for one year before returning to New Amsterdam to consolidate with other Dutch colonies against external domestic and foreign threats. The Dutch returned a year later in 1626 and constructed Fort Nassau in present-day Gloucester City.

Today, waterfowling boats, rigs, and decoys are found in many museums, including some reed-stuffed and duck-skin-covered indigenous people's decoys, and Tommy Fitzpatrick's Delaware River decoys. There are numerous articles written in hunting books, magazines, and newspapers about Tommy Fitzpatrick and his prized Delaware River decoys. This article includes information obtained from some of these prior texts and highlights interviews with others who are fortunate to own some of his decoys, knew him, or were hunters and carvers themselves. They live or lived along the verifiably 3½ square-mile peninsula of Delanco and are part of the upper river portion of a 20-mile[6] decoy and sculling region on the Delaware River from Delanco to Trenton, New Jersey.

In the 1800s, the Delaware River "provided the migrating ducks with approximately 4,500 acres of tidal marsh, with extensive areas where wild rice and wild celery grew...."[7] Over the years, this perfect habitat that attracted the ducks provided continued stimulation for the waterman to take an innovative approach for creating better boats, better rigging, and new methods to outwit the waterfowl.

In the 1860 federal decennial census for Delanco, the enumeration included a steamboat pilot, boatmen, and fishermen among the inhabitants of this town, bounded by the Rancocas Creek and the Delaware River.[8] These waterways provided a livelihood and subsistence for many community residents. If not out of necessity, the rivers provided many of the residents with a diversion from daily routines or, like the people listed in its census, river activities were a daily occurrence for their occupation.

Scullers, Decoy Carvers, and River Rats

Figure 3. Tommy Fitzpatrick in his sculling boat with the day's harvest. Courtesy of Kate Fitzpatrick.

and hunt ducks on the Delaware River. One interviewee shared what could have been a life-changing experience because of his dedication to the sport! Throughout the article are interspersed stories shared by interviewees about comrades now deceased.

Thomas "Tommy" Fitzpatrick

Earlier in Fitzpatrick's life, he worked as a cordwainer [shoemaker] in Philadelphia and, during the war years of 1917–1919, he worked at a shipyard, probably the Philadelphia Naval Shipyard. In 1916, Tommy married Kathryn "Katie" Rogers Whitsell.[10] They lived for 42 years on a floating houseboat that he constructed at the "foot of Willow Street along the Delaware River,"[11] between Willow and Cedar streets in Delanco. The Fitzpatricks rented the waterfront property from the Stockton family. Their floating home was often tied to a utility pole to protect it from being carried away during extreme high tides. The photograph below was taken in 1956 after a nor'easter storm slammed the shoreline along Delaware Avenue in Delanco, New Jersey.

Kate Fitzpatrick and her brother Tom, grandchildren of Tommy and Kate, shared their recollections of the houseboat and their grandfather:

> A narrow open decking wrapped around the houseboat.[12] To enter their home, a person stepped down into darkened houseboat with two daybeds, area oriental carpets, hardwood floors, pot belly and coal burning cookstoves,

A few decades later, Thomas "Tommy" Joseph Fitzpatrick, born in 1887, would become another name added to the list of the town's early fishermen. Tommy was also "noted for his small boatbuilding skills and his duck decoys."[9] Fitzpatrick's decoys and photographs, along with other images of Delanco and Delaware River town watermen, were celebrated over a century later at the centennial celebration of Zurbrugg Mansion.

For this article, oral history interviews (personal communications) with family members of scullers and decoy carvers occurred to learn more about their decoy carvings, boats, and sporting techniques. Other interviews included those who have or still continue to carve, rig decoys, scull,

Figure 4. Entrance to the Fitzpatrick houseboat at high tide along the Delaware River. Courtesy of Kate Fitzpatrick.

kitchen table, three chairs and cast-iron frying skillets with no running water. Catfish, sturgeon, duck, and apple pie were just some of the smells that permeated throughout their home. Their grandmother was a great cook and made the best pies.

A three-foot, knee-high railing extended around the back porch with a Pine-Sol smelling outhouse in the corner. A few steps down from the porch stood a free-standing, one-windowed shanty, opened to the houseboat where he kept his handmade carving tools and decoys. A 2x10 four-foot-long bench with a small table attached is where he worked on his creations. The smell of paints, wood, and Granger tobacco filled the shanty.

Docks extended from the shanty with slips and boats anchored in the river. His own duck boat, covered with Delaware River reeds with a pointed bow and stern, made it effortless for him to go in both directions. He sculled his boat when he was in close range of his targeted area, with his loaded 10-gauge double barrel shotgun.

They loved watching their grandfather go about his day. If the weather was agreeable and the river still, young Tommy rowed out into the Delaware River to fish, his boat always tied to the dock! Their grandfather is remembered as a sweet, calm, talented musician, and carver; fond childhood memories of a simpler time in the 1950s.[13]

Tommy Fitzpatrick "made his living off of the river and by repairing and repainting rigs of decoys for the hunters on the river."[14] The Delaware River provided "River Rat" Fitzpatrick his livelihood—"renting rowboats, mooring and renting boat slips, selling bait, trapping and hunting ducks for market, selling fish and turtles, and carving decoys."[15]

If Fitzpatrick copied an earlier decoy carver, it is thought that his work can be compared to that of John English (1849–1915). "The English style is the Delaware River style and John English set the standard against which other Delaware River makers have been measured and compared ever since."[16]

David Giannetto shares his father's recollections, Vincent Giannetto III, a duck decoy carver and hunter himself, in his book *The Decoy Artist*. Here is part of Vince Giannetto's narrative about Tommy Fitzpatrick.

Upon meeting Tommy "Fitzy" Fitzpatrick for the first time when Vincent was a young boy, Vincent recalls that moment and gives a physical description of Fitzpatrick and his workspace in his duck decoy carving shelter (workshop) on the Delaware River:

Figure 5 (left). Tommy Fitzpatrick's Draft Card that lists his occupation as a fisherman. **Figure 6** (above). Tommy working on the hull of his boat. Courtesy of Kate Fitzpatrick.

Scullers, Decoy Carvers, and River Rats

His stature was "not much over five feet tall" and he had an "old man's face. His clothing was dull, worn-out color, his boots dark-brown leather" were weathered with "heavy water stains and caked with sandy mud." Typical clothing becoming of a River Rat!

Unassembled decoy heads and bodies rested on a high shelf above in the workshop and his work bench consisted of wooden planks. When his decoys were assembled and carved, they fetched Fitzpatrick 50 cents. His hunting boat tied to the dock rolled with the river waves at the end of the dock.[17]

Fitzpatrick did not always sign his decoys. When he did, he used initials comprising a capital "T" sharing a common continuous top stroke with a capital "F."[18]

Mark Fenimore recalls that Tommy Fitzpatrick had a "double-ended boat that rode the river in a 'putt-putt-putt bang, putt-putt-putt bang' motion [probably a one-cylinder hit-and-miss engine adapted for boating use]. He had been up to Perkie's Meadow[19] catching shad."[20] When he didn't use the boat's motor, he knelt down on his knees in the bottom of his boat and rowed, showing not a ripple in sight from the oar's movement. The ducks did not see the oar because Fitzpatrick tied a line to the shortened oar and let it float in the water as he approached the ducks.[21]

Beyond the house were his docks and a woodshed with a woodstove where he would burn the excess driftwood used for his decoys. When the weather was nice you would see him down on his knees between the boathouse and shop carving driftwood decoys with a hatchet and sandpaper.

Figure 9. Boys on the beach with the Fitzpatrick houseboat facing the river. Courtesy of Kate Fitzpatrick.

Figures 7–8 (top). An example of Tommy's decoy carving talent. Courtesy of Kate Fitzpatrick. (Below) Another example of Tommy's decoy carving talent. Both images dated September 1954. Courtesy of Kate Fitzpatrick.

Fitzpatrick worked "in an open shop shaded by the low overhang of his house" and what appeared to be "the hull of his houseboat."[22] Vince Giannetto did not get a close look at what he was carving. "Few men would reveal the techniques they used to create their decoys, and as a result, each man's work was uniquely his own ... his rig of decoys often marked what type of hunter he was ... defining his reputation along the river."[23]

The job of his decoys was "to lure in the real thing."[24] On the Delaware River in the 1950s, the "real thing" were mallards, black ducks, pintails, mergansers, buffleheads, and teals.[25] The realism of Fitzpatrick's decoys is expressed in this old saying, passed down through Clare Hamlin's family, that when he "painted the heads and before they dried the cats were chewing on them."[26]

Fitzpatrick made his decoys "with the typical raised wing carving peculiar to the Delaware River birds."[27] "The heads and bills were carved in proportion to the hollowed-out bodies. He hammered the nostrils in with a screwdriver and the eyes varied: shoe buttons, tacks, glass, and some were painted."[28] "Fitzpatrick originally carved round-bottom decoys, but later changed his carving style to flat-bottoms. The flat-bottom decoys kept the duck from rolling side to side" with the movement of the water on the river.[29]

In September 1953, fourteen-year-old Bob White remembers visiting Louis Steel at his Pine Street workshop behind his vernacular nineteenth-century dwelling with gothic design elements on Rancocas Avenue in Delanco. Steel built a scull boat for White's friend, Donald O'Hara. Bob vividly recalls Mr. Steel having sculling oars, push poles, and four peach baskets, each filled with about ten of Fitzpatrick's mallard decoys, that were selling for $2.00. White purchased one of the push poles.

They heard shotguns echoing off the Rancocas Creek and when White inquired about the shooting. Steel told him that they were shooting railbirds. Before they left for their return trip to Trenton, Mr. Steel encouraged them to stop and visit with Fitzpatrick. They did not do so and simply returned to Trenton. Bob White resents not visiting Tommy Fitzpatrick and not purchasing a decoy. At 13, Bob White started carving his own decoys. He begrudges having missed a valuable opportunity to meet one of the best carvers along the Delaware River. Today, White makes a living selling his hand-carved decoys, too, and is considered the "best contemporary decoy carver working today."[30]

Tommy Fitzpatrick died December 11, 1958. Not one word is written in his obituary about his decoys. The article mentions that he lived at 426 Delaware Avenue and that he was "a retired shipbuilding carpenter."[31] Upon his death, the houseboat was sold, towed upriver, and used by a dredging company.[32] In 2011, 53 years after his death, one of Fitzpatrick's pristine, colorfully painted feathered black ducks, sold for $5,000.[33] Fitzpatrick carved over 2000 decoys during his lifetime using just a small hatchet and sandpaper as his main carving tools.

Figure 10. A Tommy Fitzpatrick decoy that sold for $5,000 decoy. "The monetary value for an old hunting decoy generally takes into account authenticity and history, condition, and of course the form and paint of the bird. Most Fitzpatrick decoys check a lot of boxes and we're fortunate a handful of his ducks have survived the perils of hunting and time." Colin S. McNair, Decoy Specialist, Copley Fine Art Auctions, LLC. Courtesy of Copley Fine Arts Museum.

Frank Astemborski

Frank Astemborski, now deceased, knew Tommy Fitzpatrick and owned several of Fitzpatrick's duck decoys. During a meeting on Tuesday, December 7, 2021, with Astemborski's widow Shirley, she located a large expanding brown file with flap and cord closure. Written across the front of the file were the words "Delaware River Decoy Carvers," which held the names and photographs of many Delaware River decoy carvers, rivermen and hunters. Frank Astemborski knew them well, being an avid hunter and fisherman, too. He participated in a centennial celebration event for and at the Zurbrugg Mansion on Delaware Avenue in Delanco on September 25, 2011, with other decoy collectors and carvers: Ed Stickel, George Shaffer, Ray Pestridge, and Bill Hamlin.[34] Frank's table displayed decoys and information about some of his contemporaries and earlier watermen, and boatbuilder Louis Steel. Tommy Fitzpatrick was one of these men, along with the others named: Fred Alfred, Howard Bacon, Ed Bintliff, Warren "Eagle" Dewson, Charles Ercol, Mark Fenimore, Fred Fuhrer Jr. and Sr., Bill Hamlin, Jess Heisler, John Killen, John Perkins, Silvan "Sub" Rapagna, Ralph Ulissi, Bill VanNess, and Jim Vogelmann.

Frank Astermborski's father, PFC Frank Astermborski, died on November 22, 1944, from

Scullers, Decoy Carvers, and River Rats

wounds received during the Battle of the Bulge. He left a son and daughter who barely remembered him. At age 14, an uncle took Frank duck hunting and the young man became hooked and his passion grew into a lifetime of sculling on the river and carving decoys. "The things he did at a young age would never have flown in today's world. He grew up quick."[35]

Frank Astemborski, like Fitzpatrick, was a self-taught decoy carver. Before carving his decoy, Frank measured the duck, then drew a diagram on paper for a template. Shirley said Frank had his own style, first working with cork and then wood. Frank amassed a sizeable collection of decoys. His decoys were working birds: floating decoys in the Delaware and Rancocas. Below are a few decoys from Frank's collection.

Not only a collector of duck decoys, Astemborski's eight duck boats occupied his garage, lean-to, and basement. The boat count is higher according to his son Frank Jr., who recalls there being as many as 14 boats. "Most of the boats he intended to use and/or fix up and never did. After his passing, we were able to sell most of them to others who wanted to fix them up and use again."[36]

According to Frank Jr., he "had a great childhood with him and it was always an adventure. Our difference was he loved anything duck hunting and it was his passion. I just enjoyed hanging out with him and 'liked' it. I had so many other interests growing up: baseball, riding my dirt bike, working on my Chevelles, etc."

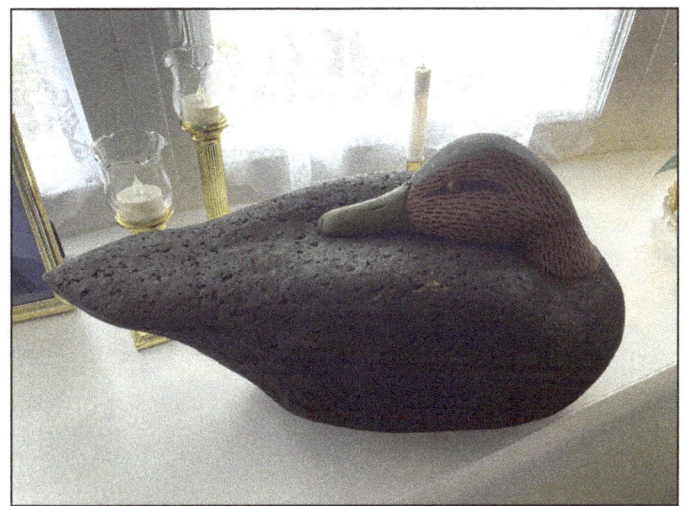

Figures 11–14 (clockwise from upper left). One of Frank Astemborkski's cork-bodied decoys. Another view of the cork-bodied decoy turned on its side to show how it was weighted to keep it upright in the water. Carved decoy heads ready for attaching to the decoy bodies. Templates and wood parts for assembling Astemborski decoys

The two Franks had a great relationship which is exemplified in his son's recollection of sculling on the Delaware River with his father:

> To be very honest, sculling a boat is an art. It is not an easy endeavor. The oar is taken usually from old, large oars from lifeboats and shaved down to the desired thickness to allow for flex and bending. The ideal is to have a sculling oar that has slight curvature to it yet be strong enough to allow movement in the water. The motion used to propel the duck boat is unique and takes plenty of practice. However, once you get good at it, this allows the boat to be propelled through the stern quietly. If you are really good, the boat goes straight at the ducks in the decoys, no sound, and it looks like some large driftwood following the current.
>
> My dad taught me as a young kid and I could do well just in front of the house by myself. But, under the full weight of a loaded boat, two people, wind, current, cold, nerves, etc., it's a whole new dynamic. I was probably 12 or 13 and was determined to scull my dad into the ducks. Well, I did fine for the first half of the journey. When we got closer, my arm got tired and I started to lose control of the scull. We ended up literally going in circles a few times and my dad just kept laughing. He was cool about it and not upset. I was ticked off and wouldn't stop—ha-ha. Amazingly, several ducks stayed in the decoys and we ended up getting two.
>
> My dad was the best at sculling—period. Sometimes ducks would fray off when you approached them and you had to make a decision on whether to shoot or focus on a smaller group and keep sculling to get into better range. He would sometimes have to scull for 10–15 minutes as the duck would simply leave the decoys and keep swimming away. His passion about the whole experience of the chase gave him that focus to make it a successful hunt. I never quite understood any of this until I was much older.[37]

Figure 15. Brian Caffery, Frank Astemborski, and Ralph Ulissi taken at Perkins' Meadow. Photograph courtesy of the Astemborski family.

Ralph Ulissi is 89 years old and lives on Perkins Lane in Edgewater Park and was instrumental in identifying Brian Caffery in the circa 1978 photograph taken of him and Frank. He insisted that his backyard is within the Delanco Township bounds and it should qualify him for mention in this article as a Delanco sculler and boatbuilder!

Ralph grew up on Magnolia Street in Beverly and rode his bike to buy his $3.00 hunting license from William Hookstra, who sold licenses from his farmhouse on Charleston Road near present-day Kennedy Way in Willingboro. Sub Rapagna and Jim Vogelman were the two men who inspired him and Astemborski to hunt and carve.

Ulissi carved balsawood working decoys. "Vogelmann's pintail decoys were oversized, about 18 inches and fabricated out of cedar. Oversized carved decoys made it easier for the ducks to see them than the life-sized decoys. The idea caught on as these larger decoys definitely attracted the ducks."[38] Ulissi owned several of Fitzpatrick's decoys that he purchased from Delanco resident John Killen for $5.00 when he sold off his hunting rig.

Ulissi quoted one of Frank's favorite sayings when meeting a fellow hunter—"You don't know anyone unless they have their hip boots on."

In 1974, Zack Taylor interviewed and photographed Frank while sculling on the Delaware River for his publication *Successful Waterfowling*. Five photographs

Figures 16–17. Sculling action on the Delaware River with Frank Astemborski ready for action. Both photos courtesy of the Astemborski family.

appear in Taylor's book depicting Frank in his sculling boat draped with "strands of manila rope that stand up better than grass."[39] Frank is pictured in his sculling boat with Charlie Ercol on the Delaware River. Frank Astemborski is the last known sculler on the Delaware River at Delanco, New Jersey.

Frank recorded his hunting adventures in his journal and enumerated the names of persons he partnered with in New Jersey and Pennsylvania. In New Jersey, Frank's hunting partners included Stanley and Coke Yansick, Bob and Burt Bowker, Fred Fuhrer, Charles Ercol, Warren "Eagle" Dewson, Jim Vogelman, Sub Ragana, Tom Perkins and Allan Nicola. In Pennsylvania, directly across the river at Mud Island, also known as Biddle Island, he hunted with Mercer and Charles Biddle, Dr. George Seifert, Ed Henshal, Dutch Kubernus, Bud and Charlie Rose, Jim and Joe Dunner, Frank Sidebottom, and Bill Rossbaurer. New York, Connecticut, Maine, Canada, Illinois, Delaware, Virginia, Maryland, North Carolina, Arkansas, and Argentina were his out-of-state and country gaming territories.

I (the author) had the pleasure of knowing Frank Astemborski. He possessed a kind and gentle spirit and served as one of the crew on my Alligator (submarine) Armada on the Rancocas Creek [*SoJourn*, Summer 2017, 15–21]. On many occasions, he'd trek through the reeds of the marsh, an area he knew well, searching for signs of the pre-civil war era submarine prototype. Below is a photograph of Frank taken in 2007 during one of our excursions on the Rancocas Creek with Vince Capone of Black Laser Learning. Frank Astemborski died June 18, 2015.

"There were days Frank would go out and could have shot his limit. He never picked up the gun. Just sat there and absorbed the beauty of it all."[40]

Marcus "Mark" Fenimore

Mark Fenimore, now 92 years old, hunted ducks in the late 1940s with Dick Hamlin on the Delaware River. Mark remembers the river appearing "black with ducks" from Hazel Avenue towards Beverly."[41]

Figure 19. A current photo of Mark Fenimore taken February 8, 2022. Photograph courtesy of Bill Hamlin.

Ralph Ulissi fabricated Fenimore's duck boat from a Jess Heisler pattern. Fenimore never sculled. They entered the river at the Union Avenue Wharf area, where all that was left of the wharf at this time were the pilings. Mark remembers his father telling him that the wharf had two landings or ramps so produce could be loaded and unloaded at both low and high tides. After putting in on the river, they would set their Fitzpatrick decoys and handmade cork decoys between the sandbar

Figure 18. Frank Astemborski in his hunting garb, photo taken in 2007. Photograph courtesy of Alice M. Smith.

and the Delanco shoreline off Oakford Avenue and wait. They would be on the river for hours.

Before Mark's father, William Fenimore, taught him how to handle a gun, they would hunt for rabbits at his uncle's farm on Sandtown Road, Southampton Township, Burlington County, near Medford, New Jersey. Here is Mark's hunting lesson account:

> My first time out with my father, we walked the farm fields and I simply walked behind my father... the next time my father gave me a stick and told me to beat the brush... then I got my first BB-gun but no BBs... the next trip out, finally, my father gave me a loaded gun!

Mark spoke about the common courtesy of duck hunters and the mutual respect of distancing from one another when setting their rigs of decoys. Some would hunt the lower, middle, and upper sandbar or "Perkie's Meadows" (Perkins). Donald Jones and Doctor J. George Wagner hunted at the lower end of the Delanco waterfront, in the vicinity of what was once called White Sheet Bay, located on the upriver side of Hawk Island. They sculled the river before and during the years of the Second World War. Other names remembered by Mark were Chester Hoffman, Elwood Knight, Norm Harding, Bill VanNess, and Bill Michalsky. George Shaffer, and Howard Miner hunted in the Rancocas Creek near Anderson's Farm in Delran.

Fenimore's decoys were made from long sheets of cork purchased at Armstrong Cork in Gloucester City. He fabricated the bodies in cork and purchased the heads at Herter's. Flat bottom decoys seemed to perform better in the river. The rounded decoys were boxier and would bounce and topple in the tidewaters.

While discussing the changes that took place on the Delaware River during the interview, a question triggered a memory from the 1930s when he lived at 314 Vine Street. Mark remembered hearing the sound of gravel traveling through large pipes. Vine Street was several blocks from the Delaware River. In the 1930s, the Army Corps of Engineers began dredging the Upper Delaware to a depth of 25 feet to Trenton."[42] The dredging of the river affected the hunt as the meadows at Perkins and the West Avenue area were filled in with the dredge spoils. Twenty years later, a hurricane in the mid-1950s destroyed the river vegetation on the sandbars.

Mark loved hunting, and in 1953, he missed the dress rehearsal for his wedding because of an emergency at his Public Service job out of Burlington. The next day, the lure of the river and hunting called on his wedding day. While on the Delaware River early Saturday morning with Dick Hamlin, the wind tossed and the waves pounded and swept against and over the side of the boat, making it difficult to navigate back to the dock. Mark worried whether he would get to church on time, but he made it just in time and married Bette on that November day.

Mark Fenimore died on September 26, 2022, at the age of 92. I am thankful that I had the opportunity to interview him and grateful that a portion of his memories will live on through the narrative in this article.

Figure 20. Dr. Wagner's "if-found tag" ("please return-to tag") appears on the bottom of one of Tommy Fitzpatrick's black ducks. Courtesy of Bob White.

Figure 21. Mark Fenimore's wedding picture with full bridal party. Courtesy of Mark Fenimore.

Terry McNulty

Terry McNulty, a contemporary of Frank Astemborski, now 80 years old, has been duck hunting and sculling for 65 years and knew Tommy Fitzpatrick who "carved many nice black and pintail duck decoys."[43] Terry has some of Fitzpatrick's decoys.

When Terry McNulty resided at 725 Delaware Avenue in Delanco, New Jersey, the decoys they used during the 1970s comprised oversized decoys for visibility when sculling on the Delaware River. Terry started hand-carving decoys in the 1960s. He competed and won world-class carving competitions. In 1976, he was a celebrated carver with Ducks Unlimited. He also carves shorebirds, and the Curlew is his best seller. Terry is still carving, but no longer enters competitions.

Our phone conversation on December 13, 2021, prompted Terry to discuss the sighting of a Drake Canvasback in Delanco. He recently found the April 1978 letter he had written to the United States Fish and Wildlife Service about this rare sighting. Terry sighted the duck, with an unusual red marking on its feathers, on the Delaware River in the vicinity of Astemborski's house. Canvasback were federally protected migratory birds. The Fish and Wildlife Service sprayed the red markings on the Canvasback to identify the birds. The red and blue markings on the birds determined their weight. The Drake Canvasback ducks originated in the Mississippi area.

Terry McNulty owned and operated the Delaware River Decoy Company in Riverside, New Jersey. The Delaware River Decoy Company, nationally known for their products, started operations in 1983 at a shop/garage located at the corner of Lincoln and Pulaski avenues in Riverside. His company employed three carvers and two full-time toll painters. The decoy company mass produced machine-made ducks made from his molds. He sold his company in 1987 to Jim and Joan Seibert of Cape May and it became known as The Delaware River Decoy Company of Cape May. The Seiberts resold the company after ten years to buyers in Nebraska.

McNulty recently traveled to North Dakota for a hunting trip and stated it was his worst year ever. Members of a 100-year-old hunting club in Washington State have invited Terry to hunt with them in the new year. Hopefully, 2022 will be a better year.

Samuel William "Bill" Hamlin and his son Bill Hamlin

In the afternoon of December 13, 2021, I met with Bill Hamlin, the eldest son of the late Samuel William "Bill" Hamlin. Bill, the son, contacted and organized the duck carvers who participated at the Zurbrugg Mansion festivities. He brought along pieces from his father's collection to the interview, which he had previously showcased at the mansion event. We spent the afternoon discussing his father's collection, his father's recollections of Tommy Fitzpatrick, and hunting stories.

The Hamlin family were duck hunters and owned several of Fitzpatrick's black duck and pintail decoys. Uncle John Richard "Dick" Hamlin, like his brothers, was called by his middle name, too. In the mid-1940s, Bill and Dick lived at 408 Iowa Avenue in a section of town known as Delanco Gardens. The men would cross Burlington Avenue from home, go through the Perkins Farm, and on out to Perkie's Meadow along the Delaware River. They waded into the marsh area in front of the meadow, their favorite hunting spot, and almost directly in line with their house. They built a double-ender sneakbox and took a 14-foot-long whaling boat oar and shaved it down to size for their sculling boat. Hot water was applied to the oar and then it was hung with weights to form a bend at the wide end to create a long sweeping curve. The oar/paddle was worked with the hand in a figure eight motion to move the boat in a straight line as the hunters laid flat in the boat to keep out of the sightline of the drakes and hens.

The next generation of Hamlin boys learned the craft from their father and uncles. By the time they became of age to hunt ducks, the Delaware River was dredged again in the 1950s and the dredge spoils filled in Perkie's Meadow. That did not deter the Hamlin boys. John, Bill, Steve, and Paul being boys, decided to freshen up the decoys which had faded over time during their

Figure 22. One of McNulty's mass-produced decoys. Courtesy of the Riverside Historical Society.

dad's many hunting outings. They applied black paint to some of Fitzpatrick's black ducks, but they did not paint the heads of the ducks. This is visible in the following photograph as you can see in the photograph. Oh well, the auction price for the sale of Fitzpatrick black duck decoy just dropped 90 percent![44] If you come across one of these decoys, repainted, it just might be one of Fitzpatrick's decoys.

Figure 23. Photo of a repainted Fitzpatrick decoy (children's artwork).

According to Bill, Tommy Fitzpatrick roughed out his decoys using a hatchet on driftwood found along the riverbanks. His life-sized decoys were cut in half and hallowed out. He nailed lead onto the bottom to make sure the decoy sat upright in the water. Many of his decoys were sleepers, meaning that no space exists between the head and body of the duck: contented ducks. Fitzpatrick did not scull but used a short paddle as he crouched down in his duck boat to paddle out to the ducks.

Bill started hunting at age fourteen. The Hamlin boys worked on Allen "Pappy" Stuart's farm, where Mark Fenimore grew mums near Perkins Lane and West Avenue along the railroad. The Riverwinds residential development occupies this land today with its nineteen two-story houses. The boys saved their money to buy model decoys—Model #72 was the oversized decoy and Model #63 was a life-sized duck. Bill and his brother Steve walked pushing and pulling their boat trailer from their home on Burlington Avenue next to the Joan Pearson School to the end of Magnolia Lane. They launched their scull boat on the Delaware River at low or high tides when the wind was still and the river calm. Drifting and rigging decoys, they would string two decoys together on one long anchor and another decoy on a single anchor off the side of the scull boat.

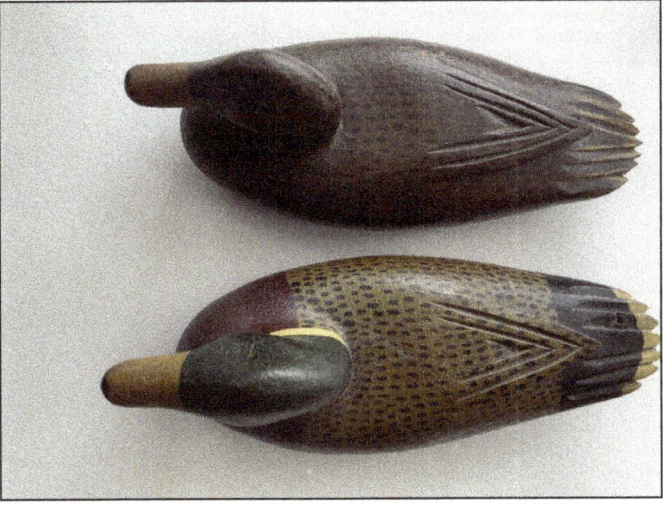

Figure 24. A photo of two Fitzpatrick painted duck decoys in the Astemborski Collection. Courtesy of the Astemborski Family.

The rig of decoys was arranged 4, 6, and 10 feet apart to make the decoys look natural. The rig of decoys floated 200/300 yards up or down the river depending on the tide. They would lure in and hold the ducks while they sculled towards them for shots. Steve would lay flat on his back in the front of the boat. Bill laid on his left hip, sculling the oar with his right arm in a figure eight motion. He remembers his arm burning after sculling. With their heads down, the boat looked like a log on the river or floating debris. The sculling boat had two small holes cut in the front of the boat for visuals. Sculling toward the raft of calm, sleeping ducks, they'd sit up, holler and shoot with their 12-gauge shotguns.[45]

In the 1970s, they purchased Styrofoam decoys for $70.00 from Herter's Sports Catalog. Herter's Sporting Goods was the Cabela's of today. The Styrofoam decoys did not work well so they decided to cut off the decoys' heads to make sleeping decoys and their duck numbers increased on their next hunting adventure. During that same decade, Bill sighted many white Drake pintails, "bull sprigs," on the Delaware River at the end of Union Avenue that colored Mud Island white. During Bill's duck hunting career, he has not seen that many pintails in one place. When asked why the pintails do not return to Mud Island, Bill stated that 50 years ago grass or wild rice covered the island; all that remains today is the mud.

Their mother Helen forbade duck hunting on the Delaware River on Christmas Day. Forbidden not because of the holiday, but because of a family tragedy that occurred in 1924 on the icy Delaware River. William and James Major received a shotgun as their Christmas gift from their father. William and James could not wait to get out on the river. On that day, high

winds and waves overturned their canoe and dumped the two boys into the icy waters. "Their cries carried to the Major home"[46] and their father shouted to hold on to the capsized canoe. When the father returned with help "the boys were nowhere seen."[47] Tragedy for the family would strike again seventeen years later on the Rancocas Creek. On June 30, 1941, Stephen Leland Hamlin, a distant cousin, drowned when his rowboat "capsized from backwash of a speed boat."[48] Boating on these waterways, and particularly with their confluence waterways can be treacherous.

Samuel William "Bill" Hamlin was a duck carver, too. He carved his decoys, however, to be decorative. Doug Atkinson, a local artist and fisherman, showed Bill the art of shadowing on his painted decorative birds. In 1977 Bill participated in the Waterfowl Festival, sponsored by the Ward Foundation in Easton, Maryland, and won first prize for one of his ducks. The Ward Foundation's Museum included a decoy labeled Delaware River Style. Knowing Fitzpatrick's work, Bill, identified the decoy as one of Fitzpatrick's decoys.

How many other museums have unidentified decoys sitting in their showcases? How many other unidentified decoys sit in basements and retired hunting boats and garages? You might have a Tommy Fitzpatrick decoy in an old cabinet drawer—a decoy priceless to the beholder. Tommy Fitzpatrick's "duck dynasty" continues today in his prized decoys sought after by many collectors.

"Each man's personality came out in the decoys he made. There were no patterns, no schools for these men, just hard lessons learned on the river. They approached making a decoy the same way they approached making a hunt, the same way they approached life."[49]

Figures 25–27. Three sequential views of Bill Hamlin's scull boat being launched and out on the river with Hamlin on the hunt for ducks and geese. Courtesy of Bill Hamlin.

Figure 28. Photo courtesy of Kate Fitzpatrick.

AUTHOR'S BIOGRAPHICAL SKETCH

Mrs. Alice M. Smith, a local historian, has lived in the triple-town area of Delanco, Riverside, and Delran for over 74 years. For the past thirteen years, she has served as the President of the Riverside Historical Society. She states that she is out of her element in knowing the subject matter for this article, but she found it challenging, enjoys interviewing people, encouraging others to participate in the process, and loves learning new subject material! Her woodworking accomplishments to-date have been with popsicle sticks, tongue depressors, and clothes pins for a 1980s nativity set, although she has added decoy carving to her bucket list!

Since 2000, Delanco, her hometown, has added 962 new homes.[50] While interviewing people for this article, she has heard from many of them how progress can produce changes that are not necessarily good for the wildlife. Dredging changed the landscape of Perkie's Meadow, which is now River's Edge, a residential development containing 265 condominiums. Many wildlife habitats are filled in and built up. There seems to be fewer ducks on the river, but not fewer ducks overall. She, however, remains hopeful. To attract more wildlife, she wants to replant Mud Island with wild rice, wild celery, and other edible plants for wildlife; not for the shoot, but for celebration of their beauty and viewing of their habitats.

Shirley Astemborski witnessed such tranquility in December when she observed a dozen buffleheads bobbing between the white caps on the river. Kate Fitzpatrick lives along the Rancocas Creek where mallards, swans, and mergansers are seen swimming in its frigid, partially frozen waters. Several years ago, Alice stood under a bald eagle's nest at the magnolias along the riverbank. In the fall, while resting on a park bench during her morning "Team Fitness" riverbank walk, a bald eagle flew over the treetops and crossed the Delaware River into Andalusia, Pennsylvania. During the quiet, peaceful, not-a-ripple-on-the-water experience, she remembers hearing the flapping of the eagle's wings and its call—the river is coming back, it is blanketed again with flocks of black ducks and white patched buffleheads!

There is something about the river people of Delanco; their friendliness and willingness to share their stories, photographs, and their generous hospitality that contributed to the completion of this article after several months of enjoyable storytelling interviews. I apologize in advance for missing the names of other Delanco hunters and decoy carvers not mentioned in this article. That will be another story or even an entirely separate work.

ACKNOWLEDGMENTS

I'd like to extend my warmest appreciation to Tommy Fitzpatrick's grandchildren, Kate Fitzpatrick and Tom Fitzpatrick; the late Frank Astemborski's wife, Shirley; Frank Astemborski Jr.; Terry McNulty; Mark Fenimore; Jay Cohen; Ralph Ulissi; Lou Stickel; Mal Anderson; and Don Hamlin, son of Dick Hamlin, for sharing their stories, photographs, and decoys. Bill Hamlin, son of Samuel "Bill" Hamlin, for helping with research materials and obtaining photographs for this article. Bob White of Tullytown, Pennsylvania, for welcoming me into his home, sharing stories and allowing me to photograph and handle his decoys. Colin McNair of Copley Fine Arts Auctions for sharing his decoy expertise; Michelle Dwyer and Copley Fine Art Auctions, Hingham, Massachusetts, for the use of a Tommy Fitzpatrick's decoy photograph, and Paul W. Schopp for his encouragement, editing skills, and making me look good!

Thank you, South Jersey Culture & History Center at Stockton University, for this opportunity to write another article for *SoJourn*. Little did I realize how much I missed the face-to-face human contact that this article's interview process afforded me. It's nice to be back!

Endnotes

1. *Raft* is a term used to describe waterfowl floating and drifting in the river.
2. Zack Taylor, *Successful Waterfowling* (New York: Crown Publishing, Inc., 1974), 233, 237.
3. Frank Harris Moyer, *The Delaware River: History, Traditions and Legends* (Charleston, SC: History Press, 2019), 136.
4. Colin McNair, decoy specialist, Copley Fine Arts Auctions, Hingham, MA, specializing in antique decoys and 19th and 20th century American, sporting and wildlife paintings, personal communication.
5. Marfy Goodspeed, "By Their Names You Shall Know Them, Part 2," *Goodspeed Histories, New Jersey, and Genealogy*, http://www.goodspeedhistories.com, 2013.
6. Paul W. Schopp, personal communication, January 4, 2022. Distance of 20 miles, measured from the tip of Hawk Island, Delanco to just short of the Capital City Yacht Club, a section of the river historically considered the Upper Delaware. Not to be confused with the non-tidal portion of the Delaware River above the falls in Trenton.
7. Moyer, *The Delaware River*, 136.
8. Charles A. Frush, Adair Herbst, Margaret Hunter and Agnes Perkins, the Delanco Bicentennial Book Committee, Delanco, New Jersey, *The Delanco Story—Its Past and Present* (The Kingswood Group, 1977), 48.
9. Ibid.
10. Kate Fitzpatrick, "Delanco Movers and Shakers: Tommy Fitzpatrick," *The Positive Press—News about YOUR Neighborhood* 7, no. 6, August (Riverside, NJ: The Positive Press, 2010), 10.
11. *The Delanco Story*, 25.
12. Proof of the decking can be seen in a photograph found in H. Harrison Huster and Doug Knight, *Floating Sculpture—The Decoys of the Delaware River* (Spanish Fork, UT: Hillcrest Publication, 1982), 67.
13. Kate Fitzpatrick and Tom Fitzpatrick, personal communication, December 2021.
14. Henry A. Fleckenstein Jr., *New Jersey Decoys* (Exton, PA: Schiffer Publishing, Ltd., 1983), 186.
15. Fitzpatrick, *The Positive Press*, 10.
16. Kenneth L. Gosner, *Working Decoys of Jersey Coast and Delaware Valley* (Rosemont, PA: Rosemont Publishing & Printing Corporation, 1985), 186.
17. David F. Giannetto, *The Decoy Artist—America's Last Hunter-Carver* (Gretana, LA: Pelican Publishing Company, Inc., 2012), 60, 61.
18. Kate Fitzpatrick, granddaughter of Tommy Fitzpatrick, personal communication, January 26, 2022.
19. Perkie's [Perkins] Meadow was also known as Perkins Point and the cove. The property belonged to Charles Perkins, who grew beans, corn and, across the road, stood his cherry and apple orchards. Today, Rivers Edge, a 265-unit housing development, stands on the infilled meadow.
20. Marcus "Mark" Fenimore, personal communication, January 4, 2022, with Bill Hamlin in attendance.
21. Kate Fitzpatrick, personal communication, op. cit.
22. Giannetto, op. cit., 60, 61.
23. Ibid., 42.
24. Ibid., 20.
25. Ibid., 41.
26. Don Hamlin, personal communication with Bill Hamlin in attendance, February 1, 2022.
27. Kate Fitzpatrick, *The Positive Press*, 10.
28. Ibid.
29. Ralph Ulissi, personal communication, February 10, 2022.
30. Rod Taylor, *Hunting & Fishing Collectibles Magazine*, "History and Artifacts from America's Sporting Past," 5, no. 6, November–December, 2005, 10.
31. "Obituaries: Thomas J. Fitzpatrick," *Courier Post* (Delaware Township, NJ), December 13 1958 (microform edition), 2.
32. Kate Fitzpatrick, personal communication, op. cit.
33. Colin McNair, decoy specialist for Copley Fine Arts Museum, personal communication, January 12, 2022.
34. Joseph Busler and Peter Silverberg, *The Zurbrugg Mansion Centennial Celebration* (Delanco Historic Preservation Advisory Board and Riverside Historical Society), September 25, 2011, 12.
35. Frank Astemborski Jr., personal communication, February 13, 2022.
36. Ibid.
37. Ibid.
38. Ralph Ulissi, op. cit.
39. Zack Taylor, op. cit., 241.
40. Frank Astemborski Jr., personal communication, February 13, 2022.
41. Marcus "Mark" Fenimore, op. cit.
42. The Delaware River Valley Association, *The Truth about the proposed 40-Foot Channel in the Upper Delaware River*, pamphlet Distributed in the Interest of the Taxpayers, [c.1950?], 9.
43. Terry McNulty, personal communication, December 13, 2021.
44. Colin McNair, op. cit.
45. Bill Hamlin—In the 1970s when Bill started hunting, he used lead shot in his 12-gauge shotgun. By the 1990s, lead shot was outlawed and replaced with non-toxic or steel

shot. Personal communication, January 9, 2022.
46 "Christmas Gift is Responsible for Death of 2," *Courier Post*, December 26, 1924, 1.
47 Ibid.
48 *Trenton Evening Times*, "Boat Capsizes, Youth Drowns," June 30, 1941, 13.
49 Giannetto, op. cit., 102, 103.
50 Kate Fitzpatrick, personal communication, op cit.

This hunting scene is typical of the lithographic illustrations found in mid to late nineteenth-century journals and magazines. Often these illustrations accompanied a companion published article. This image has been colorized.

Front cover of *The Sphere*, a British magazine showing a German U-boat attacking a British merchant ship. The cover demonstrates the fear of German U-boats that gripped the allied nations. Montague Dawson, artist, *The Sphere* (London, United Kingdom), LX, no. 787, February 20, 1915.

The Great War and the Jersey Shore:
The U-151's Gamble Hits Atlantic City

Zachary Baer

In the late spring of 1918, throngs of vacationers gathered in Atlantic City, New Jersey, to frolic on the beach and visit the city's seaside amusements. At that time, Atlantic City offered countless distractions from the everyday toils of working-class life. The city most importantly provided a haven of escape from the disruptions that the Great War, more commonly known as the First World War, brought to life. As most Americans could well explain by 1918, the war commenced in 1914 and the United States officially joined in the fray during 1917.

Despite the war in Europe, the summer of 1918 brought record crowds of visitors to the city that had long gained the nickname the "Queen of Resorts."[1] Accommodations, like the glamorous Traymore Hotel, located at Park Place and The Boardwalk, expanded their operations throughout the war years helping to cement the city's reputation as a premier resort destination.[2] The small Jitney Line Buses began operating one year after the war started, and moved holidaymakers around the city.

City officials even focused their attention on non-war related issues. "Girls may go without sleeves, but not without stockings," began a decree concerning the proper attire for female beachgoers from Beach Director Dr. Charles L. Bossart in 1917. "All skirts must approach the knees. Just how near the knees depends on the 'architecture' of the wearer ... thin girls will be allowed more liberty in this line than plump maids."[3]

In the minds of many citizens, the war was "over there," as the George M. Cohan song goes. Despite Walter Evans Edge, Governor of New Jersey, calling New Jersey a "centre of war activities," the average citizen maintained a generally positive and patriotic view of the events in Europe. After all, the federal government and the War Department had not issued any warnings or reports on imminent threats. For its part, the government carefully controlled all war news to keep the American public in a state of ignorance. Not only did the government engage in widespread censorship of the press, but it also spread propaganda in support of the American viewpoint. Hence, the public lived in a state of bliss, believing that the war could not possibly reach the United States, but that belief and sense of isolation from the war would soon change.

On the morning of June 4, 1918, Beach Patrolman Edward Shaw noticed a small bobbing vessel on the horizon. Shaw turned toward lifeguard Captain Alexis Miller and stated, "this looks like another boatload of survivors." Shaw was referencing the newspaper headlines from the previous day, "U-Boats Sink Seven American Vessels off Coast of New Jersey; Submarine Raider Shells Steamship CAROLINA."[4] The headline sent shockwaves of fear throughout the eastern seaboard and put men like Shaw and Miller on high alert. Pushing his fear aside, Miller immediately led a team into a lifeboat and rowed out towards the survivors. The scene Miller and his men found was stark: two exhausted men slowly rowed a lifeboat full of survivors.

Excitement on the beach mounted as Miller and his team embarked on the rescue. Within a short period, the survivors came ashore to cheers from those on the beach. A celebratory mood filled the beach as a full band playing on the boardwalk rushed to the scene. Quickly the "Lulu Shriner Temple" band struck up a rousing rendition of "The Star-Spangled Banner" to welcome the wayward survivors of the S.S. CAROLINA.[5]

Postcard from 1918 showing the Carolina's Lifeboat No. 5 as it arrives onshore. From left to right in the background is the Hotel Alamac with the Alamac Pier jutting out (extreme left), Tennessee Avenue, the Hotel Schlitz (center), Ocean Avenue, and the Hotel La Marne (right). The image was most likely taken by one of the lifeguards that went on the rescue mission with Captain Alexis Miller. The original photograph was black and white but then colorized by the postcard publisher when printing the card. Courtesy of the Paul W. Schopp Collection.

The shock and awe of this scene is captured in the rare postcard above. As the image makes evident, those on the beach experienced a remarkable wave of excitement and thrill; it would not be until later that the grim reality set in . . . the war had officially arrived on the shores of the United States.

The conflict that many beachgoers likely believed only took place in Europe had crossed the seemingly impenetrable natural barrier of the Atlantic Ocean and arrived for the first time in Atlantic City. The citizens failed to realize, however, that the attack by the U-151 on Sunday, June 2, which sank 6 ships, was only the beginning. In fact, five more U-boat submarines would arrive along the Atlantic Coast in the following months, sinking in total over 100 ships.[6]

The following article outlines the story of the U-151 and its terror campaign along the Atlantic coast. As the events demonstrated, the voyage of the U-151 and the sinking of the S.S. Carolina served as a wake-up call to American citizens and ultimately mobilized domestic support for the Great War. The U-151 and the sinking of the Carolina also shows how U.S. Federal Government efforts to diminish fear led to unfettered destruction at the hands of U-boats and encouraged the spread of misinformation.

Setting the Scene: The War "Over There"

The passengers who walked onto the S.S. Carolina in New York City could not have realized that the most vivid thrill of the First World War off the coast of the United States was about to unfold before their eyes. By the spring of 1918, the Great War that consumed Europe was well underway. Most informed citizens who decided to travel on the Carolina to Puerto Rico likely understood how the 1914 assassination of Austro-Hungarian Archduke Franz Ferdinand sparked a chain of events that divided European nations into two alliances: the Triple Entente, consisting of Russia, France, Serbia, and Britain, and the Triple Alliance consisting of Italy, Austria-Hungary, Bulgaria, and Germany. Within months, Europe plunged into all-out war as troops mobilized for both sides.

The Great War and the Jersey Shore

From 1914 to 1917, American citizens watched as President Woodrow Wilson kept the United States politically neutral, while simultaneously bolstering the U.S. economy by supplying both sides with war matériel. Even after 128 Americans died during the tragic sinking of the British passenger liner LUSITANIA in 1915 at the hands of a German U-boat, President Wilson remained neutral. During the 1916 election, President Wilson ran on a simple slogan, "He Kept Us Out of War," highlighting his first term accomplishment. With Wilson at the helm, Americans, like those who traveled on the CAROLINA, believed that United States would remain involved in the conflict only at a distance.

The tides of war began to change, however. Many United States citizens supported England and France in their efforts to defeat Germany, in part due to the nation's long historical and diplomatic relationship with the two nations. In addition, U.S. media outlets published frequent propaganda encouraging anti-German sentiments. The sinking of the LUSITANIA reminded those on the CAROLINA of the potential horrors when traveling via ship.

Among the many military innovations derived from the First World War, the U-boat most captured America's attention. Germany's use of U-boats was out of necessity. Since the early stages of the war, Britain declared the North Sea a war zone, which effectively blockaded Germany from importing goods at their ports; all ships attempting to reach any port would first be inspected by the British Navy. The impact on Germany was staggering. "By 1916, the German population was forced to eat only bread and potatoes . . ." recalls Paul Hodos in his book *The Kaiser's Lost Kreuzer*.[7]

Germany relied heavily on imports to provide food and other supplies and the blockade left Germans wanting.[8] To break the blockade, Germany invested heavily in U-boats as they offered the ability to circumvent British Naval forces by skulking underwater. Moreover, Germany used U-boats to enact their own blockade of Britain in 1915 and began to develop long-range submarines to trade with neutral nations around the world.[9]

U-BOATS AND THE ATLANTIC COAST

The concept of a submarine was not new to the United States, especially New Jerseyans. The state holds a long-standing connection to such underwater vessels dating back to the American Revolution.[10]

At the start of the First World War, Germany's use of U-boats both fascinated and caused dismay among Americans. They were fascinated because U-boats represented a new age of innovation: individuals had read about submersibles in books by authors like Jules Verne or seen them on the silver screen, such as in the 1916 silent film *20,000 Leagues Under the Sea*. Now they were real. They were dismayed, however, at Germany's use of U-boats to terrorize enemy shipping, leading to catastrophic events like the sinking of the LUSITANIA.

Yet Americans rested at ease in a belief that their stance as a neutral nation would keep them safe. They believed that the natural border of the Atlantic Coast and the protection of the U.S. Navy would prevent any harm from coming to the United States. In an August 1915 article in *The Daily Record* of Long Branch, New Jersey, the U.S. Navy assured readers, "The last vestige of danger of war with Germany over the submarine issue seems to be fading away with certainty."[11]

As the war progressed, however, both the Atlantic barrier and neutrality would crumble. In July 1916, Germany proved that the Atlantic Ocean was not a barrier when two merchant submarines reached the shores of the neutral United States. The first, the DEUTSCHLAND, arrived in Baltimore Harbor. Considered a "dare-devil" journey, American media outlets at first celebrated the sub's arrival.[12] The second U-boat to shatter Americans' sense of safety was the merchant vessel U-53. This submarine arrived in Newport, Rhode Island, on the afternoon of October 7, 1916, and almost immediately, the U-53's commanding officer, Kapitänleutnant Hans Rose, paid a visit to United States Naval authorities.[13] The arrival of the U-boat caused a commotion.[14] Although the visit only lasted about three hours, the U-boat demonstrated its damaging prowess by sinking five enemy merchant vessels, including three British ships, off the Atlantic Coast before arriving in American waters.[15]

While the sinkings included no American casualties, the presence of the U-boats interrupted shipping along the coast sent shockwaves among the American populace. The headline of *The Philadelphia Inquirer* speculated, "U-Boat Visit May Mean Warfare on This Side of the Atlantic."[16] Congress responded to the visits by authorizing the construction of numerous ships to bolster their naval presence.[17] The only hope the United States now had to avoid submarines on their shores was its neutrality stance.

But neutrality did not endure. "I have called the Congress into extraordinary session," stated Woodrow Wilson in an address to Congress on April 2, 1917, "because there are serious, very serious, choices of policy to be made."[18] The Commander-In-Chief emphatically asked Congress for something many Americans hoped to avoid: a war declaration. Wilson held ample justification, including a now infamous declassified telegram, known as the Zimmerman Note, sent from Germany to Mexico. The gist of the telegram involved Germany offering Texas, New Mexico, and Arizona to Mexico in exchange for their help to defeat the United States.[19] Equally significant among Wilson's reasons for a declaration of war was the "reckless and lawless submarine warfare" in which Germany engaged in unrestricted manner months earlier.[20] This meant that any ship in the Atlantic believed to be supporting the Allied war effort would be sunk by German submarines.

The United States' entry into the war meant confronting fears that U-boats would terrorize the Atlantic coast. "There was every expectation that Germany would send submarines to the Western Atlantic, where they could prey upon our shipping and could possibly bombard our ports," remarked rear-Admiral William Sims.[21] In Germany, a debate over whether to send U-boats to the United States began in earnest, as this would require diverting the vessels away from the British-French war zone. Germany, desperate to turn the tide of the war, decided to convert seven U-boats originally built as unarmed "merchant" submarines into a "Flotilla" that could maneuver around the British naval blockade and begin to raid Uncle Sam's shoreline.[22] Yet the question remained, would this gamble pay-off?

The U-151 Arrives

On Sunday April 14, 1918, the crew of the first U-cruiser, the U-151, scrambled like ants to make last minute preparations before launching the 213-foot vessel out to sea. As the men worked, their captain looked on, eagerly awaiting their departure. Heinrich von Nostitz was no stranger to the sea. A man of medium build standing about 5 foot 6 inches, with dark hair and a thick beard, he had a reputation among his subordinates as a serious, studious man with meticulous attention to detail.[23]

Von Nostitz was ordered by his superiors to hand select a crew of "dare devils" who would be willing to take a "Jules Verne" style undersea journey.[24] The crew who joined remained unaware of the larger mission, only that they expected to be gone for 5 months.

S.S. CAROLINA entering port, most likely in Puerto Rico, c. 1916. Courtesy of the Paul W. Schopp Collection.

Specifications of U-151

Measurements	Length	213 feet 3 inches
	Beam	29 feet 2 inches
	Height	30 feet 4 inches
	Draught	17 feet 5 inches
Displacement	Surfaced	1,512 tonnes
	Submerged	1,875 tonnes
Test Depth		160 feet
Engine Propulsion	Two Diesel	800 Horsepower
	Two Electric	800 Horsepower
	2 propellers	5 foot 3 inches
Speed & Range	Surfaced Speed	12.4 knots (14.3 mph)
	Submerged Speed	5.2 knots (6.0 mph)
	Surfaced Range	25,000 nautical miles (29,000 miles)
	Submerged Range	65 nautical miles (75 miles)

"Fine," recalled the ship's boarding officer, "we were ready for anything in those days."[25]

Approximately ten days prior to departure, the Chief of the German Navy's Admiralty Staff provided von Nostitz with the top-secret orders for their mission. The first goal was to lay mines at the entrances to the Chesapeake and Delaware bays. Second, observe shipping and ocean courses in as clandestine a manner as possible. Third, the crew of the U-boat was to cut the transatlantic cable.[26] When the men learned their mission was to cross the Atlantic, one crewmember recalled it "exceeded all of our imaginings."[27]

Journeying across the Atlantic Ocean in 1918 in a submarine was no easy task. A hellish trinity of heat, odor, and tight quarters met the sailors. Hatchways were between one and a half to three feet in diameter.[28] Food was another inconvenience of undersea travel. For the most part, the crew relied on canned provisions.

The U-151's journey across the Atlantic was uneventful. U.S. naval forces based in Europe became aware of the U-boat about two weeks into the boat's journey and sent a telegram to officials back home to expect a submarine by the end of May.[29] U.S. intelligence was right on the money.

On May 25, the U-151 engaged in its first naval action, sinking the ship HATTIE DUN. Over the next few hours of May 25, the U-151 went on to capture and sink two schooners, HAUPPAUGE and EDNA. Before sinking a boat, the U-151 followed an internationally agreed upon protocol known as "prize rules," which involved firing across the bow to warn the ship of their presence, boarding the ship and directing all crewmembers to depart the ship, at which point the U-boat could sink the vessel. This was much different from the style of unrestricted submarine warfare used in the European theater. This was due to the Kaiser not declaring a "sperrgebiet" or war zone off the United States coast. As a result, all U-boats off America had to observe the prize rules. Most of the ships targeted by the U-boats, like the three already sunk, were smaller wooden vessels with no armaments that would not have been large enough to travel in a convoy.

Beyond following prize rules, the U-151 did everything in their power to maintain their secrecy from the United States as long as possible. As a result, the crews of all three ships became prisoners of the undersea raiders. A motley crew of 23 prisoners, consisting of "elderly men" of German descent from the HATTIE DUN, young men of Danish and Norwegian origins from the HAUPPAUGE, along with black crew members of unknown origin and Portuguese crewmen, joined the crew of the U-151. In an amusing twist of fate, the captain of the HATTIE DUN and EDNA were old friends and a reunion commenced "in the bowels of a German submarine."[30]

One key piece of information gathered from the prisoners was that the three captains had no warning of a U-Boat from the Navy. This was welcome news to the U-boat crew. They now wondered, however, would their presence be detected and reported in the press?

"100% AMERICANISM"

Within two days of the attack, newspapers began to report the missing ships. Fortunately for the U-151, the press failed to report that submarine attacks caused their disappearance. Instead, newspapers cited naval reports that played down the presence of a U-boat along America's shores. In one article addressing the possibility of a submarine attack, the Navy responded to an eyewitness telegram spotting the U-151 by stating that "The day was misty and the Navy is fully convinced that the master was nervous at the sight of some unusual object, which, however, was not a U-boat."[31]

The Navy went on to state there was "nothing to indicate" that a U-boat was involved in the sinking and disappearance of the crew from the three vessels. "The Navy today finished checking up on last week's feverish rumors of raiders and submarines off the Atlantic coast and found them to be entirely unfounded."[32] Instead, newspapers called the disappearance of the three ships a "sea mystery," blaming the wreckage of the three ships on "rough weather along the coast."[33]

The Navy withheld the presence of the U-151 as a wartime measure. In a dispatch dated May 15, 1918, the Naval Force commander in Europe laid out the strategy of a future attack:

> There are circumstances which render it highly important that nothing whatever should be given out which would lead the enemy even to surmise that we have had any advance information concerning this submarine, even in the event of our sinking her, and that such measures as are taken by the department be taken as secretly as possible and without public disclosure of the specific reasons.[34]

Despite knowing that, indeed, the attacks resulted from a submarine attack, the Navy had no difficulty ensuring this information would not become public. By 1918, the United States Government held a strong clamp over what was published and reported in the press. As historian John M. Barry writes, "the government compelled conformity, controlled speech in ways, frightening ways, not known in America before or since" under President Wilson.[35] To this end, President Wilson empowered the postmaster general with the right to refuse delivery of any unpatriotic or critical newspapers or other print media. Journalists could also be charged with up to twenty years in prison for writing anything disparaging about the government under a new sedition law.[36]

Wilson additionally signed executive order 2594, which created the Committee on Public Information (CPI) under the leadership of George Creel. The CPI's main goal was to keep unpatriotic information out of the press. Creel demanded "100% Americanism." To do this, he created a network of thousands of individuals to give brief speeches before meetings, movies, and shows to promote cohesion around the war effort.[37] The CPI also demanded that their press releases be printed unedited in every newspaper. Americans were encouraged to report anyone who "spreads pessimistic stories" or "confidential military information."[38] Reporting the location of a U-boat would most certainly bring trouble for any newspaper.

With the press muzzled, the U-151 traveled unimpeded. Korvikapitan von Nostitz ordered the crew to New York, where the U-151 spent three days "fishing" for transatlantic cables to cut. Despite now roaming up and down the coast for well over a week, no newspaper reports warned any vessels of the U-boats' presence or whereabouts.

The U-151 Wreaks Havoc

As the U-151 roamed the coast of the Atlantic seaboard on the morning of Sunday, June 2, 1918, numerous commercial and private vessels traveled about, carrying on with business as usual. Weather reports indicated smooth seas and a beautiful, sunny late spring day. Among the ships that continued to maintain a normal schedule was the S.S. Carolina, which continued operation between New York and Puerto Rico. Unbeknownst to the Carolina's captain, a menace lurked beneath the surface. Having left the New York shoreline, the U-151 traveled south toward New Jersey. Terror then ensued.

The first victim of the U-151 was the Isa B. Wiley, departing from Philadelphia. The attack occurred at 6:50 a.m. As the takeover occurred, the U-151 captured another passing vessel, the S.S. Winneconne, leaving from New York City. By day's end, the U-151 would capture and sink six ships. This would go down as the single greatest loss of shipping on the east coast up to that point in the war. The six ships totaled 14,517 tons. The American press dubbed June 2, "Black Sunday." Boarding officer Dr. Frederick Körner remembered the day differently, calling it the U-151's "lucky day."[39] Among the ships sunk was the S.S. Carolina, traveling from New York City to San Juan, Puerto Rico.

Mrs. Charles Seymour Westbrook, from New York City, was sitting on the deck of the Carolina when she spotted a periscope coming out of the water. Before long, a shot from the U-151's deck gun was fired across the bow of the Carolina and the vessel cut its engines. German officers boarded the Carolina, informed the ship's captain they would sink the passenger liner, and that all passengers would have time to gather provisions and get into lifeboats. Most passengers left behind nearly all their possessions and money.

Mrs. Westbrook was placed on lifeboat #5, the last to leave the Carolina. As the lifeboats left the Carolina, the U-151 fired their torpedoes. A great conflagration engulfed the ship as it slid underwater. For a short time, one of the lifeboats with a motor tugged lifeboat no. 5 along until it broke free in the middle of the night. A lifeboat crew member had a compass, but when that failed, the boat relied on the north star for guidance. After nearly forty hours at sea, the lifeboat crew guided the boat towards the top of a large building, later determined to be the Hotel Traymore. The *Atlantic City Daily Press* states the survivors were "taken to the Hotel Thurber, where they were provided with food and drink." Mrs. Hamilton, one of the lifeboat survivors, considered the ordeal a "nightmare."[40]

Within a short period, the other survivors of the CAROLINA reached shore up and down the coast. The schooner EVA P. DOUGLAS rescued nearly 250 victims. Other lifeboats landed in Lewes, Delaware, and Barnegat, New Jersey.[41] For those victims that lost their belongings and money, charitable organizations like the Shriners and the American Red Cross provided funds to help the victims get back on their feet.[42] The postcard on the following page shows beachgoers in Atlantic City sitting in the lifeboat. The words, CAROLINA, can be seen on the boat's oar. Although those in the picture appear to be happy Atlantic City visitors, for the passengers on the CAROLINA, hysteria and fear would grip them during the Black Sunday attacks, especially after boarding lifeboat no. 5.

Lifeboat Number 5 Passengers	
Name	Address
F. Anderson	No address
J. Barber	No address
C. Blank	No address
Felix Capbegville (Capegille)	Baton Rouge, Louisiana
Anita E. Cheney	San Juan, Puerto Rico
B. A. Cheney	San Juan, Puerto Rico
John Connoly	New Orleans, Louisiana
Lillian Dickinson	Arlington, Massachusetts
R. Fernandez	No address
Juan Garcia	No address
P. Goulpan	No address
Rachel B. (PJ) Hamilton	San Juan, Puerto Rico
Charlotta Hamilton	San Juan, Puerto Rico
C. Haseth	No address
Caroline D. Higgins	Cambridge, Massachusetts
Samuel Johnson	Woodhaven, New York
A. Kruppenbach	New Orleans, Louisiana
L. Levy	No address
B. E. Lewis	No address
Gertrude Lucian	San Juan, Puerto Rico
Lieutenant J. C. McClaren	422 Sterling Place, Brooklyn
T. A. Merte (Purser for Carolina)	Jamaica, Long Island
Charlotte A. Perkins	Boston, Massachusetts
F. Quirino	No address
D. Rodriguez	No address
M. Rodriguez	No address
J. P. Torren	No address
Mrs. Clarence Seymour Westbrook	83 West 56th Street, New York

HYSTERIA AND FEAR

Most newspapers attempted to quell hysteria from the attacks by explaining the U-boat's appearance as a sign of Germany's desperation. "By striking with her submarines on this side of the Atlantic," begins one article, "Germany has admitted to the world that the American army will turn the tide against her on the battlefields of France."[43] Newspaper reports also provided Americans with a story of revenge. "America Delivers Stinging Reply to U-boat Raids," read one headline in the *Atlantic City Daily Press*. "United States Marines . . . gained two and a half miles of territory . . . a prompt and bloody reply to German U-boat raids."[44]

American men responded to the U-151's attack in a variety of patriotic ways. In most major eastern cities, men waited in long lines at recruiting stations. The "recruiting fever" proved so great that more men enlisted in the days following the attack than at any other time up to that point in the war.[45] Others responded by working swiftly to hunt down the U-boat. In the immediate aftermath, the Navy Department made official statements expressing that Germany had as many as three U-boats off the coast of the United States.[46] The following day, "unconfirmed reports" suggested American destroyers had "surrounded and captured" the U-Boat.[47] Both reports would ultimately turn out to be untrue. The U-151 would go on to attack three more ships on June 3, one ship on June 4, two ships on June 5, and ten more ships by the end of the month. President Wilson called the attacks, "distressing things."[48]

This view of Atlantic City comes from a real photo postcard, c. 1915. Although no images exist taken from the actual lifeboat, this image portrays the oceanfront vista survivors of the CAROLINA would have seen as they arrived on shore.

Postcard from 1918 showing the CAROLINA's Lifeboat No. 5 on the beach. In the days following the landing, the lifeboat became a novel tourist attraction and beachgoers, like those shown here, regularly visited the craft until its removal. Both images courtesy of the Paul W. Schopp Collection.

As the Navy hunted for the U-boat, others on shore hunted down alleged spies and traitors believed to have helped the U-boat along the coast. One report speculated that Germany landed spies in Cape May to infiltrate the country.[49] Other reports emerged about "mysterious flashes of light" from the Jersey shoreline. Newspapers spread rumors that "a system of light signals in code" allowed a "band" of individuals, led by a "woman with keen mind and high intelligence" to direct the U-boat.[50] Despite never uncovering the traitors, the hysteria did lead to at least one innocent German American citizen being harassed and arrested.

Anti-German discrimination was at a fever pitch during the war. Americans became suspicious of anything German. Historian John Barry recounts that, "conversing in German on the street" might cause people to question a person's loyalty. Fritz Flage found this out the hard way. Flage was reading a German newspaper on the street in Atlantic City when a crowd surrounded him and began to question him. As the crowd grew, Flage "took to his heels" and the crowd chased him through the streets as they yelled "spy." Flage was arrested but was later released when the charges were dropped.

Another theory influencing the hysteria surrounding the attacks was that U-boats were using germ warfare to spread disease. "Blame U-boats for the Epidemic," reads the headline of Philadelphia's *Evening Public Ledger*, "... the mysterious epidemic which has spread over the country ... was brought to Spain by German submarines."[51] In reality, the epidemic originated in the United States but due to U.S. Government censorship through the Committee on Public Information, most Americans were unaware of its true origins. The influenza pandemic was widely misunderstood by the country at this time and would go on to infect nearly one third of the world population.[52]

In total, the U-151 would spend just over six weeks on the Atlantic Coast. During that time, the ship would attack 24 ships.

THE IMPORTANCE OF THE U-151

In 2001, the S.S. CAROLINA and the U-151 captured national headlines once again. This time, news reports recounted acclaimed diver John Chatterton's successful identification of the S.S. CAROLINA in the mid to late 1990s.[53] "I spent 5 or 6 years researching the ship," Chatterton recalled in an interview.[54] Chatterton dove on the wreck after identifying the location from translated German U-boat log books. Diving on the wreck was not a simple task. Chatterton stated that "If it is easy, someone else has already found it."[55] Among Chatterton's major achievements was identifying the lettering "CAROLINA" on the fantail of the wreck. He brought this information to one of the descendants of a survivor of the CAROLINA, Joseph Rodriguez, who is a Senior United States District Judge of the United States District Court for the District of New Jersey.

Judge Rodriguez granted Chatterton salvaging rights to the CAROLINA. Chatterton's dives on the Carolina have provided him with countless artifacts. His work is documented as a virtual museum on the website njscuba.com.

The U-151 was one of 329 submarines that served under the German flag during WWI. Since its fateful voyage, numerous historians and academics interested in the study of World War I have recounted the submarine's story. In the general population, however, most Americans are unaware of the havoc the U-boats caused on the Jersey coast. Understanding the impact of the U-151 is essential to understanding why the United States entered the war with such vigor. As renowned naval historian William Bell Clark wrote in 1929, "... the single action of one U-boat in sinking the New York-Porto Rico liner CAROLINA, with the loss of thirteen lives, did more to awaken the 'will to win' in this country than all the paid publicity of the Committee on Public Information."[56] Despite the importance of the CAROLINA, neither history textbooks nor state standards for New Jersey require students to analyze the impact of U-boat raids on the United States during the First World War.

U-Boat Tonnage Scores for North American Raids			
U-Boat	# of Ships Sunk or Damaged	Gross Registered Tons	Warship Tonnage
U-151	23*	58,028	0
U-152	3	7,975	0
U-155	8	17,525	0
U-156	36	27,293	13,680
U-117	23	35,020	16,000 damaged
U-140	7	30,594	0
Totals	102	176,435	29,680
Source: Hodos, *The Kaiser's Lost Kreuzer*, 192			
*Excluding SS HERBERT PRATT			

Wreckage Caused by U-151 on Atlantic Voyage				
Boat Name (None are Warships)	Date	Position/ Location	Country	Details
HATTIE DUN	May 25, 1918	37° 40'N, 74° 58'W	United States	435 tons; sunk
HAUPPAUGE	May 25, 1918	Off coast of Maryland	United States	1,446 tons; salvaged
EDNA	May 25, 1918	Salvaged	United States	325 tons; salvaged
ISABEL B. WILEY	June 2, 1918	Off coast of Barnegat	United States	776 tons; sunk
WINNECONNE	June 2, 1918	39° 26'N, 72° 50'W	United States	1,869 tons; sunk
JACOB M. HASKELL	June 2, 1918	Sunk 50 miles ExS of Barnegat, New Jersey	United States	1,778 tons; sunk
EDWARD H. COLE	June 2, 1918	Sunk 50 miles ExS of Barnegat, New Jersey	United States	1,791 tons; sunk
TEXEL	June 2, 1918	Off coast of NJ; 38° 57'N, 73° 13'W	United States	3,210 tons; sunk
CAROLINA	June 2, 1918	Off coast of NJ; 39°0'00"N 73°28'00"W	United States	5,093 tons; sunk
SAMUEL C. MENGEL	June 3, 1918	Off coast of NJ; 38° 07'N, 73° 46'W	United States	915 tons; sunk
HERBERT L. PRATT	June 3. 1918	Cape Henlopen, Delaware	United States	7,145 tons; hit mine; salvaged
EDWARD R. BAIRD, JR.	June 3, 1918	Salvaged	United States	279 tons; salvaged
EIDSVOLD	June 4, 1918	Off coast of Virginia; 37° 12'N, 73° 55'W	Norway	1,570 tons; Sunk
HARPATHIAN	June 5, 1918	80 Miles off coast of Virginia	Britain	4,588 tons; sunk
VINLAND	June 5, 1918	About 50 miles off coast of Virginia; 36° 32'N, 73° 58'W	Norway	1,143 tons; sunk
PINAR DEL RIO	June 8, 1918	36° 15'N, 73° 55'W	United States	2,504 tons; sunk
HENRIK LUND	June 10, 1918	36° 30'N, 71° 29'W	Norway	4,226 tons; sunk
VINDEGGEN	Captured June 8, Sunk June 10, 1918	36° 25'N, 71° 20'W	Norway	3,179 tons; sunk
KRINGSJAA	June 14, 1918	Off Virginia Coast, 38° 02'N, 71° 40'W	Norway	1,750 tons; sunk
SAMOA	June 14, 1918	90 Miles off coast of Virginia; 37° 30'N, 72° 10'W	Norway	1,138 tons; sunk
DWINSK	June 18, 1918	39° 10'N, 63° 10'W	Britain	8,173 tons; sunk
CHILIER	June 22, 1918	39° 30'N, 53° 40'W	Belgium	2,966 tons; sunk
AUGVALD	June 23, 1918	38° 30'N, 53° 42'W	Norway	3,406 tons; sunk
DICTATOR	June 28, 1918		Britain	125 tons; sunk
Sources: Merril, 182–85; https://uboat.net/wwi/boats/successes/u151.html; *A History of Submarine Warfare Along the Jersey Coast*				
Locations are approximate and not exact. This was given based on the results acquired from uboat.net				

The Great War and the Jersey Shore

An official postcard available onboard the S.S. Carolina for passengers to send to friends, the New York and Porto [sic] Rico Steamship Company supplied these cards on each of its vessels as a courtesy. With the sinking of the Carolina, many of these postcards likely drifted on the ocean's surface before becoming waterlogged and sinking to the bottom. Courtesy of the Paul W. Schopp Collection.

Acknowledgements

This article would not have been possible without the help of three people. Paul Schopp sparked my curiosity to write this article by showing me the postcard of Lifeboat No. 5 arriving in Atlantic City. Paul also provided assistance during the researching, writing, and editing phases of the article, as well as all of the images. Additionally, after reading Paul Hodos wonderful book, *The Kaiser's Lost Kreuzer*, we emailed back and forth. He was extremely generous with his time, knowledge, and advice on source material. Lastly, the world-renowned diver John Chatterton was gracious enough to answer numerous emails and meet via zoom for a lengthy interview on his experience researching and diving on the Carolina. His knowledge and personal contact with the Carolina offered a rare and unique perspective. Thank you to all three individuals for your kindness and selflessness in assisting this article.

About the Author

Zachary Baer is a history teacher at Shawnee High School. He is a member of the West Jersey History Roundtable and holds a deep, abiding interest in writing and teaching about local history. Zachary looks forward to receiving feedback and comments from *SoJourn* readers. Comments can be sent directly to the author at zacharytbaer@gmail.com. An accompanying digital lesson plan about U-boat attacks off the Atlantic coast for high school classrooms can be downloaded on Zachary's website: https://sites.google.com/lrhsd.org/baer-history

Endnotes

1 James D. Ristine, *Atlantic City* (Charleston: Arcadia Publishing, 2008), 9.
2 "25 story Hotel At Resort," *The New York Times*, September 8, 1916.
3 "No More Bare Legs At Shore," *Harrisburg Telegraph* (Harrisburg, Pennsylvania), January 27, 1917, 6; for more, see "Cops Now Armed with Tape Liners to Measure Skirts of Bathers," *The Evening World* (New York, New York), July 22, 1915, 5.
4 "U-BOATS SINK SEVEN AMERICAN VESSELS OFF COAST OF NEW JERSEY; SUBMARINE RAIDER SHELLS STEAMSHIP CAROLINA," *Evening Public Ledger* (Philadelphia, Pennsylvania), June 3, 1918.
5 "73 Carolina Survivors at Atlantic City," *Evening Public Ledger* (Philadelphia, Pennsylvania), June 4, 1918.
6 U-boat stands for Unterseeboot in German, meaning

undersea boat.
7. Hodos, *The Kaiser's Lost Kreuzer: A History of U-156 and Germany's Long-Range*, 10–11.
8. Ibid, 11; As Hodos identifies, Germany relied heavily on imports. In 1912 and 1913, Germany's imports exceeded exports by over 640 million US Dollars.
9. Ibid.
10. Joseph G. Bilby, Harry Ziegler, *A History of Submarine Warfare along the Jersey Shore*; https://www.ussnautilus.org/fultons-torpedos/; http://www.delancotownship.com/content/5300/5919/5951/default.aspx. The first submarine used to sink an enemy ship was the TURTLE, a small barrel-shaped submarine used by the Continental Army during the war for American independence. The TURTLE attacked British vessels during the defense of New York in 1776 and during the Philadelphia campaign of 1777. Prior to building a career in the steamship industry, Robert Fulton built the first practical submarine under commission from Napoleon in 1801. Fulton's submarine, the NAUTILUS, was ultimately not utilized by the French Navy, though it did conceptualize numerous design principles used in later submarines—such as the torpedo. More germain to New Jersey, during the Civil War the French inventor and immigrant, Brutus de Villeroi, designed the first submarine for the United States Navy known as the ALLIGATOR that was built in Philadelphia and tested on the Rancocas Creek in New Jersey near Delanco Township. Another Civil War era submarine, the INTELLIGENT WHALE, was built in Newark. Though never used by the Navy, the submarine can be seen on display in Sea Girt at the National Guard Militia Museum of New Jersey.
11. "Germany Sends Words of Peace," *The Daily Record* (Long Branch, New Jersey), August 27, 1915, 13.
12. "German Submarine Eludes Allied Warship Fleets and Docks At Baltimore," *The Morning Post* (Camden, New Jersey), July 10, 1916.
13. The trip to Newport took 17 days; "U-Boat Visit May Mean Warfare on This Side of the Atlantic," *The Philadelphia Inquirer*, October 8, 1916, 1.
14. For a complete account of the U-53, read *The Kaiser Strikes America: The U-boat War Off America's Coast in WWI*, 39–40.
15. "Ships Hit By U-53," u-boat.net; Tane Casserley and Debrorah Marx, "The Enemy in Home Waters—How World War I Came Home to North Carolina," *National Marine Sanctuaries Monitor*, 9.
16. "U-Boat Visit May Mean Warfare on This Side of the Atlantic," *The Philadelphia Inquirer*, October 8, 1916, 1.
17. William Bell Clark, *When the U-Boats Came to America* (Boston, MA: Little, Brown, and Company, 1929), 12.
18. Woodrow Wilson, War Messages, 65th Cong., 1st Sess. Senate Doc. No. 5, Serial No. 7264, Washington, D.C., 1917, 3–8.
19. "U.S. Entry into World War I, 1917," Office of the Historian, United States Department of State, https://history.state.gov/milestones/1914-1920/.
20. Woodrow Wilson, War Messages, 65th Cong., 1st Sess. Senate Doc. No. 5, Serial No. 7264, Washington, D.C., 1917, 3–8.
21. Rear Admiral William Sowden Sims, "The Victory At Sea," *The World Works*, ed. Walter Hines Page (New York, NY: Doubleday, Page, & Company), 510.
22. Samuel J. Cox, "H-019-5: 'Black Sunday' and the Battle of Orleans," *Naval History and Heritage Command*, June 2018, https://www.history.navy.mil/content/history/nhhc/about-us/leadership/director/directors-corner/h-grams/h-gram-019/h-019-5.html.
23. Hans Joachim Koerver, *German Submarine Warfare in the Eyes of British Intelligence 1914–1918* (Berlin, Germany: Schaltungsdienst Lang, 2012), 616.
24. Lowell Thomas, *Raiders of the Deep* (New York, NY: The Sun Dial Press, 1940), 287; *Raiders of the Deep* provides an excellent first-person account of the U-151's boarding officer, Dr. Frederick Korner.
25. Thomas, *Raiders*, 287.
26. Translated German orders from German archives; Der chef des Admiralstabes der Marine, 6304 op.IV, Nur durch Offizier, Berlin den 4, April 1918.
27. Thomas, *Raiders*, 287.
28. Koerver, *German Submarine Warfare*, 615.
29. James M. Merrill, "Submarine Scare, 1918," *Military Affairs* 17, no. 4 (Winter, 1953): 181–90.
30. Thomas, *Raiders*, 298.
31. "Submarines Off Coast," *The Brooklyn Citizen* (New York, NY), Monday May 27, 1918.
32. "UBoats Sent Far Out to Sea to Sink US Transports," *The Evening World* (Philadelphia, PA), May 27, 1918.
33. "Philadelphians Missing at Sea," *Evening Public Ledger* (Philadelphia, PA), May 27, 1918.
34. German Submarine Activities on the Atlantic Coast of the United States and Canada, Navy Department, Office of Naval Records and Library, 1920.
35. John M. Barry, *The Great Influenza* (New York, NY: Penguin Books, 2018), 123.
36. Ibid, 124.
37. Ibid, 126.
38. Stephen L. Vaughn, *Holding Fast the Inner Lines* (Chapel Hill, North Carolina: UNC Press, 2011),155.
39. Thomas, *Raiders*, 307.
40. "Survivors of U-Boat Victim Carolina," *Atlantic City Daily Press*, June 5, 1918.
41. "Survivors of Liner Carolina Land at Atlantic Ports," *Evening Public Ledger* (Philadelphia, PA), June 4, 1918.
42. "Local Red Cross Helps Survivors," *Atlantic City Daily Press*, June 6, 1918, 1.
43. Raid Shows Fear of American Army," *Atlantic City Daily Press*, June 4, 1918.
44. "America Deliver Stinging Reply to U-boat Raids," *Atlantic City Daily Press*, June 7, 1918.

45 Merril, "Submarine Scare," 184.
46 "Washington Gets No Reports of New Raids of Sinking," *Evening Public Ledger* (Philadelphia, PA), June 4, 1918.
47 "Believed Submarine Captured or Sunk off Delaware Capes," *Evening Public Ledger* (Philadelphia, PA), June 5, 1918.
48 Merril, "Submarine Scare," 183.
49 Ibid.
50 "Spies Sought Who Guided Sea Raiders," *Atlantic City Daily Press*, June 7, 1918.
51 "Blame U-boats for the Epidemic," *Evening Public Ledger* (Philadelphia, PA), May 30, 1918.
52 "History of 1918 Flu Pandemic," Centers for Disease Control and Prevention, https://www.cdc.gov/flu/pandemic-resources/1918-commemoration/1918-pandemic-history.htm.
53 Brendan Schurr, "A Personal History Beneath the Waves," *Los Angeles Times* (Los Angeles, CA), June 10, 2001.
54 Personal Communication, John Chatterton, September 8, 2021.
55 Ibid.
56 William Bell Clark, *When the U-Boats Came to America*, 5.

This hunting scene is typical of the lithographic illustrations found in mid to late nineteenth-century journals and magazines. Often these illustrations accompanied a companion published article. This image has been colorized.

Wading River at Bridgeport in the fog.

Railbirding and Rice on the Wading River:

Recollections, Anecdotes, and Natural History

Horace Somes Jr., Stephen Eichinger, and Peter H. Stemmer

Hunting of "railbirds" was an early fall tradition on the Wading River and was considered a "warm-up" for the following waterfowl season. A time to test the gun, a boat, the hunter's "eye" (or aim), and to get out on the water and tidemarsh which was probably last seen the previous winter during the late season before freeze-up or during the trapping season for muskrat. The hunting blind might be inspected for needed repairs and "grassing" for the upcoming duck season due to months of weather, tides, and ice floes, which occurred before global warming greatly reduced the ice overs on the river.

Even if the birds were absent, the seasonal splendor of the freshwater marshes could be enjoyed. The plant growth was diverse with "wild oats" *Ehinochloa walteri* (Coast Cockspur Grass) producing larger heads of seed, compared to the rice, but equally beneficial food for waterfowl, either the migrating sora or the overwintering ducks. Flowering plants also could be vibrant, including the richly-red Cardinal Flower, *Lobelia cardinalis*, and showy Swamp Rose Mallow, *Hibiscus moscheutos*. Resident wood ducks also could be flushed, and the opened top of a "rat-house" might reveal sunning by young "kit" muskrats.

The local game was the widespread Sora Rail, *Porzana carolina*, although the diminutive Virginia Rail, *Rallus limicola*, that could reside into the winter, might also be "flushed" but not shot—unless by mistake. The larger King Rail, *R. elegance*, might also be occasionally encountered locally, but the hunter might "pass-up" on a shot, thinking it to be a small duck of the early fall that was not yet in-season. The similarly large Clapper Rail, *R. crepitans*, however, was not found on the local freshwater marshes, preferring the brackish and salty marshes along the lower river and coast.

Railbirding continues where the preferred food wild rice, *Zizania aquatica*, still flourishes, such as the Maurice River. Rising sea level, increased salinity of local tidewater, and past over-grazing by population influxes of Whistling/Tundra Swans and Canada Geese contributed to the decline of the rice beds along the Wading and nearby Mullica Rivers during recent decades. The rice is small-seeded but edible also for humans, although it is not botanically related to the store-bought rice that is a commercial staple in Asia. When pushing a railbird boat through the dense growth, a substantial amount of seeds might inadvertently be collected in the bottom of the

Sora Rail, *Porzana carolina*. Photo by Elaine R. Wilson, www.naturespicsonline.com.

boat. For a rare but laborious treat, the seeds could be extracted by winnowing and served as a small bed of rice for the small breast meat of the sora.

A historic anecdote involves Native Americans along the river with the family/tribal name of Ashatamarus. They may have been among the last in the Little Egg Harbor area which historically was considered to extend west to Wading River. The small seeds of wild rice could be collected in the early fall by bending the stalks over the sides of a canoe and beating them loose from the stalk. This would have been very productive in the largest rice beds that grew on the extensive mudflats

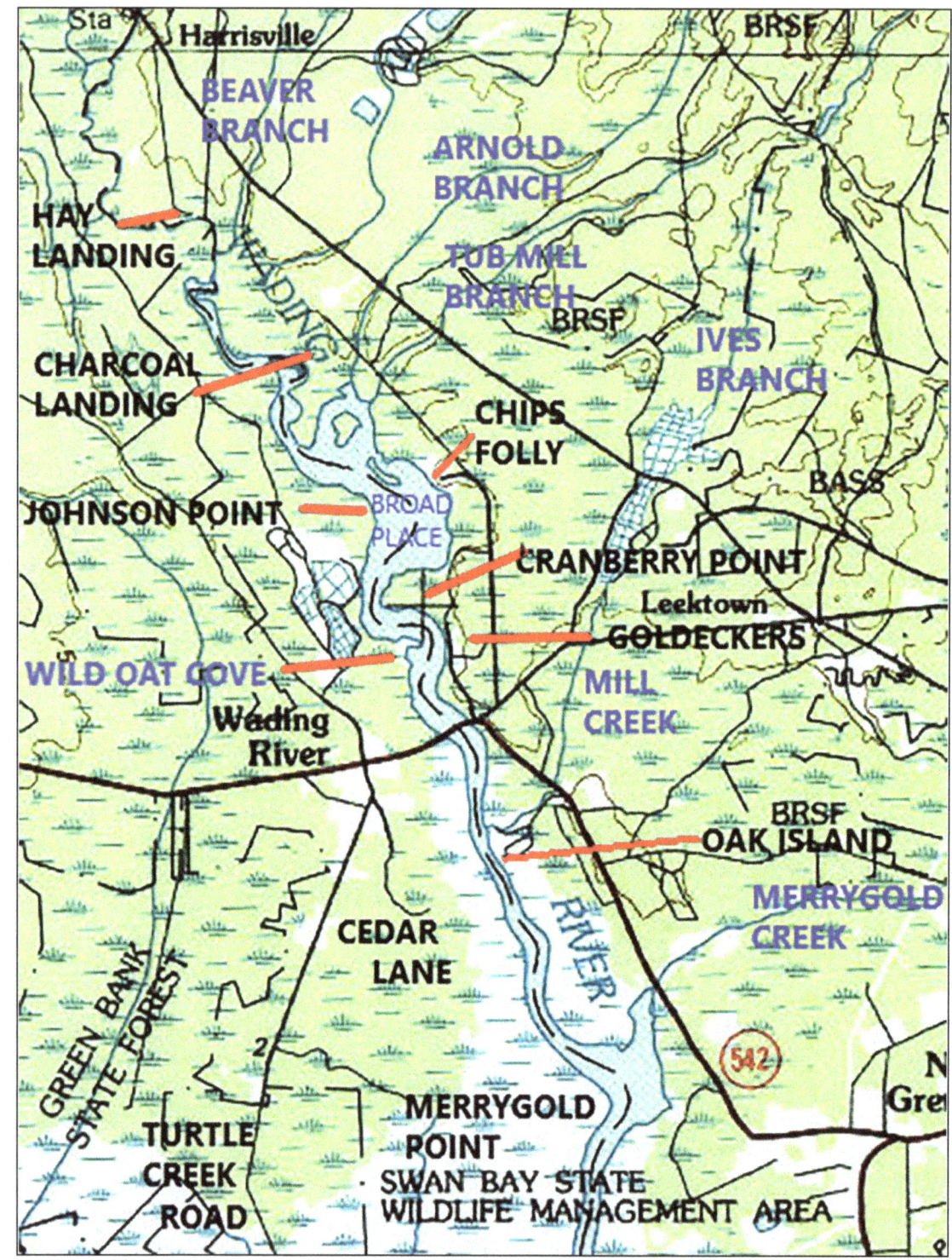

Place names on the Wading River for railbirding and rice. Adapted from USGS, Hammonton, 1984.

Railbirding

of the Broad Place, where Chips Folly Campground now occupies the eastern shore. The curvature to the shoreline created a moon-like shape, and local tradition is that the Native Americans called those wide waters Half Moon. A number of small streams and swales drain through the eastern shoreline, from Cranberry Point in the south to Beaver Branch, which extends far into the Pinelands and the historic forgotten towns of Martha Furnace and Calico. The animal name for the northernmost tributary is an old reference appearing in grants and surveys of the West Jersey Proprietors, who first partitioned the Little Egg Harbor region for the British crown. Beaver are now troublesome to local cranberry farms on both sides of the river, but doubtlessly were present prehistorically to the benefit of the Native Americans, either for their own use or lucrative trading with the first colonists.

The area of small drainages that extend westerly across today's County Highway 679 and into the Broad Place was collectively referred to as the "Wading Runs" in early business accounts and would have furnished both White Cedar from the swamps as well as adjacent Pitch Pine of the "Barrens." Southeast of Beaver Branch

(Top) Wild rice panicle with dangling seeds, *Zizania aquatica*. (Bottom) Sunrise over goose decoy layout and former rice beds on Middle Grounds at Grape Creek between Wild Oat Cove and Wading River Bridge, October 1979.

on the upland was the "coaling grounds" where charcoal was manufactured in previous centuries from the plentiful Pitch Pine, and exported through the riverside at aptly named Charcoal Landing. Below Beaver Branch, there was Arnold Branch and then Tub Mill Branch, where an early sawmill was powered from a small impoundment. The stream with the mill also was historically referred to as Ashatama Run, although it is not known if the tribe had a village in the immediate area. Native American settlements along the river, however, are indicated by the recovery by residents of projectile points from Chips Folly southward to Oak Island at Mill Creek, south of the bridge. This coincided with the river's past distribution of the best rice growth. From the top of the riverside bank at Goldeckers, a large stone artifact was recovered and apparently was either a grinding pestle or hammerstone. With the proximity to plentiful rice kernels from the adjacent marshes, this tool could have been used to make meal either from the wild rice or home-grown maize corn.

Although rice grows in a variety of wetlands and waters, its height is greatly reduced as salinity increases and is non-existent in saltmarshes near the ocean. Locally, it could dominate the mudflats referred to as "middle grounds," between the river channel and the more-elevated but still tidal marshes that were closer to the swamps of white cedar, red maple, and scrub. Closer to the upper limit of the normal high tide, the rice was one of many herbaceous marsh plants that might extend in open water patches for a short distance into the adjacent scrub swamps if they had tidal flow.

Downriver as the water became brackish with increasing salinity, the tide marsh changed to the domain of taller perennial plants whose dense, thick

Coarse/Big Cordgrass—*Spartina cynosuroides*.

stalks persisted through the winter after frost dieback. The tall "reeds" of cordgrass, cattail and three-square could withstand the winter snow and ice that flattened much of the upriver freshwater marsh plants, including the rice. This reed land provided different habitat for wildlife such as muskrats, as well as ready-made material for camouflaging the hunting blinds that might be called "stand-ups," as they typically had a bench seat, but the hunter had to stand to shoot through the camouflaging reeds. The thick marsh cover also could shelter over-wintering ducks, but the Sora Rail were long gone to the southern coast that extended into the Caribbean.

During the winter on the middle grounds, the residual rice stalks would become broken and bent over into the water and flattened if there was an overburden of winter ice. Ultimately, decomposition would create the detritus that formed the river-bottom mud and tide marsh muck and peat, which could accumulate to a depth of a dozen feet or more along the river. The remnants of plants on the mudflats might help boaters to navigate the waterway channel, which could be both narrow and winding. Unless there is a "blow-out" low tide, the mudflats would remain hidden by only inches

Grinding pestle or hammerstone recovered by Horace Somes Jr. from crest of high riverbank at Goldeckers.

Railbirding

or a few feet of water. Otherwise, the overall waterway may appear to be up to a half-mile wide, although the channel is less than 50 feet and very winding. This would be challenging to navigate, even for canoers unless they arrived at high tide. Boaters needed to avoid the flats where the mud could be churned and clog water pumps, and an occasional hidden stump or log was a definite danger for the propeller. In areas of underwater plants and remnants, the underwater stalks could become a tightly wrapped "ball" that had to be cleared by hand from the propeller—an undesirable task when a hunter had to regain propulsion on a cold, windy day in the late duck season.

The following anecdotes were provided by Steve Eichinger to Pete Stemmer for the History Committee of the Bass River Community Library:

"I remember in my early teens that railbird season started on September 1st. It seemed there was always a Nor' Easter or a shore storm brewing that would create high tides up the Wading River. This was good for railbird gunning.

"For those who may not know what a railbird is, following is a description of the elusive little bird whose formal name is Sora Rail—*Porzana carolina*. It's a small quail-sized bird from eight to ten inches long. They are a migrating bird, have a high reproductive rate, and like fresh water on rice and oat covered meadows.

"The sport of gunning these birds comes when you are pushed, by boat, over the marshes at high tide. You need the high water to be able to move the boat fast enough to jump the birds. If you can't move fast enough, they will run through the reeds, won't jump. If everything is in your favor, high water, a good pusher at the stern, and a good shot on the bow, you'll get a good amount of birds and will have a lot of fun.

Steve Eichinger Sr. with double-ender boat, October 1962.

"When the railbirds jump, they will fly about 25 feet and drop very quickly, providing a challenge to the hunter. They kind of remind you of a whiffle ball with wings. The limit on railbirds is 25 birds a day. You need about 25 of the small birds to have a good railbird pot pie which was similar to chicken and dumplings.

"I lived in the old McKeen Hotel in the 1940s with my father, Steve; mother, Martina; and brother Lee, "Chubby." We rented half of the house from my aunt, Alice Weber. The old hotel sat alongside the Wading River, at the bridge, so I got a first-hand look at railbirding along the river.

"The best area for hunting was a 100–150 acres piece of meadow on the west side of the river and south of the bridge. There had to be up to fifteen boats there at a time.

"Everybody respected one another's range. I don't remember someone ever being shot. If quarters got too close there were other places to go, including Mill Creek, Teal Creek, Head of Straight Ditch on Cove Creek, and Merrygold Cove. Those were downriver on the Bass River Township side.

"You could also go upriver along the edges and in Wild Oat Cove at Cranberry Point. The further upriver you got, the harder it was to push. The water got pretty deep, and you didn't have enough pole to push, so you didn't have the speed.

"The boat I used was called a double ender that had sharp bows on both ends. It was built from Jersey cedar. It was built by Wade Lippincott, known as Capt. Wade, who lived in a houseboat by the old wreck of the ship ARGO. Several gunners kept their boats at his houseboat. Capt. Wade also built other boats for duck hunting and open rowboats for fishing.

"The railbird boat was not rowed. The pusher would stand on the stern and use a long pole about twelve feet long. Most were made of a straight cedar sapling slightly tapered from about two inches at the bottom to one and a half inches at the top. The bottom had cleat-like wedges nailed or screwed to the bottom and sides up about two and a half inches. Some had two and others had three of these wedges.

"The gunners would start gathering about two hours before high tide. They parked their cars along the shoulder of the road on the west end of the Wading River bridge approach. There wasn't much room for cars passing on the road to get by, as the gunners milled around, showing their gunning trophies. I remember seeing silver plates, vases, and other awards for local, state, and national skeet shooting events.

"I remember the guns were L. C. Smith, Parkers, and some foreign makes. They ranged from 12, 16, 28, 20 to 410 gauge. I believe the 20 gauge was the favorite gun. Some were pump, automatic, single, and double barrels. Number 9 and number 10 shot was generally used.

"They headed out about a half hour before high tide and gunned until the birds stopped jumping. This was about when the tide started dropping. Some used flat sterned canoes and some had double enders that were built out of state. You had to be very careful with these, as they tipped over rather easily. I didn't like them. The old flat bottom cedar double ender was just fine with me. There was a man from Berlin that used to walk the meadows on low water, but he never had much luck.

"Captain Wade's nephew, Bob Lippincott, was my teacher. One afternoon he said, 'Come on. We'll take the double ender. Here's the deal. I'll push you and you shoot till you miss. Then you push and I'll shoot until I miss.' We used his

Horace Somes Jr. with push poles and marker buoys for downed birds: (left) vintage McAnney pole—20 feet long with 3 prong toes; (center) historic pole crafted from oyster-tong handle—15 feet with keeled rudder for pushing, steerage and short-distance paddling; (right) homemade pole crafted for Horace by Jeff Lamb of Pemberton.

12 gauge. I told him that I didn't have a license. He told me not to worry about that. If we saw somebody coming and I had the gun that we would change places. I learned a lot from that first trip.

"After that, Captain Wade used to let me take one of the boats and practice. The boats that I liked belonged to a man from Red Bank. He would pay me $15.00 to push for him. The rest of the pushers got $25.00, but I was a kid and he owned the boat. The limit was 25 birds. If you had good water and good birds, you could take two parties, or you could come in, put the birds in your vehicle and go out for a second trip.

"I remember pushers Charlie DeBow from Lower Bank; Chet Downs from Tuckerton; Steve Eichinger, my father, from Wading River; Bob Lippincott from Turtle Creek; Buckie Mercintainie from Bordentown; Dr. Moon from Tuckerton; Paul Mower and Mr. Green from Pennington. Fred Winterbottom and Ronnie Senn are the last railbird gunners that I know of. Their last season was 2008.

"The days of railbirding are gone for good in this area. The phragmites started in this area in the 1950s and 1960s and have taken over the areas where we used to push our boats. They have also taken over areas north on the river making less food available for the birds."

While small in stature, railbirds contributed, in their time, to the lifestyle and livelihood that benefited from the waters and wetlands along the river. In addition to pay from pushing the double-enders for visiting sportsmen, there also was income from guiding duck hunters and the rentals of prime shooting spots for concealment blinds. There also was the wetland opportunity for trapping of fur-bearing muskrats which might have either been skinned locally and sold to local "buyers," or sold whole-bodied for their dark, fatty meat as "marsh rabbits." Beneath the waters, fishing for a variety of species offered both subsistence food and commercial sales, including the heavy spring influx of anadromous fish such as herring and shad that would arrive for a month to spawn in the upriver near the Pinelands. Another denizen of both water and marsh was the snapping turtle whose body of more than a dozen pounds could be trapped and sold live for its fresh meat—although the animals' appearance did not seem to offer a food "delicacy."

Brian Detrick of Turtle Creek Neck has recollections from the Updike family of his mother Marguerite and her relatives. Uncle Henry Updike of New Gretna was a fur-buyer for "rats" and their skins, and owned marshland at the bridge approach, which offered both prime rail hunting and historically was dotted in the winter with muskrat houses that offered trapping. Grandfather Jim Updike, who knew how to build small boats for the river, provided railbirding anecdotes in November 1965, as well as the names of small tidewater creeks where the rice flourished and there was good hunting.

Such place names may seem to be inconsequential today for the reed-covered marshland and streams; however, geographical references were then significant for hunting guides, local landowners, and visiting sportsmen. These place names indicated who owned or utilized what and where for hunting, trapping, and fishing. Prime railbird locations might be distinctively and colorfully named as Merrygold and Cove Creeks in Bass River Township, Straight Ditch opposite Stump Creek across the river in Washington Township, Cove and Teal Creeks opposite Bills Creek, Cattail Point near Oak Island, Mill Creek at the mouth of Ives Branch near the old Leeks Lower Landing, Grape Creek that drained from the cranberry bogs on the western shore above the bridge, and Wild Oat Cove opposite Goldeckers.

Jim related that several businessmen from Hammonton would bring their shotguns as well as money to rent boats and hire local "polers" in the 1920s. One hunter owned a garage and sold Chevrolets and Buicks, but "he liked rails and ducks." The offering might be two dollars for a high tide, which could be good pay in the rural community of Wading River. The work was hard, particularly when there was not "much of a tide," such as between the full and new moons when the astronomical highs flooded the marshes with less water than at the peak of the lunar cycles. Over a period of years, the rate increased and Jim's last work was for $7 tides—a good supplement to his farming and boatbuilding.

On a small former knoll next to the marsh at the approach to the bridge, another resident "Wad" (Watson) Lippincott also would build and sell river boats under the shade of a long-gone willow tree. His houseboat and "boatworks" were abandoned decades ago, and the site is now covered with tidewater and reed grass. However, he handcrafted both double-ender railbird boats designed for the rice marshes, as well as local hunting skiffs that were preferred for the river waters and not suited for the coastal bays, where the bet-

Abandoned houseboat or floating cabin of Wad Lippincott, who built double-enders and other river boats on a former knoll and under a long-gone willow tree at the bridge approach. Photo by Steve Echinger, April 1963.

ter-known sneakboxes were used. One design was the short garvey style of approximately ten feet in length, without a pointed bow but a shortened, squared front that allowed easy navigation and turning in a narrow marsh creek. It did have fore and aft decking and could be accessorized with marsh grass for camouflage—similarly to the Barnegat sneakbox of the saltwaters. Both vessels could carry a hunter, decoys, and his gear. Manufactured with light, buoyant, and durable white cedar from local swamps, both types rowed admirably before outboard motors became prevalent. Horace Somes Sr. recollected buying such a boat from Wad with a small spread of black-duck decoys for the sum of $35 before World War II, which curtailed its use when he went into Army service.

A receipt from Lippincott on August 12, 1892, indicted the purchase of a "sail scow" by Howard McAnney of Turtle Creek Neck who would use it for a wetland form of "farming." Such flat-bottomed, blunt-ended vessels served as barge-like scows, which might also be termed "row garveys." They alternatively could be sailed or poled with favorable tidal current and wind direction.

Locally, these "freight" vessels could be used in the harvesting of Salt Hay, *Spartina patens*, from the downriver, short-grass marshlands of more-saline brackish waters near Swan Bay on the Mullica River. This marsh grass could be used as pasturage for livestock where the marsh "muck" was firmer or harvested for storage in a hay barn as silage to feed livestock. Historically, it also would have been "scowed" upriver through the meandering channel of the middle grounds at Wading River. At the head of tide, the fibrous plant material would have been off-loaded at the Hay Landing near Beaver Branch for paper production at the nearby "forgotten" industrial town of Harrisville. Import loads of ten tons of old rags and ships' rigging also could be rendered into fiber for the coarse paper products from the mill. Cargoes on the returning scows would have included paper materials, as well as bog-iron products, charcoal, lumber, barrels, and other produce from the "forgotten towns" of the Pinelands. Exports would be transferred onto sailing ships that could navigate the Wading River only as far as the river-crossing that was then named "Bridgeport." The shipping, scowing, and railbirding

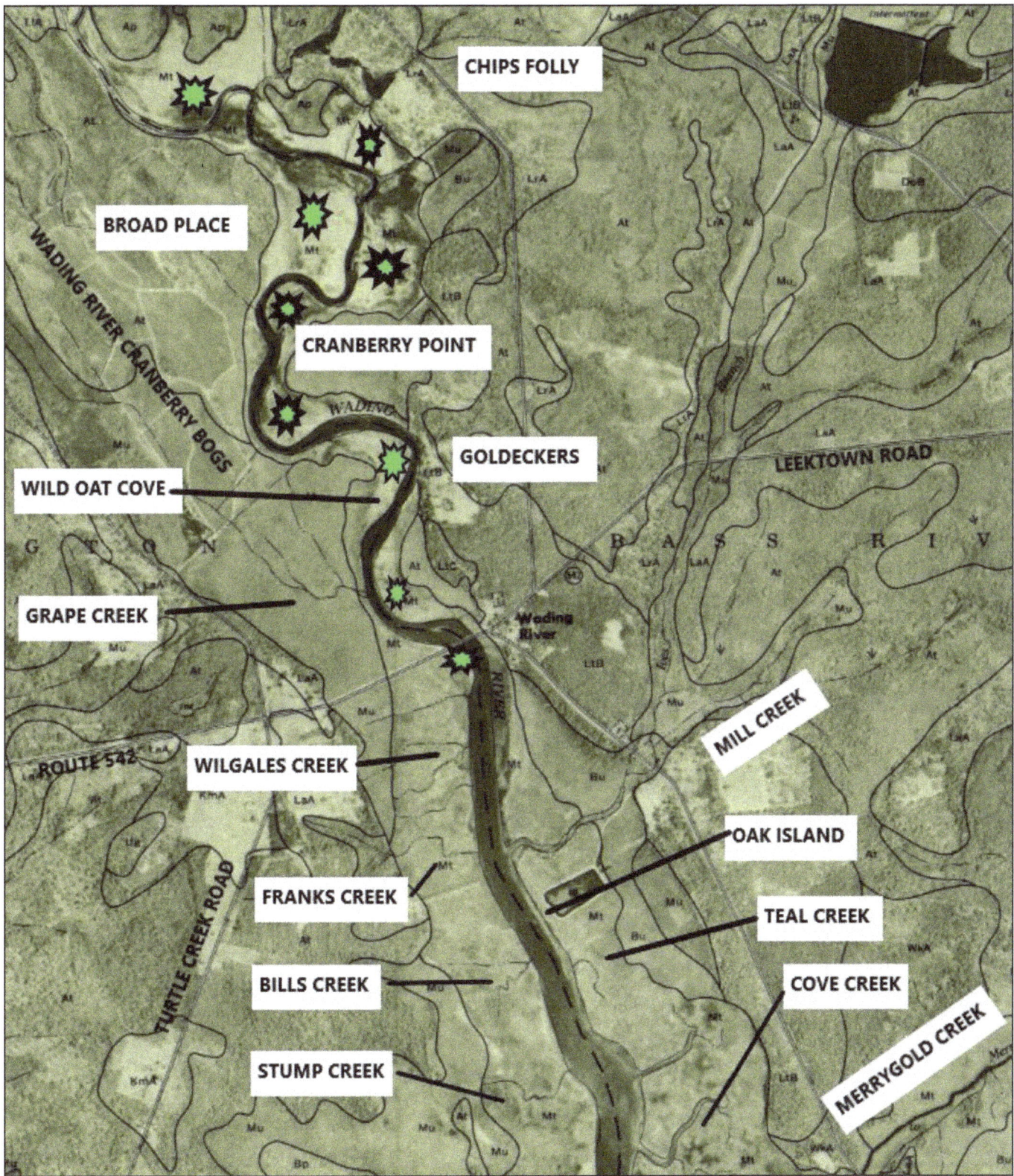

1971 Wading River wild-rice middle grounds highlighted in green. Rice beds in tidal marshes (Mt) with other plant species, extended along both riverbanks and along tributary creeks. (USDA-SCS Soil Survey of Burlington County, sheet 96.)

Howard McAnney hunting with 20-gauge and black ducks, October 13, 1945.

Dorothy McAnney Somes hunting with 20-gauge and black ducks, October 13, 1945.

Horace Somes Jr. with hunted black ducks.

are now gone, but reflected the benefits of the natural resources of water, wetlands, and Pinelands to the historical culture.

The 1910 annual report of the State Museum contained the following interesting information concerning wild rice based upon the observations of Witmer Stone:

> Plentiful in water along the larger rivers and swamps of the Middle and Cape May districts and the Coastal Strip, running well up into the Pine Barrens along the principal water courses, but not strictly speaking, a member of the Pine Barrens flora . . . In September it has become the shelter of thousands of reed birds and rail, and the gunners soon begin to beat and trample it down in pursuit of game. The storms of autumn complete the work and by winter the acres of swaying and fluttering foliage are reduced to a dense brown mat which covers the marsh, and through which, in the following spring, the tender green sprouts of the next year's crop push their way and once again give color to the meadows. The rice follows the courses of small streams for many miles back from the rivers and coast. I have found it on Cooper's Creek, twelve miles from its mouth, while it follows the larger streams as far as the head of tidewater. Very often a dam makes a sharp line of demarcation between the tidewater and Pine Barrens floras, as at Toms River, Batsto, Mays Landing, Millville, etc., and checks abruptly the range of the wild rice.

Aerial photography, nature observations, and hunting activity all indicate the ecological changes that have impacted the rice beds, associated waterfowl, and hunting traditions. Historically, the local Wading River and freshwater marshlands offered a varied and rich resource for both waterfowl and hunting. While the small Sora Rail occur across the continent, they were almost exclusively dependent on the rice during their early fall migrations down the Wading. Formerly numerous and varied ducks also were dependent on various plants and their fruit during both migrations and overwintering, unless "pushed out" by freezing weather and water to areas further south.

The railbirding would announce the beginning of the fall migrations of many waterfowl, although locally raised wood ducks would already be present from spring nesting. Beyond the grassy seeds, the sora and "woodies"

Railbirding

Rail Skiff races at Tuckerton Seaport's annual Baymen's Seafood and Music Festival the fourth weekend in June 2005. Photo by Sandra Anton.

also eat another freshwater plant that may grow with the rice and along small streams—Green Arrow Arum/Tuckahoe, *Peltandra virginica*. With distinctive broad, fleshy and arrow-shaped leaves, it may grow among the rice in deeper-flooded wetlands and stream sides. In contrast to the tall rice flower and seed panicle, it has an inconspicuous spikelike floral structure and produces a large bulb-like seed pod that can remain submerged into the winter, after the leaf structure has vanished into the mud. It contains a number of large, fleshy, purple/black seeds that the "woodies" eat. Interestingly, these may be referred to as "duck corn"—which is not illegal to hunt over. Unfortunately, the arum prefers fresher waters and increased salinity has sharply curtailed its growth along with other marsh plants that benefited the waterfowl. In brackish reed land, it would form a dense skirt of fleshy growth on the sloping streambanks, which were topped by a berm of dense, tall Coarse Cordgrass, with an occasional muskrat hole where those animals accessed the waterway from their lodges through an under-mud tunnel. Many of these tidal streams now have barren muddy banks that are overtopped by very dense foxtail reed. For the hunter or trapper these reed meadows are now very difficult to penetrate and contain few muskrat houses—if they can even be seen or found.

Blue-winged teal also would be early travelers and would add to the challenges for a rail hunter being pushed through the rice beds by a poler in the rear of the boat. These and other ducks were not open to hunting in September. Both Sora Rail and ducks might be unaware of the approach and "kick out" with a jump near the boat—with the rail sometimes appearing in the last second and almost from under the gunwale. To shoot a duck now would be "out of season" and a game-law violation. However, these small ducks with their distinctive blue wing patches would depart soon with the rail. They would rapidly be replaced by the hardier Green-Winged Teal, who also would "push south" when the cold arrived and be replaced by large-bodied ducks, such as Pintail and Mallards that were most sought by hunters in the past. Black Ducks would arrive and remain the longest and into the winter, risking being caught by freeze-ups when those that could not escape by further migration would be confined to small areas of open water due to the current—as the freshwater of the Wading River had none of the coastal salinity of the lower Mullica and Great Bay that prevented freezing until temperatures in the teens and colder. The last of the Black Ducks to be shot might appear to be conspicuously large birds that were referred to as "red leggers" due to their colorful legs and feet.

When railbirding, it might be more interesting to be standing in the stern with the push pole than seated in the lurching and wobbling boat. At mid-century, when the hunting was heavy, visiting sportsmen would pay to rent a boat and local man to pole for a high tide of only a single or few short hours of the highest water. A watermelon might also be rolling on the floorboards for refreshment during the hunt. It was obvious that the local guide needed to know the waterways, marshes, and "honey-pots" of cover that were the hotspots for both birds and shooting. As reduced demand made poling less lucrative, both persons on-board might be fellow sportsmen and take turns between shooting and pushing.

There were two aspects to the otherwise hard work of pushing the boat through the rice beds, sometimes only after a row either upriver or downriver to a hunting area—as an outboard was out of the question on a small "poke-boat." First, there was the satisfaction of putting the shooter over the birds and not flushing them before coming into range. This involved not only navigating the narrow, winding streams, but also "reading" the landscape—or more correctly, the "marshscape." Decision-making included whether the water was deep enough to pole through and whether the tide was going in or out. The hunt ended as the tide ebbed, particularly "between the moons" when the astronomical tides peaked at lower levels, unless there was storm flooding with wind that was not excessive. Also, was the vegetation thin enough to push through or a no-go for reeds and cattails—even if they might provide cover for resting birds? Rail might be among the plants between the flooded shrubs at the edge of the marsh, but a boat could not go there. And finally, did the cover offer food from rice or other plants that were favored food? The poler was in a position to see this and plot a course for the boat. He might first circle an area and then proceed to sweep it with a grid pattern. Generally, one would start at the streamside and go to the back of the patch, before looping back to the stream. As the rail preferred to stay in the grass and not fly over open water, this would keep them in the patch until the area had been worked over in a grid pattern.

Another aspect for the poler was the "view of the action" for the person standing in the stern—although care had to be taken not only to navigate correctly, but also to maintain one's balance while moving the boat as quietly and stably as possible. It was often possible to spot a flushing bird before it was seen by the shooter, whose view was to the front, right or left—but not all at the same time. A bird might do a reversal and fly past the rear of the boat, where the gun barrel could not be swung without jeopardizing the man with the heavy pole, which could also serve as part of the weaponry. When the boat could proceed no further through the vegetation, but birds might be present, the pole could be used to reach out and slap the water and plants, and possibly flush a sora from cover.

Spotting also was important, as a call of either "right" or "left" would indicate a flush when the shooter was looking a different way. If the bird flushed or flew too far or the shot missed, it might land quickly but out of range. The poler would decide whether to attempt to reach the spot and re-jump the bird again. A pair of small sharply colored wood blocks might be kept in the stern and could be used as buoy markers that could be thrown in the direction that a bird was shot and dropped. This would assist in the retrieval if the bird had fallen a distance from the boat or out of sight. There also was the possibility that another bird would jump and be shot, and the bearing to the first drop might become confusing.

The hunter's position was not as easy as it would have appeared. Seated low in the lurching boat was a different and more difficult position than normal shooting from a standing position. One was in a floating boat that could bobble if the water was deep or the grass growth was very thin. It might lurch to a stop at the end of the push when the length of the pole had been reached, or if a submerged stump was encountered. Also, swinging the barrel for a left-side shot might be easiest for a right-handed person, and caution was needed to not swing too far and shoot near the poler behind you. Care also had to be taken to not move too far and fast, tipping the boat and balance for the poler—who did need to stay on-board. The birds tended to jump only when closely approached and might suddenly appear airborne within feet of the boat. A shot too quick and close would destroy the small body and meat, leaving a puff of feathers in the air or on the water. The wad of plastic or cardboard from the shot shell would be a bad sign if found to be lodged in what remained of a small body. But a relatively quick shot would be needed as the birds tended to not fly far before folding their wings, and dropping back into the grass, where they might not be seen or jumped again.

An occasional hunter might want the challenge of going by himself as both the shooter and poler. This would necessitate a cradle rack across the seat to hold the shotgun, with the barrel facing the bow. A larger 12-gauge might be used for the stronger pellet charge

Railbirding

1925 hunting license of Orville McAnney. The cost was $1.50.

as a bird might have flown far before the gun could be picked up, aimed and fired safely, without the standing hunter upsetting the boat or falling overboard, with the gun and shells. A recollection of Aunt Alice, who rented several boats from the landing, was of a particular hunter who preferred to go it alone. On one occasion, overreaction or bad timing resulted in the gun discharging as it was being raised, and before the muzzle cleared the gunwale. The result was a neat 12-gauge hole in the bow that had to be patched. Fortunately, no one else was on board and in the front of the boat. It is not known who did the repair or if Alice rented another boat to this avid hunter.

Safety also had to be exercised if several boats were in a single area and were seeking the same game in the same habitat, but possibly with intervening patches of taller plants. Although camouflaged hunting clothes were not used (other than possibly a light vest with shell holders), hunter-orange safety material on a hat or light coat was necessary. The poler watched to keep a safe and respectful distance—and definitely out of range of another boat—and preferably out of line with the shooter in the bow to minimize the noise of a muzzle blast, even if out of range for the actual lead (and later steel) shot. Some very good meadows were near the bridge and some extended to the edge of the embanked approach. It is not known whether any railbirds knew of the public right-of-way and used it as protective cover or a safety zone. But care had to be taken near the traveled highway to prevent a gunshot or pellets into or across the roadway. A good poler could make sure of a gap in traffic and safe time to fire in that direction. Precaution also was needed for other boating on the river channel, but that was generally unlikely, as there was much less traffic in the past, particularly in the late season of mid-September to early October during the best hunting.

When the birds were plentiful at the height of the migration, the hunter might make a quick go/no-go decision for a shot that might be too close or too far or too difficult. It might always be possible to re-flush a bird from a better vantage position and with a better likelihood of dropping it for recovery—particularly if it was flying near thick cover, such as cattails or reed grass. After a shot, it was necessary to always be ready for another bird to jump, particularly if a distance had to be traversed for the retrieval. Several birds might take flight, but it was unwise to drop more than two at a time and lose their locations for retrieval. When the population was very high, many birds might be in a small area of an acre or less; and the bag limit of twenty-five could be reached easily. It might be time to switch between the shooting and poling positions so that both could get their turn. As the weather tended to be fair and warm, clothing would be light—possibly only a T-shirt. After several shots even with the light shell loads (compared to the duck season magnum loads with the thick padding of a hunting coat), the shoulder might become sore or even bruised. It was then time to switch off and take a turn with the pole—and maybe see your companion miss an "easy shot."

As good as it had been in the "glory days" of thick rice loaded with many birds, things were changing towards the end of the twentieth century. The slow rise in sea level was bringing brackish water with higher salinity. Although the rice beds might be imperceptibly thinner or smaller from one season to the next, the adjacent swamp line was retreating or thinning, particularly for the white cedar that were most sensitive, and particularly after a coastal storm brought flooding of saltier tidewater in from the coast and upriver. Aerial imagery provided evidence of the slow and barely perceptible change over recent decades, when the photography was taken at suitable seasons and tide heights.

The soils mapping for Burlington County in 1971 by the U.S. Department of Agriculture's Soil Conservation Service clearly indicates the narrower river channel and broad bordering rice beds on the middle grounds, although there is no distinction in the "MT"/Tide Marsh between the middle grounds and the higher marshland where the rice mixed with a variety of other species.

Another change came with the Tundra or Whistling Swans that first appeared in small flocks or numbers from their trans-continental migration from the Pacific Northwest. Horace Somes recollects, as a juvenile member of the former Pemberton Bird Club, going to be shown one of the first pairs of swans (not Mute Swans as introduced from Europe) that had arrived on a lake in that area. It was a novelty and a new addition to the birdwatching life-list. As the population grew, they found the rice beds of the Wading to be perfect for both floating and feeding, and there must have been advertising, as their numbers surged.

It would be awesome on an early November day for weather to arrive with a strong northwesterly wind and to see a major flight at high altitude after the birds had crossed the Appalachians, which did not offer such habitat. The swans would spiral down with their characteristic "whistling" to rest and feed and drink the fresh water. Their landings might be in small family groups of a half-dozen birds, but their total numbers quickly grew until hundreds could be seen on the rice beds in the fall or early winter until the waters iced over. The feeding would pull large amounts of rice and other river-bottom plants out of the mud—complicating decoy sets for

Whistling swan in flight with long outstretched neck, Wikipedia.

Former rice bed on riverbank with exposed ancient cedar stumps opposite Goldeckers and north of Wild Oat Cove.

duck hunters when floating mats would "load up the lines with trash."

If a decoy was not pulled out of position by the tide current on the floating debris, it would appear that the fake-duck was nesting and not natural. If a heavy decoy anchor did hold, it was possible for the decoy to be either tipped unnaturally or even pulled under water. When the drifting of debris was heavy, this could entail boat trips for a hunter out of the gunning blind. Clearing the lines wrapped in plant stalks could be difficult and required hands to be over the side of the boat and underwater—and in suitable waterproof gloves, hopefully with insulation and waterproof wristlets or long gauntlets that could also be used in trapping to keep cold water from leaking into the fingertips. The engineering construction of the county bridge was also put to the test when river flooding came from heavy upstream rain and reservoir release from the cranberry bogs. A heavy "beard" of floating grasses could accumulate across the upriver side of the structure at the water line. The county highway foreman observed that a number of railbirds were seen picking through the "salad bar" to pick out the rice seeds.

The swans were not alone, as the increasing population of non-migratory Canada Geese also visited the rice beds. The large high-altitude "V"s of coastal migrants no longer overflew with the fall northerly breeze, but the "golf-course" geese stayed year-round in the region, taking advantage of the manicured grasses of the lawns on athletic fields, shopping malls, large corporate properties, and dangerously, around airports. In the winter, when retention ponds and landscape pools froze over, the geese would visit and add to the uprooting of rice. This did not benefit the migrating rail or ducks that had depended upon the rice beds for foraging, as well as the adjacent tall-grass marshes where food and cover were increasingly being displaced by the intrusive reed grass blanket of Phragmites, which did not provide food seeds.

There was an unanticipated benefit for hunters who had seen the accompanying reduction in migrant and resident ducks that had used the rice beds. Waterfowl hunting locally had only taken geese occasionally in the past, and decoy layouts might only contain a pair or several goose "stools." When the geese arrived, however, it brought flocks that might be numerous and contained

Exposed dock remnants and ballast piles along west shore of Leeks Lower Landing, opposite Oak Island and downriver of Cedar Lane. Note the receding shoreline of tide marsh vegetation.

Horace Somes Sr. and son Frank poling rice bed on Middle Ground at Cranberry Point, September 1966.

large-bodied game. Successful hunters might now have layouts of a dozen or more geese, with only a couple of duck decoys—and maybe a high-necked goose decoy painted entirely white as a "confidence" bird to resemble a swan and make the overall layout appear to more in-keeping with the mix of live waterfowl that now used the area.

There was spillover depredation on the commercial cranberry bogs both locally and upriver, which also offered large water bodies for resting when flooded for the winter but not frozen over. While neither the swans or geese eat the berries or vines, their long necks and body tip-ups allowed them to reach the bottom of the shallow bog waters. A byproduct of their scavenging for herbaceous weeds that grew among the cranberries was the uprooting of vines that would produce the next-year's valuable berries. As a deterrent, farmers would utilize carbide-fueled noise "cannons" to scare off the birds, or string long "clotheslines" of light but visible twine on posts across bogs to deter flight approaches and landings by the large flocks of large-bodied birds that required a long landing path, comparable to a large "jumbo" jet at an airport.

As the rice beds disappeared, the large population of visiting swans also disappeared, although an occasional family group might pass through in the fall. The numbers of geese were reduced, but still could visit and take advantage of residual marshes—particularly along the edge of the dense reed grass, where palatable short plants could continue to be grazed. However, the remaining plant growth and sod along the riverbanks were subjected to foraging for roots, leaving a pock-marked pattern of mini "bomb craters." The bottom muck now was destabilized due to the absence of plant cover and roots and was subject to erosion—in places exposing large areas of underlying gravel and sand. This in turn exposed areas of ancient cedar stumps and logs from the "ghost swamps" that had existed thousands of years ago, when the sea level was much lower and the river was bordered by forests and not by marshland. Coincidentally, historic docks, boat wrecks and ballast evidence of shipping might also be exposed from the mud, indicating the era when there was a Bridgeport where sailing ships could traverse as far as the old low-level drawbridge. Cargoes could be loaded from local produce, or off-loaded onto lighter, smaller, shallow-draft scows that could navigate the winding and narrowing channel through the rice beds. Ultimately, these barge-like vessels could reach the Beaver Branch/Hay Landing near the head of tide below Bodine Field, on the old colonial-era stage route from the major port-of-entry at Tuckerton, through the Pinelands and to Philadelphia in the Delaware valley. This allowed for both import of supplies to the interior, to the now-forgotten towns and industries of the Pine Barrens, as well as export of iron, paper, and forest products via the so-called Wading River.

More recently, traffic of increasingly powerful but small boats and personal watercraft have contributed to further erosion of the mud that covered the riverbanks and flats. "Jet skis" now routinely travel, right-or-wrong, to and beyond the head of tide through the narrowing waterway. At higher tides, the deeper winding channel may not be distinguishable for safe navigation from the much-broader area of shallows with only a foot or several inches of water. This may not be a problem for a rowboat, canoe, kayak, or float tube; however, it can be unforgiving for the propeller of a deeper-draft outboard—even of minimal horsepower.

For several years, a former rice bed that was immediately downstream of the west end of the bridge provided the witness to misadventure. Inscribed through the muddy bottom was a narrow plow-line that proceeded from the open channel and across the middle ground, which at the time must have been covered with water, but shallowly. The dug line and outboard path ended abruptly at the largest old stump that extended out of the mudflat, but not far enough to be seen above the water. The outcome is not known, but could not have been good for the motor's lower unit or propeller —or the person's wallet. It should be noted that the Wading River has not had channel markers for normal, safe navigation; and precautions also must be exercised when passing over the extensive, hard-rock piles of ballast at the old Leeks Lower Landing, downstream of the bridge at the mouth of Ives Branch/Mill Creek.

In recent years, wild rice has extended upriver along the Pine Barrens streams of both the Oswego (East Branch) and West Branch of the Wading River. Scattered plants may occasionally be seen on the broader unshaded riverbanks among native cranberries and a variety of other Pinelands flora. It may only become apparent in the late summer with the distinctive large, branching structure of flowers and seeds, and yellowish-green of the late-season foliage of the rice. This distinguishes it from the many other grasses, sedges and bulrushes. Most recently, it has spread and flourished in Martha Pond, which furnished the waterpower from the Oswego River for the historic Martha Furnace and village. After the dam for the former impoundment was abandoned, the old pond bottom had evolved into a botanical "treasure" bog of many noteworthy species, including orchids and several insectivores: pitcher plants, bladderworts and three species of sundews. This has now largely changed into a grassy complex with scattered stands of cedar islands and remnants of the former open channels. From an initial large stand of rice at the head of the pond near the ruins of the abandoned lift pumphouse for the nearby Martha/Calico cranberry bogs, the rice now extends over large areas of the old pond and downstream to the outlet at the former spillway for the dam that powered the furnace to the east and sawmill to the west. It may not be favorable for the canoers who venture downriver from Oswego Lake on the paddleable, wadeable portion of the river to encounter the rice beds now in the old pond. The biblical parable of "Moses in the bulrushes on the Nile" might seem applicable, as they try to "pole" with their paddles through the rice stalks—which may rise several feet above the water and hide a channel-way or deepest water.

This may be advantageous, however, to the waterfowl that continue to migrate down the tributary Wading River to the tidewaters and marshes to the south. Doubtlessly the diminutive Sora Rail will take advantage of the natural resource of this new habitat of wild rice. And they will not be subject to the "railbirding" that historically existed and was part of the local culture for both visiting sportsmen and local residents.

Acknowledgments

This article would not have been possible without the documentation by Peter Stemmer of the recollections and anecdotes of Steve Eichinger, who resides, hunted, fished and trapped from his home at the eastern end of the highway span at old Bridgeport. Thanks also to Rob Auermuller for his foggy-morning vista of old Bridgeport at the Wading River Bridge (on page 138).

About the Author

Horace A. Somes Jr., a lifelong resident of the coastal New Jersey Pinelands, spent his career working for the New Jersey Forest Fire Service as an environmental consultant and in various NJDEP positions. Though retired, he is currently a member of the Tuckerton Historical Society and is a business partner with his brother Frank for Wading River Christmas Tree Farm.

Reference Literature

Able, Kenneth W. *Beneath the Surface: Understanding Nature in the Mullica River Estuary* (Rutgers University Press,

2020).

Able, Kenneth W., J. Walker and B. P. Horton, "Ghost Forests in the Mullica Valley: Indicators of Sea-Level Rise," *SoJourn* (Winter 2017-2018), 87–96.

Annual Report of the New Jersey State Museum: Including a Report of the Plants of Southern New Jersey, with Especial Reference to the Flora of the Pine Barrens, 1910.

Bass River: A Newsletter from the History Committee of the Bass River Community Library; contributions by Steve Eichinger and Herrintown Poet:

    # 2, October 1998: A place called "Goldacker"
    # 3, January 1999: A place called Chips Folly: Hen Updike and the "Marsh Rabbit" (Herrintown Poet)
    # 4, May 1999: A place called Tub Mill Run
    # 5, December 1999: A place called Bodine Field
    # 8, December 2000: Wading River Landings
    # 9, January 2001: Wading River Landings, Part II, The McKeens
    # 10, May 2001: Wading River Landings, Part III, The McKeens
    # 12, June 2002: The Stage Road
    # 23. March 2009: Duck Hunting on the Wading River

Blackman, Leah, *History of Little Egg Harbor Township, New Jersey from Its Settlement to the Present Time* (Tuckerton, 1963).

Dellomo, Angelo N., *Harrisville, A Journey Down the Sugar Sand Roads of Yesteryear* (Atlantic City: Angelo Publishing Co., 1977).

Markley, Marco L. "Soil Survey, Burlington County, New Jersey," US Department of Agriculture, Soil Conservation Service, 1971.

Moerman, Daniel E. *Native American Medicinal Plants: An Ethnobotanical Encyclopedia* (Portland, OR: Timber Press, 2009).

Mounier, R. Alan, *Looking Beneath the Surface: The Story of Archaeology in New Jersey* (Rutgers University Press, 2002).

Pearce, John E., *Heart of the Pines: Ghostly Voices of the Pine Barrens*, revised edition (Hammonton, NJ: Batsto Citizens Committee, New Jersey, 2000).

Reeves, Joseph S., *Maurice River Memories*: "Introduction," "Summertime 1937" and "Tidewater," *SoJourn* (Summer 2020), 65–76.

Somes, Horace A., Jr., The "Forgotten" Port and Landings on the Wading River, Historic Overview with Illustrations, From the Saltwater of the Coast to the Cedar Water of the Pine Barrens, 2019; unpublished archival contributions to Tuckerton Historical Society and Stockton University.

(Top) Vintage McAnney Pole: twenty-feet long with three-prong toes. (Bottom) historic pole crafted from oyster-tong handle: fifteen feet with keeled rudder for pushing, steerage and short-distance paddling.

ONE PRICE TO ALL!

GO TO

Cutter's Pharmacy

TO GET YOUR

DRUGS, PATENT MEDICINES, TOILET ARTICLES, PAINTS, OILS, GLASS, &C.

TO CURE
RHEUMATISM
USE

Cutter's Rheumatic Remedy

AGENT FOR

Dr. James Still's Black Salve,

(The Celebrated Cancer Doctor of Medford, N.J.)

PRESCRIPTIONS CAREFULLY COMPOUNDED DAY OR NIGHT.

A lamp burning in front of the Store all night.

MacCrellish & Quigley, Printers, 96 East State Street, Trenton, N.J.

Dr. James Still's famous ointments and salves gained wider distribution beyond his own office at Crossroads in Meford, as attested to on this facsimile broadside from Hopewell, Mercer County, New Jersey. The original broadside, in poor condition, was found on Pinterest.com.

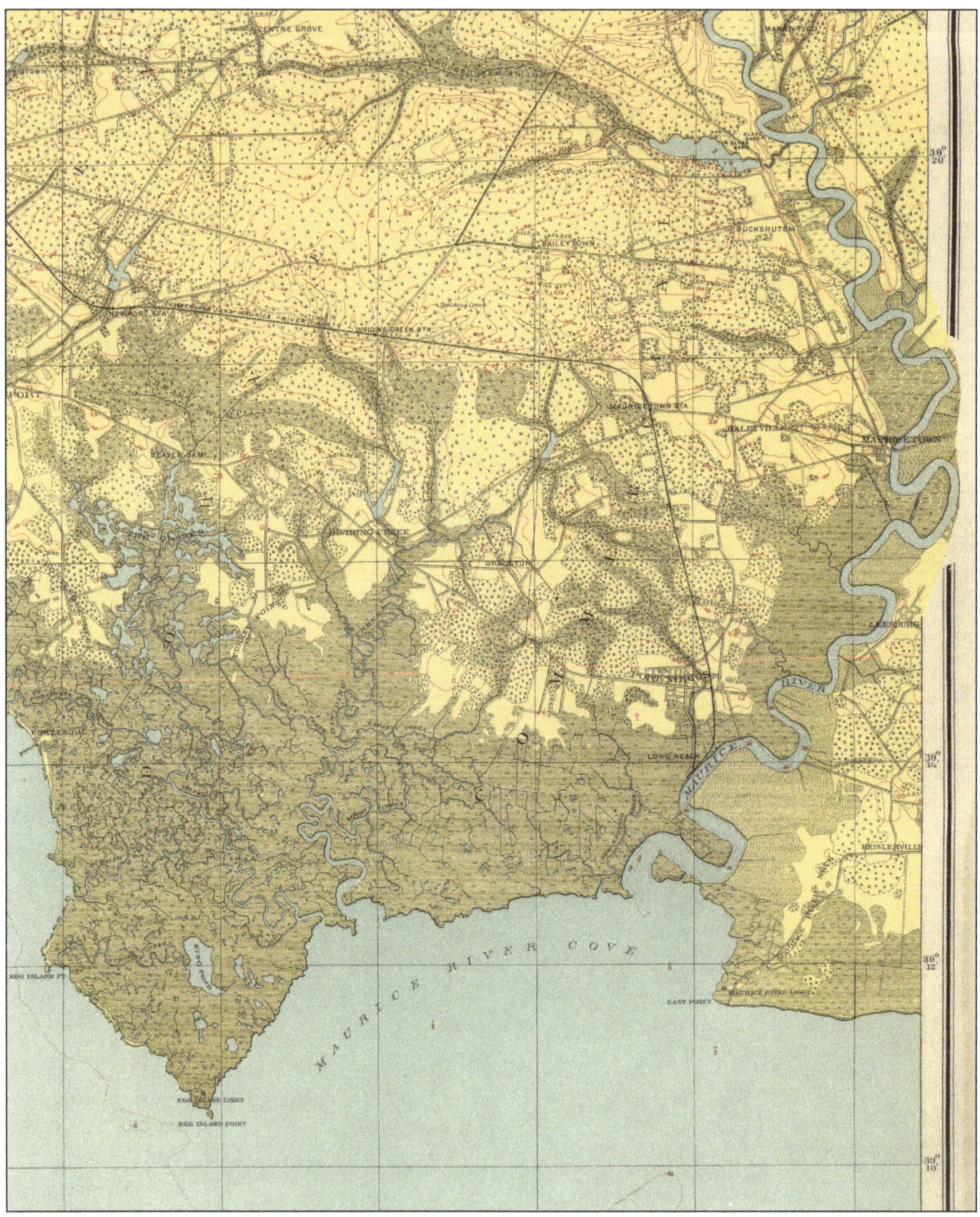

George H. Cook and Cornelius C. Vermeule, *A Topographical Map of the Vicinity of Bridgeton . . .*, Atlas Sheet no. 14, Delaware Bay (Trenton, NJ: Geological Survey of New Jersey, 1887). Courtesy of The David Rumsey Historical Map Collection.

Maurice River Memories:
"Night & Day" and "Hip Boots"

Joseph S. Reeves Jr.

Night and Day

The kitchen clock read one a.m. when my dad and I left the house for the short walk down to the river. It was a warm Friday night (actually early Saturday morning) in the second week of September, 1942. The sky was clear with stars so bright you could almost touch them. The big constellation of Orion the Hunter was rising in the east. Two of our cats started to follow us, then stopped and watched us walk into the night.

We pushed off from the wharf and headed upriver on the last of the flood tide. Dad rowed with easy strokes past the oyster schooner tied up at Bacon's dock. Our bateau was heavy with carp net and riding low in the stern so I balanced the boat by sitting toward the bow. We eased the boat through the pilings under the town side of the bridge. The sound of muffled voices came to us from the tender's shack a few yards away. Our only light was provided by the stars and a street lamp near the bridge. The sound of voices and the dim light faded as we cleared the bridge and rowed steadily and silently upstream.

Dad angled the boat out into midstream to take advantage of the favoring current through Upper Mauricetown Reach. The wind was calm and the river was misty smooth in the darkness. The waterman feathered each oar stroke as it creased the surface. We made no sound. Rowing around the bend where Upper Mauricetown Reach turns into Bricksboro Reach we could make out the two bungalows which sat on the only high ground on that side of the river within miles. Midway through Upper Bricksboro Reach Dad carefully rewet the cloth which cushioned our steel oarlocks. You could hear our breathing but not our rowing.

We passed the big breach in the marsh which had been known as Walter Bateman's farm before the dike ruptured in 1933. Then, proceeding so carefully that the water dripping from the tips of our oars was all that could be heard, we glided into the west river bank at the south end of Old Ferry, down the river from Steep Run. Here my dad staked the net's end at the prepared spot, then let the net run quietly over the stern as we moved outboard of a line of stakes. The tall cedar stakes had been placed about fifty to seventy-five feet apart and a few feet outboard of the low watermark in late August. Now, on the peak of the flood tide, only their tips showed above the surface. No current flowed by the stakes, indicating that the waterman had timed the entrapment perfectly. With all twelve hundred feet of net away we completed the encirclement by staking the net's downriver end at the bank. The neat line of corks suspending the net extended into the darkness along the row of stakes.

My dad then sat on the stern and I took the oars and started downriver. We paused after a short distance to check the moorings on a fishcar dad had pre-positioned here the day before yesterday. The livecar was moored between two hefty stakes aligned with the current. They had been shoved hard into the river bottom about twenty feet outside the low water mark. The

This is the fourth installment of Joseph S. Reeves Jr.'s stories, first published in his Maurice River Memories *(1993). The work is a collection of his childhood experiences with his family on the Maurice River and shows a bygone era when rivermen could support a family utilizing the natural resources of river and shoreline meadowlands. These stories are republished with the kind permission of the Mauricetown Historical Society, the copyright holder. The accompanying illustrations, are from the original printing. The 1888 map of the Maurice River, to the left, is not.*

livecar would not go aground when the tide fell. With any luck we'd be putting several hundred pounds of live carp into the car in about six hours. The rugged stakes and lines were holding securely.

I rowed out into midstream to catch the first of the ebb tide for home. Our quiet movement had become routine and we kept silence although our net had been set. Somewhere close by a night bird on the wing whispered past. Rowing down Bricksboro and Upper Mauricetown Reach we spoke in hushed tones. We speculated on the size our catch might be when we returned to the net at low tide in a few hours.

Passing under the Mauricetown bridge, we heard no sounds from the tender's shack. A light ebb tide was flowing by the wharf as we tied up. From across town a dog barked. Mist was forming on the river. It must have been around four a.m. Time to catch a few hour's sleep.

When I was a boy our day-to-day existence depended on the Maurice River and on the skills of my dad, a waterman. Joe Reeves was an expert fisherman, trapper, and waterfowl hunter's guide who always treated the river and surrounding lowlands with care and respect. He was a waterman's waterman and his generation was the last to earn a living this way for an entire lifetime. I was lucky enough to accompany him for a few years as he earned our livelihood from the river. We were most fortunate to have been provided with these beautiful gifts from nature.

My dad and his brothers made their living primarily from shad fishing, carp fishing, fur trapping and acting as guides for waterfowl hunters. Shad fishing occurred only during springtime. Trapping was our only source of income in the winter months and waterfowl hunting took place in the fall. Carp fishing seasons occurred in both spring and fall. Carp fishing required a lot of hard work at various times of the day and night. Spring was more difficult because the water temperature was still cold from the winter and the weather was often unpredictable. Carp fishing in September and October was easier because the river was still warm and the weather

Upper Mauricetown Reach, November, 1942; carp are taken at low tide.

was favorable—but the timing was bad. Railbird hunting season occurred at the same time, so my dad and uncles often worked round the clock. Summertime was the low point for income, especially during the depression of the 30s. They could not afford to pass up the opportunity for earnings in the fall from any available source.

Our primary buyers of carp were the Jewish fish markets in Philadelphia and Atlantic City. We sold big quantities just before the Jewish holidays. Names of some of the buyers were Slavin, Grossman, Goldstein, Bralow and Gilfonte. Carp for sale had to be kept alive. The big buyers always showed up in tank trucks equipped with aeration devices. They would purchase hundreds of pounds at once. We kept the fish alive by placing them in pounds. Any carp judged to weigh less than 2½ to 3 pounds or so is let go. The fish, which are temporarily placed in the shallow water in the boat, will suffer if left too long, especially if the weather is warm. Several trips to the livecar while fishing out may be required.

The net must be recovered after fishing out is completed and all fish have been placed in the livecar. The net is normally quite muddy because of being in very shallow water at low tide. In fact some of the net is lying exposed on the flats. A good fisherman will try to rinse the mud from the net as he takes it in, stacking it on the boat's stern. The long heavy net is even heavier after its soaking, and is tiresome to handle. The fisherman must decide whether to return home and dry the net or leave it in the boat for the next setting. Net life is usually shortened when the net is allowed to remain stacked in a pile while wet and muddy, so the extra work of drying it on poles can be worthwhile.

We used flat-bottom wooden row boats or bateaus which were tapered in the bow and squared-off astern. Many boats served double duty; they were used for both shad and carp fishing. If a very long carp net was carried, a bigger boat, perhaps as long as 20 feet, was used. (Most rowboats were 15 to 18 feet long.) My dad did not ordinarily like to use an outboard motor, prefer-

ring to row whenever possible. When setting the net it was advisable to row and row quietly, because even the slightest noise would probably spook the feeding fish and result in a waterhaul (no catch). However, after the net has been set the work effort remaining before the entire process is done must be considered. Most carp fishing was conducted upriver from Mauricetown rather than downriver. This meant that when going back to the net to fish out, the tide was still flowing downriver and the boat had to buck the current. After fishing out, the tide would have switched to the flood and the fisherman had to return to Mauricetown with the heavy net loaded aboard, sometimes with the livecar in tow, while again bucking the current. The workload could be eased with an outboard motor. My dad and Albert got outboards around 1940. They were on the order of only 2½ or 3 horsepower. They had their disadvantages, of course. Keeping them under repair was alien to my dad and uncles who disliked tinkering with mechanical devices, so the motors were out of operation a lot. Their mounted position on the boat's stern was in the way of the net and they had to be serviced with gasoline and oil, which cost money. In the end my dad used a motor sparingly, such as when towing a heavy livecar against the tide for a long distance. Albert and Morty used theirs a bit more, probably because Albert was handier with the servicing and repairs.

My dad and uncles carp fished the Maurice River all the way up to the Coal Wharf. More often they limited operations to the reaches downriver from Acorn Gut. About the only reach fished for carp downriver from Mauricetown was Noman's Friend, and that not often. Sometimes they would position their boats and nets in Port Creek just behind my Great Grandmother Althea Reeves Sharp's house and conduct operations from there. Dad didn't have a car for the two-mile trip, which had to be made regardless of the time of day or night. He had to make sure he could get a ride from Albert, Robert or Morty, but he had to walk the distance in hip boots more than once. The arrangements for coming and going to the prepositioned boats had to be worked out in advance.

Carp fishing improved for a few years after the dike farms bordering Upper Mauricetown Reach breached, around 1933. The growth of oat-bearing reed in the newly flooded areas provided better feed and a better habitat for breeding carp. When the farm across from town flooded, around 1934, another good feed-producing area was created. The first breach to open in the dike there was located in the lower end of Noman's Friend Reach just upriver from the bend into Dorchester Reach. It didn't take long for my dad to prepare that area for carp fishing by staking it out soon after the oat-bearing reed began to grow.

My dad fished alone sometimes but was accompanied by Harry Reeves (Houk) for a time. Uncle Robert carp-fished with dad for a while in the late 40s, then Morty replaced him. Earlier, Morty had fished for several years with Albert. I was allowed to go carp fishing with my dad on only a few occasions, because of school. Mom and dad were careful to see that school came first and I suppose this was a wise decision. Nevertheless, I remember with gratitude the experiences of the times I was allowed to go. It was a pleasure to accompany my dad, who was the one the others always consulted when plans were being made.

My dad was the only one of the brothers who made his entire life's work that of being a waterman on the Maurice River. Percy abandoned fishing at an early age to sell insurance. Morty was a prison guard at the state prison farm near Leesburg, Robert served as a U.S. Postmaster; young Jack became a businessman and manager after returning from the army. Albert combined a few years working as a bridgetender with his life's work as a waterman. My dad tried to work for a few weeks at the sand plant one summer during the depression when we were hard put to get along. His temperament wouldn't stand the routine of hourly work and he didn't even last the summer.

* * * * *

It seemed as though my head had just hit the pillow when dad shook me awake. I climbed back into my work clothes and hip boots and made a quick trip to the outhouse, fighting off a few mosquitoes on the way. Dawn was breaking and a fast look at the river showed the tide was well down. Some eddies and swirls could be seen, indicating the ebb tide was still fairly strong. We ate a fast breakfast of oatmeal and headed for the river, stopping to take the outboard clamped to the back fence.

We had tied up at Haley's wharf when we returned from setting the net: our boat would have gone aground at our own wharf. Dad attached the little Johnson to the stern, set the spark and throttle, wound the pull starter and cranked. The motor was very stubborn and needed several pulls before it started. When it did it chugged along for awhile, as though it was flooded, before it ran smooth. Finally, it settled down and we swung the boat around and headed upriver into the tide. We were early and there was no one around the bridge when we passed through the draw. Dad looked at me and shook his head a couple of times and I could tell what he was thinking about the outboard.

The motor pushed us through Upper Mauricetown Reach and Bricksboro Reach in a lot less time than rowing would have taken. As we approached the net at the lower end of Old Ferry the sun had risen, so there was plenty of light. In the narrow band of shallow water between the net and the mud flat some fish were splashing. In spots where the fish had bunched up you could see their backs out of water. Dad stopped the motor and tilted it to the retracted position and we glided into the shoreline. We were definitely going to take fish, so we bailed a couple of inches of water into the boat. Dad got out and started wading along the net, picking up fish and placing them in the boat while I stood and poled the boat along with an oar. He would chase the carp into groups, cutting them off with the net in shallow pools of water just a few inches deep, then pick most of them up with his hands. He had to use both hands for the big ones, but grabbed small fish with one hand. Every so often he would throw a small one over the net into the river. There was a lot of splashing and he quickly became wet and muddy. They splashed a lot after being placed in the boat, so I took a lot of water too, although not much mud. After progressing halfway along the net we made a trip over to the livecar, still moored at the downriver end, opened the trapdoor and placed the fish inside, using a scoop net to take them out of the boat. We returned to the net and finished fishing out.

My dad never finished the eighth grade but he did very good arithmetic when it came to carp. He estimated the weight of the catch by guessing each fish's weight when placing it in the boat, while keeping a running total in his head. This morning he estimated about 750 pounds which was a good catch. We also took a few perch and white catfish and a pike which we would eat ourselves or give to people in town. We made no attempt to keep these other fish alive but planned to put them on ice.

We rowed to the upriver end of the net after loading the rest of the catch in the livecar. I handled the oars while dad brought the net into the boat. The tide had started to flood while we were fishing out and this gave him some depth to rinse the net as he took it in. Getting 1,200 feet of wet carp net back in the boat is hard work. I don't know how my dad did it alone but he had done so many times. With no one at the oars the boat gets dragged back over the net as it is hauled in. I headed for the livecar after this chore was done, while dad rotated the motor back down into position and attempted a start. It gave us trouble as before—only worse. No matter what we did, it wouldn't go. That was not good: we were going to need it to tow the livecar back down river against the current. Finally, Dad decided we would row home without the livecar and return for it on tomorrow's favorable tide. We couldn't fuss around any more because dad had a railbird-pushing engagement with Mr. Dale Fitler on this afternoon's high tide. We took turns rowing against the tide going home. The outboard motor turned out to be just so much more weight to be hauled along with the heavy net.

My dad didn't ordinarily work on Sundays but the defective outboard motor had given him no recourse. A carp buyer was due on Monday so we had to have the fish available. We hadn't done anything to fix the motor. Sunday afternoon, about 3 p.m. we caught the last of the flood tide upriver. Dad timed it so we would row with favoring tide both ways, arriving at the livecar at high water. We pulled the heavy stakes used to moor it and took it in tow downriver. Out in mid stream with the ebb tide helping us along we had a quiet row back to Mauricetown: the cumbersome livecar was no problem. My dad took it all in stride. He didn't complain, but I knew he would never use the noisy, unreliable motor any more than absolutely necessary.

Hip Boots

My dad, Joe Reeves, lived in hip boots for most of his life, wearing shoes only on rare occasions. I wore boots only when fishing or trapping. When we were away from the water we folded the boot tops down below the knee, then back up at the ankle. I used to think we looked like an old picture of Sir Walter Raleigh, except that his boots were light and dashing while ours were bulky and cumbersome.

Dad and I put on hip boots before starting our walk into the lower meadow to check muskrat traps. Boots were essential in the marsh area where the traps were located, even though they made the long walk to the traps more difficult. It was late afternoon in mid December, 1942. The weather was clear and we expected the temperature to drop to near freezing after nightfall. We both carried cotton work gloves and dressed warmly in well-worn sweaters and jackets. Dad knew we'd be returning after dark, but with a full moon there would be no trouble finding our way back out of the meadow.

After leaving the house, we saw Grandad Reeves in his yard. He told us he had letters from Jack and Albert.

Jack, Dad's youngest brother, had been drafted into the army in October. Albert was drafted a month later, at the age of forty. Both were in training in the midwest. He also told us that aunt Ethel would be visiting soon. Dad's sister Ethel was a teacher. She was the only one in the family who had managed to get a college education.

Chum waved to us from his makeshift hut, built atop the wreck of an old oyster schooner grounded along the riverbank just below town. A wisp of smoke could be seen coming from a length of stovepipe protruding from the side of the little dwelling. Chum, a tall hulking man of about forty-five, had drifted into Mauricetown during the depression, built his home on the wreck from driftwood and scrap lumber, and eked out an existence by mowing lawns and doing odd jobs. He appeared to be mentally retarded but was tolerated, even treated kindly, by the town folk. Chum made up a part of the character of our village in the 1930s and early 40s.

We paused a few yards down the road next to several wild cherry trees growing along the river bank. Using his pocket knife, Dad cut several small limbs into stakes about thirty inches long. He sharpened a point on the heavy end and left a Y-branch on the opposite end of each. He would use a stake to anchor the ring on the end of each steel trap's chain, thus preventing a trapped muskrat from escaping.

Dad carried an extra half dozen steel traps in a burlap sack slung over his shoulder. I carried Dad's double barrelled, twelve-gauge Fox Sterling. Anytime I had accompanied dad trapping over the past two seasons he'd let me bring the shotgun, on the chance we'd jump ducks. Most of the time I never fired a shot but we traveled in great duck habitat, so it was advisable to be prepared. At sixteen I'd fired the gun enough to be comfortable but still experienced some difficulty with accuracy. Any improvement had to come from shooting at live targets, because we couldn't afford to purchase shells for practice. I was fortunate to have my dad teach me how to use a shotgun. He'd been involved in bird hunting all his life and was very safety conscious.

MUSKRAT TRAPPING
WINTER OF 1938/39

Maurice River Memories

It was easy walking on the gravel road which ran just inside the seven- to eight-foot high river bank bordering the west side of Mauricetown Reach. The road and dike gradually curved eastward with the river as it changed direction into Noman's Friend Reach. The meadow we were walking through was about the only section of lowland remaining along the river which was still diked. The dikes bordering this meadow were still being maintained and had held since their construction just after the first world war.

We had passed the first big drainage canal about a quarter mile down the road and reached the second after another quarter mile. The sluice gate under the dike wasn't keeping the river out altogether: we could see a light current flowing in from outside. This resulted in a foot or two of tide in many of the waterways inside the meadow. We hitched up our boots and walked along the canal through kneehigh grass. An occasional small cedar or pine tree grew in this terrain and I scrutinized these carefully. If we spotted one with good shape and of the correct size I'd return later with a hatchet and it would become our Christmas tree. We crossed over a smaller branch canal on an old tree trunk.

A cottontail bounded through the short undergrowth ahead of us but I wasn't tempted to shoot it. We only shot game that we intended to eat and we never ate wild rabbit. After checking about twenty-five traps here we had found two muskrats, both drowned. There was enough tide in the waterways so an experienced trapper like my dad could set the traps to take advantage of it. A trap could be placed so that, when the animal wound the chain around the stake, just a few inches of water would be enough to drown it. This reduced the animal's suffering and made for a higher catch rate. The muskrats in this area built their dens by tunneling into the mudbanks along the waterways. They were creatures of habit and traveled to and from their dens in well-worn pathways or runs. Traps were set in runs where signs of recent activity could be detected. Dad could spot clawprints, droppings, even pieces of chewed roots, much easier then I could. He would move a trap if a run appeared abandoned.

The muskrat is a very prolific animal and its numbers always held up well in this meadow. I'm sure we could have overtrapped the area if we had been greedy. My dad had a good sense of how many pelts to take in the season, which ran from November 15th to March 15th. The condition of the habitat and the harshness of the winter were the main factors dictating the population level for the muskrat.

Heading back toward the tree trunk bridge, having roughly circled a quartermile area, we flushed a pheasant. The bird made a lot of racket coming out of the undergrowth nearly underfoot and flew straight away at high speed. I wasn't quite ready—got the safety off and the gun up, fired once and missed. It was a ringneck cock pheasant, the first one I'd ever fired at. I felt as though I should have hit the bird but my dad didn't mind. He thought it great that we even had the chance. It was rare to flush a pheasant without help from a dog.

Back on the road again, we folded our boots down and regained a fast walking pace for another half mile. Then we turned right on a dirt road running through Ed Fisher's tomato farm. The decayed remains of last summer's crop had been picked clean by the birds before they had flown south for the winter. The roofs on the Dorchester shipyard shops across the river were visible above the riverbank a quarter mile to our left as we walked south. This road dwindled to a narrow path and ended in an area which was no longer farmed. The land was somewhat lower here, crisscrossed with old drainage ditches and some marshy areas flooded by a foot or so. By now we had crossed the lower meadow from the Noman's Friend side to within a few hundred yards of the riverbank bordering the lower end of Dorchester Reach. Dad checked his traps along the way, taking four more muskrats. One was still alive and had to be killed. I could sense my dad didn't like this part of the job. He used a stake and dispatched the animal quickly with a sharp blow to the head.

Not far from the riverbank bordering the north side of Penny Hill Reach we entered an area of meadow which had been partially flooded for some time. The dikes hadn't given way but the land was low and the drainage ditches and sluice gates were not serving their purpose. Muskrats built houses in the flooded area, since there wasn't enough land above water for tunneling. Muskrat houses look like beaver houses except they are smaller. They are constructed from twigs, reed, marsh grasses, roots and mud. Like beavers, muskrats provide an underwater entrance to keep out predators.

Sunset comes early in December. The late-afternoon air felt chilly as the sun turned red low in the west, however no ice was forming on the shallow water as yet. The wind had dropped to a dead calm and the meadow was very quiet. Dad was removing a muskrat from a trap placed in a run which meandered through a stand of dead reed several yards away. I heard the sound of whispering wings in the still air—ducks! I turned around just in time to see a flight of pintails veering away just out of

Upper Mauricetown Reach, November, 1942 — Action in a Duck Blind

gunshot range. They had approached from the southwest and spotted me standing in the shallow water during their descent. Dad saw them too, then pointed at two more ducks a bit further out, wings set, descending fast, directly toward us. This time I was ready and downed the pair with two shots at a range of about thirty-five yards. A lone black duck veered away as I was retrieving the downed pintails. It was apparent that we had stumbled onto a place where the ducks, flying in from the Delaware Bay, planned to spend the night.

I wanted some cover but didn't have time to find it, so I tried squatting down behind one of the low muskrat houses. I mentally reviewed my supply of shells—one shot wasted on the pheasant and two spent on the pintails. I'd left home with about ten or eleven, thinking that was more than I'd ever use. I waded around and propped the pintails up on some broken reeds poking out of the shallow water to serve as makeshift decoys, then returned to my crouching stance behind the muskrat house. Dad hadn't moved from his position about fifty feet behind me in a clump of tall reed.

He was calling to a flight of three black ducks circling the marsh very low and acting as though they wanted to come down. Dad's duck call was good. He wasn't using a device, just his hands cupped over his mouth. I was watching so intently I nearly forgot to reload, but remembered as the ducks turned into a descent toward us. When they approached within thirty yards I stood up and downed two, getting the second as it flared away. I then realized I'd been squatting so low my rear end was wet and some water ran down inside my boots. Reloading and getting set for another shot took my mind off the cool water.

Two teal—small, but very fast ducks—wheeled in low just over the reed and sat down quickly, not ten yards in front of me. In an instant they saw me and took out fast. There were little blue patches on their wings. I made no attempt to shoot them. A big flight of ducks numbering about ten, wings set and descending fast, came in out of the sun. There were black, mallards, and pintails all arriving together. I downed a mallard and another pintail before my shots scared the others off.

Maurice River Memories

Groping in my pockets. I counted three more shells. I reloaded and waited, squatting again, as the sun dropped below the southwestern horizon like a beautiful red ball. Within minutes a flight of four black ducks dropped in. I got anxious and missed the first shot but downed one as they veered off. I loaded the last shell but never used it because the ducks stopped coming in and we had to round up the downed birds while we still had light to find them.

Dad finished checking the traps while I gathered the ducks, placing them in a burlap sack. By the time we started back, carrying our loads, the sun was well down but a big full moon in the east gave us plenty of light. Water, which had run down inside my left boot, squished with each step. It made my sock slip down over my heel and ball up under the arch on the walk out of the marsh. After a while, we came back out on the road, where we paused to fold our boots down and adjust our loads. I hopped around on one foot to get my left sock and boot straightened out. It was cold but we would warm up fast when we hit our pace on the walk back.

The excitement hadn't worn off and we relived each shot as we walked in the moonlight up the gravel road. About a quarter mile before reaching town a small dark object could be seen in the road. We approached within a few feet before recognizing it as a skunk. It was a black one with two white stripes down its back which showed up well in the moonlight from about ten feet. It moved off into the grass after I chucked some small stones at it. I enjoyed watching skunks walk. They move almost like a wave through water with an undulating gait.

When we arrived home we found that Uncle John McClain and Aunt Doris had dropped in for a while. They had their daughter, Kathleen, with them. She was just six months old. After a short while, they had to return home to Dorchester; we gave them two of the ducks for roasting.

Mom prepared supper and we ate while we listened to the war news on the RCA radio. The announcer, Gabriel Heater, was giving a rundown on a big naval battle in the South Pacific and on the war in North Africa. It had been a year since Pearl Harbor and it sounded as though our side was beginning to win part of the time. I'd be drafted in a year and a half so we always listened intently.

After supper, Dad started skinning the eight muskrats at post over in the corner of the backyard, using a kerosene lantern and the moonlight. A crowd of cats appeared out of nowhere for handouts. Dad could do a muskrat in just two or three minutes. He was fast but careful because a slip of the knife could easily damage the valuable fur. After the hides were removed dad stretched them over cedar roofing shingles which were rounded to a point on the thin end. With the fur side inward the hide would dry in just a few days. We always cured the hides in our "empty room," an unfinished room upstairs off one of the bedrooms. The so-called empty room was actually full of curing hides, fish nets. scrap lumber, unused furniture and almost anything else that had happened to be put there. No one could remember when the "empty room" had actually been empty.

I took a pair of ducks four houses up the street to Uncle Robert and Aunt Evelyn. My cousins Robert Jr., Elaine, and little Donald were having supper with their mom and dad. Young Robert, age twelve and the oldest of the three kids, wanted to know how we got the ducks. I didn't want to hold up their meal, so I didn't go into detail. Uncle Robert was wearing his socks at the table. His hip boots were standing over in the corner.

I came home and set about plucking the remaining ducks. I dipped the three ducks in a bucket of scalding water heated on our iron range. Dad didn't mind working in the cold evening air, but I did, so I took the ducks down in our cellar to pluck them. The feathers came off easily after the scalding. Dad came down and helped after he got all the hides mounted for curing. I dressed the ducks, using a big dishpan partly filled with water, then gave them to Mom to roast next day.

Around eight-thirty everything was done, so Dad and I finally took our boots off and relaxed. I told my sisters Irene and Louise about our day and about almost stepping on the skunk. My older sister, Irene, wasn't impressed and Louise, just thirteen, acted silly so I boned up on my algebra lessons for awhile. My dad had discovered a leak around the knee of his right boot and was trying to patch it with a bicycle innertube repair kit. There already were several patches on the boots.

I tried to study but my mind kept drifting back to the meadow and the ducks. I would remember this day for a long, long time . . . .

SoJourn
Call for Articles

The South Jersey Culture & History Center at Stockton University publishes *SoJourn*. We actively seek community members, avocational historians, and scholars to contribute essays on topics related to South Jersey. Illustrations to accompany these articles will be a plus. Articles should be written for laypersons who are interested and curious about South Jersey topics, but do not necessarily have expertise in the areas covered. Potential authors should follow the style in this issue. Journal editors will be happy to guide any would-be authors. In certain instances, Stockton's talented editing interns may be assigned to help research topics and/or assist authors with writing.

SAMPLE TOPICS MIGHT INCLUDE

Biographical sketches of important but forgotten local people; the development or succession of a community's roads, bridges or buildings; local transportation (focused by mode, area or era) and what changes it wrought in the served communities; history of community businesses and industries (wineries, garment factories, agriculture, boat building, clamming, etc.); old school houses, old hotels, or meeting halls; narrative descriptions of local geographical features; essays concerned with folklore, music, arts; and reviews of new local interest publications. Photo essays and old photograph and postcard reproductions are welcome with applicable captions. In short, if a South Jersey topic interests you, it will likely interest *SoJourn*'s readers.

PARAMETERS FOR SUBMISSIONS
• Submissions must pertain to topics bounded within the eight southernmost counties of New Jersey (Burlington & Ocean Counties and south)
• Manuscripts should be approximately 3,000–4,000 words long (5 to 7 pages of single-spaced text and 9 to 12 pages including images)
• Manuscripts, if at all possible, should be submitted in digital format (Word- or pdf-formatted documents preferred)
• Images should be submitted as high-resolution tiff- or jpeg-formatted files (editors can assist with digital conversion of photos if necessary). 300 dpi resolution, or higher, preferred
• Complete and appropriate citations printed as endnotes should be employed. If using Word, please use its automated endnote function
• Original submissions only. Copyright licenses for all images must be obtained by the author or should be copyright-free figures and/or figures in the public domain
• If essays are accepted, authors should submit a short 50 to 100 word autobiographical statement
• Articles need to be more than just a chronology of the given topic. The author should be able to properly contextualize the subject by answering such questions as: a) why is this important?; b) what is the impact on the local or regional history? and c) how does it compare to similar events/personages/changes/processes in other localities?

CALL FOR SUBMISSIONS

Submissions for forthcoming issues are accepted on a rolling basis. Send inquiries or submissions to Thomas.Kinsella@stockton.edu or Paul.Schopp@stockton.edu.

As we close out this thematic issue of *SoJourn*, this night view shows a two-masted coastal schooner tied up at a finger pier on Salem Creek in the City of Salem. All of the sails and gaffs on this fore-and-aft rigged vessel are properly lashed to their boom. It appears she is carrying a deck load of lumber. Postcard publishers contrived virtually all night scenes on early postcards, since the camera equipment then available could not produce such images.

www.ingramcontent.com/pod-product-compliance
Lightning Source LLC
Chambersburg PA
CBHW060931170426
43193CB00026B/2996